Advance Prais

"Scott McKay has written an eyes-open manifesto describing how patriotic Americans can retake their country from the race hustlers, climate fanatics and diversity ideologues who aim to destroy it. Mr. McKay makes no bones about the troubles we are in. The anti-American coalition has taken control of vast areas of American life, including the schools, colleges, journalism, and even many corporations. Yet he is convinced that Americans working together can revive and renew conservative principles, while dislodging the leftists from their cultural redoubts. The Revivalist Manifesto is an important book for many reasons, but most of all because it outlines a path forward in a time of doubt, confusion, and despair."

—James Piereson, President
William E. Simon Foundation

"A compelling trumpet blast for a muscular conservatism with no apologies. Scott McKay's *The Revivalist Manifesto* is a no-holds-barred huge helping of history and solid arguments for what a real resistance to the leftist agenda destroying America would look like. *The Revivalist Manifesto* takes on the RINOs and the apologists for the Left that explains where we are, how we got here, and what we need to do about it."

—Daniel Greenfield, Front Page Magazine

"Conservatives now have a fantastic blueprint for opposing, not only the leftists who work to hobble the people, but also the half hearted party members who simply serve as allies of the opposition. Scott McKay's The Revivalist Manifesto establishes solid grounds to get us back, beyond the MAGA path, to improve the lives of every American. Thanks to his handbook we can go ULTRA MAGA."

—Eric F. Skrmetta, co-Chairman (Louisiana), Donald J Trump for President (2016, 2020).

"Scott McKay has written a treatise on where conservatism has come from, but more importantly, where conservatism should go. His is an optimistic vision that will revitalize America if embraced. Conservative leaders take note!"

—Melissa Mackenzie, Publisher, *The American Spectator*

"Kudos to Scott McKay for exploring the times in American history where revival has meant survival. McKay articulately makes the case for the revivalism needed now to ensure America remains the greatest country in the world."

—Jeff Landry, Attorney General, Louisiana

THE REVIVALIST MANIFESTO

HOW PATRIOTS CAN WIN THE NEXT AMERICAN ERA

SCOTT McKAY

Published by Bombardier Books
An Imprint of Post Hill Press
ISBN: 978-1-63758-534-4
ISBN (eBook): 978-1-63758-535-1

The Revivalist Manifesto:
How Patriots Can Win the Next American Era

Cover Design by Tiffani Shea

Post Hill Press
New York • Nashville
posthillpress.com

Published in the United States of America
1 2 3 4 5 6 7 8 9 10

To the signers of our Declaration of Independence, who pledged their lives, fortunes, and sacred honor to bequeath us this Republic, and to those of us committed to keep it.

225-317-6300

TABLE OF CONTENTS

FOREWORD

Scott McKay presents a valuable and timely contribution with *The Revivalist Manifesto* because he has managed here to articulate well what millions of conscientious, freedom-loving Americans are sensing.

This is a pivotal moment. While our great nation has faced and overcome extraordinary challenges in the past, the crisis today is unprecedented. We are engaged now in a cataclysmic struggle on every front to defend truth, preserve our foundations, and hold fast to who we are and what we stand for. There have always been political skirmishes and policy battles, but this is different.

The fight for freedom today has entered uncharted territory because the Left has now abandoned all its ties to conscience, common sense, and the Constitution. McKay understands this clearly, and his book is an urgent and necessary call to arms.

McKay urges conservatives to take a new, accurate assessment of the battlefield and our opposition, and to recognize that the time for pulling political punches has passed. Conservatives today must speak and act with greater clarity, conviction, and consistency than ever before. As McKay says, we must become a counter-revolutionary movement against the Left and its "Progressive Democrats," communists, deep state operatives, and cultural and institutional arsonists who are advancing their scorched-earth policy through our republic.

McKay insists that the culture war must be waged and won decisively, and that it certainly can be when we reach the hearts of the American people. He also suggests a battle plan that includes resisting the onslaught of China, protecting our own hardworking citizens, fueling the engines of American entrepreneurship, cracking the powerhold of the elites, and returning to the roots of our beloved country.

The goals set forth in this book are clear, and the time is short. We desperately need an American revival, and this work can help spark it. Read it, and I think you will agree.

Congressman Mike Johnson (LA-4)
Vice Chairman, House Republican Conference

INTRODUCTION

Chances are, if you picked up this book, you're one of the millions of Americans who ingests a sizable amount of political news every day and has come to a number of conclusions about this 21st century we find ourselves in:

First, that it's unhealthy to watch as much cable news as you watch. You find yourself growling at the TV, and the daily drumbeat of crisis and turmoil is taking a sizable toll on your morale and worldview.

Second, that you're struggling with an unwanted impression that America, or at least the America you've known for your whole life, is in a steep decline and on its way out. Our culture has turned poisonous; there are radical weirdos you wouldn't trust to run a lemonade stand becoming city council members, state senators, mayors, congresspeople, and Biden appointees; and from the supply chain to your company's human resources department it doesn't seem like anybody can just do a job anymore.

Third, you've come to the realization that voting Republican just doesn't seem to fix these things—though you know that voting Democrat will surely make them worse.

And finally, you're deathly afraid that all this will result in someone else—most notably China—replacing us as the world's superpower in your lifetime, and the end of Pax Americana will bring with it a lot of nasty things you'd rather not see.

You're getting all of these things through the filter of—mostly—corporate legacy media, and it's making you a different person than you remember being fifteen years ago. You feel helpless. You're losing your civic spirit. And you're becoming distrustful of our institutions: cultural, corporate, educational, political. Polls show that even the military is losing the faith of the American people. It's not hard, given the disaster of Afghanistan and all the stories of "woke" indoctrination of the troops, to understand why.

This book will help with a lot of these thoughts and feelings if you fit the profile above. Even if you don't quite identify with all of it, I'm hoping you'll still see it as promoting a framework for analyzing current events and a blueprint for rediscovering the America you've grown up proud of.

This is, after all, not just the most successful civilization in world history. It's the most successful and noble civic experiment in the annals of mankind. America's detractors, particularly the woke variety who bombard the rest of us with various iterations of critical theory, are determined to make us believe we're a racist, exploitative society that has profited from a zero-sum game at the expense of indigenous people, African slaves, and cheap foreign labor. That our patriarchy has stood in the way of true justice. And that we're due penance for our national sins.

All of it is garbage. And in coming years we're going to litigate that question in the public sphere. Once enough of us are bold and articulate enough, and once there's enough institutional support to match the monopoly the anti-America set has fashioned out of the cultural institutions it has infiltrated and corrupted, things will turn very quickly.

In these pages you'll get an argument for why.

A racist country? America is the least racist country on earth. Virtually all of the nations of the world, with the arguable exception of the post-colonial states of Africa and the Middle East, were founded on racism—or at least, on ethnicism. The USA, by contrast, was founded on an idea, and a universal idea at that. The document at the heart of our birth as an independent society states that we're all created equal and endowed with natural rights, regardless of whether we're ethnic Scots, Hutus, Hmong, Armenians, or Sephardim.

That's a lot to live up to. Have we managed it without hiccups? Of course not. We've had racism, ethnic strife, rampant injustice, discrimination, and outright abuse of the weak and underprivileged right from the very beginning.

Fine. Now do Turkey. Or Zaire. Or China.

Every nation on earth has seen man's inhumanity to man. Every nation on earth was *founded,* one way or another, on that fact. Some countries are geographical testaments to the world's greatest genocidal murderers and their progeny. Others are testaments to the exclusion of those not pure of ethnicity. There isn't a country on earth that can bear the standard the anti-Americans demand of us.

This conversation matters. Because if the psychology described above fits you, it's because you've been demoralized by a constant cultural attack on the America you knew growing up. That demoralization isn't an accident. It's part of a playbook being put in motion by people who want you not to matter anymore.

And there's a reason for it. It's not that these people are trying to end America. It's that they're trying to dominate the America that is coming. They've thought this out in a way you haven't, and they're likely further along than you are in understanding the future to come—or, at least, the future they think is coming.

But it's all right. Understanding the game makes it easier than you think to win it. In these pages we're going to set the scene for the fight to come, describe the players, and then show how it can be won. And when we're finished, you'll see that a revival is just around the corner.

PART ONE

THE END OF AN AMERICAN ERA

CHAPTER 1

Falling Apart

It's an ugly time in America.

By virtually any metric you'd use to judge the cohesiveness and orderly function of a country, we've fallen pretty quickly over the past couple of decades. We don't like each other very much; we definitely don't like our leaders; every election cycle is The Most Important in Our History because Our Democracy Is in Peril; our influence on the rest of the world seems to be slipping; and our national confidence in, well, *everything* has fallen off significantly.

But perhaps we should pull back. To be fair, this country has dealt with much tougher times. Certainly in the aftermath of Pearl Harbor, America looked to be in a lot more peril than we are now. Few of us are dealing with starvation—obesity is a lot larger problem among the poor in this country currently than is malnutrition. In fact, poverty in America essentially means driving a beater of a car and having Roku or basic cable with no movie channels. There aren't Okies on the roads heading west, vast swaths of the country aren't absent electricity or running water, and the guys begging on the streets often climb into their SUVs at the end of a hard day of panhandling.

The behavioral pathologies you most commonly see in America aren't evidence of hard times. The opposite is true. Recreational drug use, time flushed into the abyss on video games and social media, gluttonous overeating, hyperlitigiousness, a national preoccupation with Mega Millions and Powerball—all of these are things you get in a country so used to prosperity that it's beginning to forget how the good times came in the first place.

You might know something about the Tytler Cycle. If not, here's a quick primer: Alexander Tytler, a Scottish historian who lived at the same time as the American Founding Fathers, theorized a repetitious historical cycle that leads from bondage to freedom and back again. The stages: Bondage, Spiritual Faith, Courage, Liberty, Abundance, Selfishness, Complacency, Apathy, Dependence, and Bondage again.

Another, simpler way to describe the process Tytler proposed is the old axiom that hard times makes for tough men, tough men make for good times, good times make for weak men, and weak men make for hard times.

We're dealing with a bit of that. But attitudes change much more quickly now than when Tytler lived, and weak men can grow tough quickly.

If you're being honest with yourself, you've seen the current crisis coming for years. It isn't political, it isn't economic—though it's manifesting itself in both of those ways.

It's spiritual and cultural.

While most of us still understand and remember what it is to be American, that isn't what we see on TV anymore. And it isn't what we get from our leaders. In fact, a traditional American moral viewpoint such that a mere generation ago was championed by both sides of the political aisle will get you canceled now.

And getting canceled itself is something mostly new. If you grew up in the middle part of the 20th century, you were raised on the idea that McCarthyism—generally defined as punishing people and ruining their careers for unpopular political beliefs—was one of the most un-American phenomena the nation had ever seen. But at the end of the day Joe McCarthy, the Republican senator from Wisconsin whose public anti-communist campaign in the 1950s was dedicated not to blackballing communists in Hollywood but rooting them out of the armed services in the middle of the Cold War, had nothing on the lynch mobs of Twitter today.

You aren't free to hold views the majority of Americans hold, at least not if you want to openly proclaim them while working in the public eye or in corporate America. Organizations and institutions that were formerly crucial in upholding the values and culture of the country as passed from generation to generation are mostly unrecognizable. Sporting goods stores run commercials during college football games touting their corporate missions as the promotion of women's athletics—all while remaining silent on the fast encroachment by males identifying as female in track, swimming, weightlifting, and elsewhere.

Nonsense reigns supreme in America. Everyone sees it, nobody is happy.

In every single national survey recognized by RealClearPolitics from August 1, 2021, forward, at least 52 percent of those polled said America is headed in the wrong direction. The average of the last eight before the end of 2021 had only 29.8 of respondents giving a thumbs-up; 62.4 percent gave a negative response.

This isn't just the product of a bad electoral result in 2020. Americans have been in a pretty sour mood for more than a decade—at least since it became obvious that the Iraq and Afghanistan wars wouldn't be won decisively. Our recent elections are exercises in rejection—Barack Obama was elected as a rejection of old white guy leadership, mostly due to those wars and the economic mismanagement that brought on the 2008 financial crisis, then Donald Trump won as a rejection of the Washington status quo, then Joe Biden won as a rejection (if you'll allow the point) of Trump.

And Biden's approval ratings—negative by a 43.1–53.3 margin according to the RealClearPolitics average at the end of 2021 and trending continuously worse after that—indicate that the 2024 election will be a rejection of Biden, as the 2022 midterm election will likely be a rejection of the Democrat majority in Congress.

It isn't just the right track-wrong track number, and it isn't just the recognition that Biden isn't up to the job. The American people think America is failing.

Just after the new year, a Trafalgar Group poll found that most US likely voters believe American society and culture is in decline. That's bad enough. What's worse, the opinion is shared by large majorities of self-identified Democrats, Republicans, and independents. The survey found that 76.8 percent of respondents from all political affiliations said that "American society and culture is in a state of decay," compared to only 9.8 percent who think we're in "a state of progress." The remaining 13.4 percent said they were unsure. Trafalgar pollster Robert Cahaly said the dissatisfaction cut across a wide swath of topics and issues. "Social and cultural decline is in the eye of the beholder, but what's clear is that everyone is unhappy," he told the *Washington Times*. "People on the left think America isn't 'woke' enough despite the pushback and people on the right think America is too 'woke' in a way that's being pushed on them." There's also a middle segment of voters, Cahaly said, whose views are reflected by comedians like Jerry Seinfeld, who has announced he won't perform on college campuses anymore for fear of getting "canceled."

What we're getting isn't any good, and we don't like it. We're casting about for a way to fix this and put America back on solid footing, but as we make that effort, we find things keep getting worse.

The federal deficit is now so high and our national debt so crushing that we've spent ourselves into a dangerous inflationary spiral. The federal reserve is expected to start raising interest rates in order to rein in inflation, but the federal government can't afford to service the national debt at high interest rates. Only a severe period of austerity can reverse the cycle.

The loss of the war in Afghanistan, precipitated by a willy-nilly pullout of American forces even before civilians and equipment could be evacuated, has gutted American geopolitical prestige. War has already broken out in Ukraine as of this writing and looms in Taiwan and other places as China and Russia seek to divide the spoils from the loss of Pax Americana.

The dollar's status as the world's reserve currency is fraying and might soon be lost—an eventuality that will lead to a severe turndown in the American standard of living. Our people aren't prepared for it. Civil unrest, or the threat of it, lingers in the air.

We're riven by differences over things none of us can control. Our elites insist on pigeonholing us based on race, ethnicity, sex. We thought we had a consensus for a colorblind society where opportunity for all, not guaranteed outcomes for all, was the core value. In a nanosecond, it seems, that was gone.

And of course many of us were horrified to see Two Weeks to Flatten the Curve turn into two years of medical tyranny where COVID-19 was concerned, as economic lockdowns and infringements on civil liberties in the name of "science" that cannot be questioned have changed American life in quite unwelcome ways while proving wholly ineffective in beating the virus.

We yearn for a return to normal. We worry, as we see triumphant statists boast, that this is what will pass for normal. And we worry we don't have the power to take our lives back from unelected bureaucrats at the state capitol, in Washington, and in far-off offices where oligarchs like Bill Gates and George Soros overwhelm the system with funding for things we reject.

Joe Biden's presidency looks and feels different from any other in recent memory because it is. Biden didn't run a presidential campaign in 2020, or at least not one any of us would recognize as normal, and he doesn't run his own White House. We careen from crisis to crisis, our economy and society rest on wobbling wheels, and the public knows something is seriously wrong—something we don't have the leadership to fix.

What we have, instead, are Joe Biden's Four Zeroes.

These are zeroes we don't want, can't afford, and will suffer horribly from the pursuit of. What are they?

COVID ZERO

If you paid attention to what happened in Australia in 2020 and 2021, you saw the utter destruction of a free society by sheer mass hysteria weaponized by psychotics with political power. The Aussies instituted draconian measures like strict lockdowns, alcohol rationing, and quarantine camps, which you would think would have to be the result of mass deaths and overwhelmed hospitals.

And you'd be wrong. COVID deaths in Australia were among the lowest in the world, but locking down Down Under didn't stop the Delta variant from tearing through the country and humiliating the tyrants in charge.

Why are we talking about Australia and its massive COVID overreaction? Because that dystopian reality was exactly what the Biden regime and the Democrat Party clearly wanted from the very beginning of the pandemic. When Biden demanded everybody be vaccinated and when he was willing to shred the Constitution in pursuit of cockamamie COVID mandates for masks and vaccines, that's what his handlers were pushing for.

It was always about political power. It was never about public health.

Don't think so? Then explain why the regime began rationing monoclonal antibodies—the one universally accepted treatment for COVID infections—so as to deny them from states like Florida and Texas, where the state officials committed to making them available to treat COVID patients. Arguments over other treatments like hydroxychloroquine and ivermectin and the rest notwithstanding (common antiviral drugs should never have been blackballed from use; it's criminal that they have been), the actions on monoclonal antibodies made unmistakably true what should have never been more than a heinous conspiracy theory.

This administration clearly doesn't want to treat you if you get COVID. You getting it and getting over it doesn't work for them.

They want you to take that vaccine. The vaccine is a marker for compliance, and it's also a bright-line dividing point between Americans who will accept their narratives and Americans who will not.

So it's hardly a surprise that Biden otherizes the unvaccinated. In his Christmas 2021 address to the nation, after all, he babbled about a "winter of severe illness and death" among those who didn't take the jab.

And in the meantime, the Omicron variant burned through the entire nation, inflicting essentially a bad cold on vaccinated and unvaccinated alike.

Omicron was a sad wake-up call for the administration, which wanted so badly to set a "COVID Zero" goal like the Australians attempted. Team Biden thought COVID was a killer app for the perpetuation of government power and a way to bring about the "new world order" one of the dumber bureaucrats down under was chatty enough to let slip back in the fall of 2021.

An honest government would recognize COVID as a coronavirus with an animal reservoir that can never be eradicated, push herd immunity by vaccinating senior citizens and other at-risk folks as much as possible, and then focus on treating the virus with everybody else who gets it as efficiently (common antiviral drugs openly available) and as effectively (monoclonal antibodies for everybody who still has symptoms if antivirals don't work) as possible.

But that isn't what we have, and as Sen. John Kennedy said in November 2021, "The American people, from bitter experience, have learned not to trust the federal government." Who can trust a government that foisted this campaign of lies and nonsense on us?

CARBON ZERO

This was something that slipped out of Biden's mouth as he warbled about getting to net zero carbon emissions in America by 2050. Of course, during the second presidential debate in 2020, he said he wanted it in 2025, which would essentially result in forcing Americans to pull plows and hammer steel by hand.

Biden denied during the 2020 presidential campaign that he had adopted the idiotic Green New Deal agenda. He said his was better. And he nearly made himself so toxic that his people wouldn't have been able to swipe the election away from Trump in oil-producing states like Pennsylvania when he gaffed that he would eliminate fracking. Biden managed to walk that back, sort of, but once he got elected, he went full speed into assailing the domestic fossil fuel energy sector.

And we went from being a net energy exporter in 2020 to an importer in 2021. By the summer, gasoline prices had skyrocketed, and Biden was begging OPEC and Russia to sell us more oil. The sheikhs and tin-pot dictators in that cartel couldn't believe the idiocy. And you know what Vladimir Putin's reaction was.

Everything about the shortage of oil is a predictable effect of government policy, both thanks to Biden's having kneecapped the domestic production sector and his runaway deficit spending, and the resulting inflationary effect of that. Therefore it was entirely within the Biden administration's power and portfolio to address that shortage through sound policy and management. It abjectly, deliberately failed in that regard and was therefore forced to go begging to our adversaries.

Essentially, the cartel shined Biden on, declaring higher production quotas that its members then failed to meet. From an economic standpoint, nobody at OPEC is obligated to the United States or even acting in their own interests in satisfying those quotas—not when it's obvious prices will go higher as demand outstrips supply. Make enough oil to keep the shortages from killing the global economy, sure, but not enough to resolve those shortages.

Do that and the price will continue to rise—and with it, so will the profits from that oil production.

There's an extremely simple solution to this, which is to put the domestic oil industry back to work. American supply fixes all kinds of problems vis-à-vis oil prices, economic growth, capital investment, and so on. But politically for the Democrats, domestic oil is bad—a strong oil industry in states like Pennsylvania, Colorado, and New Mexico, not to mention independent oil producers in Texas and Oklahoma getting rich, makes for a bad electoral map for them. And perhaps most importantly, the environmental groups who own this administration's energy policy won't be getting what they paid for.

So politics wins out over economics with this administration as always, and the price of oil keeps going up. Instead of Texas oilmen getting rich off that higher price, Biden was then attempting to make Russian oligarchs and Saudi sheikhs the beneficiaries by going begging at OPEC's table.

At this point it might be almost insufficient to say that this administration is blitheringly incompetent on the issue of oil and gas. That's obvious, unless you want to say that all of this was being done on purpose. I'd agree with that if this was something closer to their core competencies; they're not incompetent on the border, for example—they're evil.

But nobody in the Biden administration knows anything about how the energy business works. Proof of that was found when Biden's energy secretary, a failed former governor of Michigan named Jennifer Granholm, showed her derriere during a CNBC appearance in the fall of 2021 by laughing when asked what the administration could do to relieve market shortages in oil. Granholm, apparently oblivious to the fact that just before she took office America was a net exporter of oil, claimed that it was OPEC who set oil markets, not the US of A.

That was, as the old saying goes, shocking but not surprising. Nobody expected Granholm to have the first clue about energy policy; she had zero practical experience with energy markets.

Just like nobody in the administration knows anything about how transportation and logistics work, something else that was made unmistakably obvious when the supply chain disintegrated in the summer on Gay Mayor Pete Buttigieg's watch.

You can look at the resumes of the people in charge of the agencies regulating those things, and you can see clearly that they lack expertise. They think they can try to implement this Carbon Zero/ Green New Deal stuff, and hammer (and sickle) all these industries with fantasyland policy, and there won't be any measurable negative impact.

And they spent 2021 finding out that they were wrong.

The real question is whether Biden's camp is as intelligent as Bill Clinton's was when the bottom fell out of their first year. Clinton changed course, triangulated, and claimed credit for the successes of the GOP majority that took office in the House after the 1994 elections.

There is no evidence Team Biden has that same flexibility.

BORDER ZERO

Border? What border? There hasn't been one since Biden took office, and it's quite clearly not his intention to have one ever again while he's in power.

The illegal immigration crisis is the single worst breach of faith by a presidential administration with the founding documents and public trust of its citizenry in American history, and that includes Afghanistan. Biden did everything he could to incentivize illegal immigration for the obvious purpose of embedding as many illegals into our population and onto our government assistance rolls as possible before ultimately granting them amnesty and eventual citizenship and/or voting rights (they don't care if the illegals end up citizens so long as their vote can cancel yours out).

The proof of that came when shortly after the flood of illegals went into full deluge mode, several Democrat-run jurisdictions, New York City perhaps most prominent among them, declared that illegals would be eligible to vote in local and state elections. Technically, that can be done without violating federal law requiring that federal elections for Congress, the Senate, and the presidency be restricted to citizens, but there will be local races decided during those federal cycles, and anybody who thinks those cities and states will effectively separate out the illegals from the eligible electorate for those races is kidding himself.

And it's worth recognizing that touching off the border invasion is essentially the only thing Biden's administration has done in its first year that actually worked. Because how could it not? There are nonprofit groups facilitating the invasion into our southern border, and the president first gives an open invitation to the illegals, complete with the promise of free health care and other public-teat bennies, then sends his vice president out to explore "root causes" once regular Americans become aghast at the waves of trespassers wading across the Rio Grande.

The root cause is Joe Biden. Everybody knows that, including the leaders of the Central American countries whose citizens are migrating here. They told Kamala Harris so, which should have been the end of the border crisis. Had she listened, and the administration reversed its open-border policies, the current flood would have slowed to a trickle.

But it's only going to get worse, because the word is out, and American citizenship is being degraded as fast as our currency is debased.

It's so insultingly maddening that Biden is mandating vaccinations and negative COVID tests for business travelers from London and The Hague while giving free bus rides to red states for COVID patients from Tegucigalpa and Herat. This is what Border Zero looks like, and it's up to states like Texas to essentially nullify federal immigration law, or at least to nullify the illegal refusal to enforce federal immigration law, in order to put a stop to it.

INFLUENCE ZERO

Let's recognize that Joe Biden is a longtime peddler of influence and trader-out of American interests. That's what was clearly evident throughout the suppressed scandal surrounding his crackhead son Hunter's abandoned laptop, and its implications are nothing short of horrific.

Was the pullout of Afghanistan truly the product of incompetence or something worse? It's going to take hearings, the kind of hearings an impeachment trial can generate, for example, to know for sure. But the fact is that nothing about our Afghanistan denouement is suggestive of the ordinary idiocy of the American government. The reason the American people reacted so strongly to that debacle was that it's a break even from our "bitter experience" as Kennedy puts it.

You're surely aware of the fact that had Joe Biden set out to destroy American influence with our allies and our credibility with those with whom we'd like to make common cause, not to mention to destroy any deterrent effect we might still have with our international adversaries, he couldn't have furthered those aims any more completely than he did with the Afghanistan pullout.

We're at a point of international influence we haven't been since the 19th century, when America didn't generally even have any interest in overseas affairs. And what does that do? Well, it validates the Left's view of America. We don't have international influence because we don't deserve it. We're a racist, homophobic, misogynist country whose founding documents are invalid and whose powerful, influential, and productive must wear a hair shirt of wokeness.

So when Putin wanted to invade Ukraine, weeks went by with weak American diplomacy aimed at deterring him. And he invaded Ukraine anyway. American influence kept Europe from erupting in full-on warfare for three quarters of a century, but it only took a year of Biden's presidency and its attendant Influence Zero policies to break that streak.

It makes you wonder if this is what the Chinese bought with that investment capital Hunter finagled during his trip with the Big Guy to Beijing. Or the seven figures he picked up from the mayor of Moscow's wife.

Those are the four zeroes. But they don't add up to zero. They add up to trouble. We're in a lot of it. God help us.

How did we get here, and what can be done to get us off this sinking ship? Let's start by understanding that we've been on this trajectory for quite some time.

For example, it's a lucky thing the driver wasn't crushed when a three-story-tall lamppost fell on top of a car stopped on the corner of Pine and Taylor Streets in San Francisco on a Monday evening in August 2015.

The base of the lamppost had been corroded after countless soakings with urine from San Francisco's ubiquitous homeless, prompting a spokesman for the city's Public Utilities Commission to encourage people and dogs alike to water fire hydrants rather than light poles because the fire hydrants are made of stronger cast iron.

That collapsing lamppost is a perfect metaphor for urban Democrat governance over the past four generations, a topic we'll return to often in this book. If you want to know what inevitably results from allowing the Far Left to run cities cleared of middle-class voters over decades, picture vast armies of homeless bums gleefully micturating on public infrastructure while public officials merely beg for more clichéd choices amid terror of alienating a prominent, if noisome and not quite sane, constituency until that piddle-drenched infrastructure inevitably topples.

That is, after all, what Democrat cities ultimately put on display.

It isn't just urinating bums in San Francisco, after all. San Francisco is where Kate Steinle was murdered in a senseless spray of bullets from a drug-addled illegal alien criminal five times deported to his home in Mexico. That also happened in 2015.

Don't you remember Kate Steinle? She was a beautiful girl. Her murder had a good deal to do with the immediate political relevance of Donald Trump following his decision that year to run for president.

Francisco Sanchez, the assailant, admitted shooting Steinle but denied he meant it. He said he found the gun wrapped in a T-shirt under a bench after taking sleeping pills he found from a trash can. Sanchez claimed that he was aiming at sea lions and that the killing was accidental. You can't blame him for thinking the people of San Francisco were stupid enough to believe that. After all, they were stupid enough not to get rid of Sanchez before he killed Kate Steinle.

The sheriff in San Francisco at the time, a leftist hack named Ross Mirkarimi, refused to cooperate with immigration authorities in turning Sanchez over for deportation despite holding him for a time on a local criminal warrant. Mirkarimi, who helped found the Green Party of California before turning to the Democrats in 2012, was elected to his position in 2011 but was suspended by Mayor Ed Lee after being charged with domestic violence battery, child endangerment, and dissuading a witness in connection with a December 31, 2011, New Year's Eve brawl with his wife. To be removed from office requires a vote of nine of San Francisco's eleven county supervisors, and only seven were willing to dispatch Mirkarimi.

The Steinles rightly sued the city for all they could get, which turned out to be nothing. A judge threw out the suit. Then they sued the feds, and that was similarly thrown out. Sanchez got to keep coming back after multiple deportations and felonies, and when he finally killed someone, there was no recourse available.

That's our justice system. Remember that the next time you're stuck with an IRS audit or a traffic ticket for something idiotic. Or if you're the victim of a crime.

On a similar topic, you'll remember Baltimore's atrocious former mayor Stephanie Rawlings-Blake, who in September of 2015 agreed to a staggering $6.4 million settlement for the family of Freddie Gray, the serial street criminal whose death in police custody earlier that summer touched off a spate of rioting that placed Rawlings-Blake, then the secretary of the Democratic National Committee, in the national media spotlight.

Attorneys for the six police officers charged in Gray's death were astonished at the settlement, as it would seem impossible for any of them to get a fair trial in Baltimore after such an unprecedented sum had been paid supposedly to their "victim." Amazingly enough, a local jury acquitted three of the officers, forcing then-Baltimore district attorney Marilyn Mosby, who ultimately was indicted on two counts of perjury and making false statements on mortgage applications that she allegedly used toward the purchase of two vacation properties in Florida, to drop the charges against the other three cops.

She didn't have a choice. Statements made by another prisoner in the police van in which Gray suffered his fatal injuries indicated that the deceased was throwing himself around the van in an effort at injury and thus a cause of action against the police. Word from the defense was that the prosecution tried to suppress evidence Gray had done exactly this during his past encounters with police custody. It seems that Freddie Gray might really have been killed by too many plaintiff-attorney commercials on TV.

Baltimore's taxpayers, who are sorely outmatched by the Democrat vote-farm in most of the city, could only continue decamping for the suburbs rather than stick around to be shaken down for the Gray family's blood money. Which they did; between 2010 and 2020 Baltimore's population declined by 5.7 percent, from 620,961 to 585,708.

And in New York, it's the acrid stench of urine corroding not so much light poles but public morale. During Bill de Blasio's time as mayor, the city's homeless population grew at a double-digit pace nearly every year. Homeless tourism became an epidemic, so much so that nearly one in four of the city's homeless listed an out-of-town address. Residents shortly noticed that New York's bums, many of whom are college-aged junkies sporting ironic signs with which to panhandle, were not shy about public urination. In July 2015, one of them turned up in the middle of the street on Broadway and let loose a golden stream of civilizational decline captured by a *New York Post* photographer. Given the city's move to decriminalize the use of its streets as a latrine, the display was not especially surprising.

Those with homes behaved little better under de Blasio's leadership. For example, also in 2015 the city's annual West Indian American Day Parade festivities renewed their tradition of a bloodbath of shootings and stabbings, as the pre-party for the parade known as "J'Ouvert" became the venue for one of Governor Andrew Cuomo's aides being shot in the head. The New York cops were ordered to keep a low profile at J'Ouvert, unlike their firm supervision of more high-profile affairs like the St. Patrick's Day parade; the not-so-subtle racism associated with the assumption that equal treatment would cause a riot among the darker-hued celebrants in Crown Heights not present among the pale Irish in Manhattan was hard to miss. Naturally, the result of such enlightened policies was that West Indians couldn't have nice things; but if they could, why would they vote for de Blasio?

In the classic World War II naval film *The Caine Mutiny*, Humphrey Bogart's incompetent character Captain Queeg fouls up an amphibious landing by piloting his minesweeper away from a beach to which he was supposed to escort Higgins boats; Queeg instead drops a yellow dye marker in order to point the Marines to shore while retreating to the safety of the open water. His disgusted crew members respond by singing derisive songs about "Old Yellow-Stain," with the obvious connotation that he soiled himself in the face of a fight.

Well, the Democrats who run our major cities are producing multitudinous yellow stains of their own. Those don't appear out of cowardice in the face of the fight to preserve Western civilization amid the non-potty-trained barbarians inside the city gates. It isn't cowardice afoot but instead indifference. They simply don't care about the smell—or the yellow-stained blues afflicting the rest of us.

You already knew this. You either live in or near one of our eroding cities, or you've visited one recently. It doesn't matter which. They're all the same. In 2021, an Alabama baseball dad named David Webb took his son to a travel ball tournament in New Orleans and, following his experiences, wrote an open letter to that city's mayor, LaToya Cantrell. The letter so perfectly embodies the decline we all see that it's worth reproducing in full:

> I'm just like any other visitor to your city. I came from Alabama this weekend with my 16 year old son to participate in an all-weekend travel baseball tournament at various locations around New

Orleans: Avenger Field, UNO, and Belle Chasse High School. It's been almost 10 years since we were last here. Personally, I've been to your City dozens of times since childhood, thru my high school & college years, as a business professional for seminars and shows, as a sports spectator and concert goer, as a father of a family of 4 on vacation, and now as a run-of-mill visitor here for a purpose.

While visiting this weekend, it was my intent to carve out some time to see the normal historic downtown hotspots we've always gone to in the past as a family: Canal St, Bourbon St, French Market, Riverboat, Cafe Du Mon[de], the River Walk, Aquarium, Jackson Square, etc. while also playing our baseball games. And we did. And it was eye-opening to say the least. I thought I'd put my observations together in this letter so you could grasp what a visitor sees today in the specific areas/places I mentioned above.

First, the blight you have in the downtown area is unfathomable. Entire huge buildings off of I-10 are eye sores, and the first thing visitors see driving into the City. There are numerous dilapidated buildings with no windows, no ply board, graffitied, and/or rusted beyond repair. They are abandoned tired old structures that show scars of Katrina's aftermath I'm sure; a storm from over 16 years ago.

Second, the stench is horrific. There's always been that sewage/garbage smell associated with the old sections of New Orleans. Such smells we've picked up on as a kid while visiting. And we understand why it's like that. Once conditioned to it, it's pretty much been normal, acceptable, and tolerable because that's just how it is. You know it's going to smell so you just ignore it as best you can and move along with enthusiastic intentions of enjoying the sights, the music, the food, and everything else we've fondly grown to love about NOLA. But there's one problem now that knocks ya down almost as soon as you get out of your car: WEED. Marijuana. Dope. However you want to call it. It's absolutely disgusting. Visitors and locals are smoking that trash in plain view, out in the open, on the streets, in front of kids, families, and your police. And they (police) do nothing about it. Perhaps you have a stand-down order in place to enforce drug use on your streets? Whether it's for political reasons, a thinly-stretched understaffed police force, or sheer ambivalence, it is destroying your City in my opinion. Allowing people to blatantly smoke weed on your streets is a nasty travesty. It's also going to cost NOLA in the long run. Promise. Your City has lost its way with allowing this drug trash to run rampant.

Third, your homeless are in need of attention. We walked miles thru your historic streets this weekend. While doing so, it is apparent that they have free reign. They darken the doorways of closed up shops everywhere. They sleep on dirty streets, walkways, and sidewalks and relieve themselves anywhere they choose, urinating and defecating in front of people. I saw this first hand in the side streets of The French Market. These poor folks need a helping hand. As it stands now, it looks like your City may be avoiding this problem altogether like it doesn't exist.

Lastly, I want to strongly encourage you to react. This letter may mean absolutely nothing to you seeing that I'm an out-of-towner. But I also spent a lot of money while I was here, helping NOLA's workers and presumably adding to your tax base to take care of these problems mentioned. I'm afraid if you do nothing, NOLA's visitor base will decrease significantly in the time ahead. I doubt you seek such a goal. Tourism is NOLA's bread and butter. If you don't act now, and you let this mess continue, things will deteriorate for your wonderful City.

Have some pride, be a leader, and address this now before it's too late.

Regards,
David C. Webb
A Paying Visitor

It's depressing, to be certain, and it's everywhere.

But this book brings good news. Nothing about our current situation is unprecedented. We've been through all of it before, in various colors, and we've emerged stronger—just as we will this time.

In fact, what we're really living through in many respects is a reprise of the 1970s. It's no surprise, given that we're currently led by a 1970s throwback politician.

In some ways, the 1970s wasn't the worst decade in recent American history. The music was pretty good. Between Lynyrd Skynyrd, Led Zeppelin, the Allman Brothers, Eric Clapton, and some of the other rock greats who made their mark in that decade, its soundtrack was damned solid.

At least until disco came along.

That was a pretty good metaphor for the whole thing, actually. The 1970s was a decade spent waiting around for things to either implode or get better.

Our foreign policy certainly imploded with the Iran hostage crisis, and of course from Henry Kissinger to Jimmy Carter, the post-Vietnam stance of "détente" with the Soviet Union was essentially an exercise in waiting around to lose the Cold War.

In the 1970s, folks waited around plenty—and not just to get tickets to the *Star Wars* premiere. Gas lines were a thing, and not a good thing. In the 1970s, there was a lot of talk about "peak oil," because at the time it was thought that America had mostly tapped out its oil supply, and the rest of the world would eventually follow suit.

It's funny how things that are accepted by all the smart people tend to be so wrong. Back then there was real concern about the coming Ice Age, and it was thought that the Earth couldn't sustain a population billions smaller than it is now. We've developed a strange penchant for making elites out of the morons among us.

For an example, there's Biden, our back-to-the-1970s president, who's been wrong about almost everything since he got himself elected to the Senate in 1972.

Biden's first major vote was to oppose the construction of the Trans-Alaska Pipeline, which was a curious stance to take given that his opposition came amid the 1973 Arab oil embargo.

The parallels and ironies of that set of facts alone will make you peruse your vinyl collection in search of some theme music for Biden's retrograde politics. ELO is a bit too upbeat; Engelbert Humperdinck might be just right.

That's because Biden's opposition to oil pipelines—and in fact his near-comic bumbling on that issue—is like a bad acid trip for the domestic energy industry.

Just as he opposed the Trans-Alaska Pipeline decades ago, he opposed Keystone XL in this one. This time Biden actually shut that pipeline down, which infuriated our Canadian allies and, together with a number of other moronic decisions, sent the price of oil and gasoline skyrocketing.

But then Biden dropped the US government's opposition to Russia's Nord Stream 2 pipeline, which all but gave the European energy economy over to the Russians. That happened only a couple of weeks or so after a Russian hacking club had shut down our Colonial pipeline, which supplies some 45 percent of the motor fuel in the eastern United States.

And a ransom was paid to the Russians to reopen it, which reminds one of the Iranian hostage crisis.

Biden's administration has taken almost no time to recreate the 1970s in other ways, namely juicing inflation to levels not seen since the aftermath of the Carter administration. Inflation isn't measured like it formerly was, with a lot of the most volatile prices no longer factoring into the Consumer Price Index (CPI). But in April 2021 the CPI still showed a whopping increase of more than 4 percent, and commodities like lumber, corn, and copper were through the roof. By the end of the year the CPI was scratching at the door of 8 percent, and effective inflation was well within the double-digit range. That put paid to the claim by Biden's functionaries that inflation was merely a momentary blip as the economy recovered from COVID.

Here's one difference from the 1970s: back then the liberals who ran the country simply didn't know what they were doing. That's true of Biden now, but his handlers do know. They don't believe in peak oil, but they're trying to create it by shutting down exploration and drilling. They're also working to create shortages of virtually everything as part of the idiotic Green New Deal agenda the Democrat Party has embraced. And when asked about these things, their response is to dismiss them as "first-world problems," as Psaki did in groaning about "delayed Pelotons" when asked about the supply chain collapse.

The Black Panthers are also back, though they never really went away. But this time the strident racial Marxism of the Huey Newton set is ensconced in an academic discipline of sorts called Critical Race Theory, which has the full faith and credit of the federal government pushing it from grade school to grad school. And the new gang in the streets with raised fists calls itself Black Lives Matter, though what comes out of the mouths of some of its most vocal proponents sounds almost like George Wallace.

A lot of the worst things about the 1970s are back with a vengeance.

That same year Biden voted against the Alaska pipeline, 1973, saw Israel under attack in the Yom Kippur War, a dicey affair that ended inconclusively. In 2021, Israel spent half the summer under attack by Hamas, which launched rockets from Gaza and used children as human shields to hide behind. Both in 1973 and today, the Israelis are feeling left quite a bit alone by their supposed American allies. Then it was our dependence on Arab oil that explained our tepid support; now it's Biden's dependence on efforts to get in bed with the Iranians for some strange reason.

And just like back in the 1970s, there's a "reopening" of relations with China. When Richard Nixon first broke bread with the Chinese communists, it was seen as a master stroke in international relations, sawing China off from an alliance with the Soviets. But today's thawing of relations with the ChiComs is a little less sensible given that the world is waking up to the fact that the Chinese gave us the Wuhan virus as an opening gambit.

The abject failure of the Biden administration or its Democrat allies in Congress to do something about Beijing's hosting of the "genocide Olympics" in February 2022, amid all of the horrid behavior of that regime in abusing its people in Xinjiang, Hong Kong, and elsewhere, its lack of COVID transparency, or worse, and its overt militarism and piracy of intellectual property makes the current kowtowing look a lot worse than Nixon's Cold War end run.

In the 1970s, there was hope that an opening to China would bring about freedom and prosperity there. Now? We're beginning to find a national consensus in favor of closing that door before we lose all our freedom and prosperity to Chinese dominance.

It was in the 1970s that we stopped recognizing Taiwan as a sovereign nation, though we continued treating it as one. Pretty soon there won't be a Taiwan to recognize, the way things are going.

We've gone from Billy Carter to Hunter Biden, and that's not a good trade. Nor is going from Barbara Jordan to Sheila Jackson Lee. LeBron James has found a way to be more subversive than Kareem Abdul-Jabbar without changing his name, and watching New York go bankrupt again isn't a fun experience. Nor is recognizing that the 1970s wants its murder rate back.

The *Rocky Horror Picture Show* first appeared on movie screens in 1975. There aren't too many movie screens in use right now, but you can find Dr. Frank N. Furter, or something resembling Tim Curry's intentionally awful character, at pretty much any local library during Drag Queen Story Hour or in Biden's Health and Human Services Department, where a man named Richard Levine who calls himself Rachel is our first "female" cross-dressing admiral. Other manifestations of that movie can currently be found on reality TV.

And Planned Parenthood went from cranking up the post-*Roe v. Wade* abortion machine in the 1970s to now ramping up delivery of sex-change hormones to kids. That reprise of Planned Parenthood's business model expansion isn't overly welcome either.

But we've at least managed to trade bell bottoms for skinny jeans. Whether or not that's a step up probably depends on the wearer.

The Weathermen are now Antifa, with a similar sluggishness on the part of law enforcement to do anything about their mayhem. Jim Jones's sermons are now regurgitated on college campuses and video blogs by the Squad; everybody's drinking the Kool-Aid, and the same leftist San Francisco politicians who patronized and propped up Jones are still around, more powerful than ever.

At least *The Andromeda Strain* was just a movie. It seemed more realistic than the response to COVID-19 has been.

The good news is that the 1970s begat the 1980s, as after a decade of mostly awful culture and thoroughly awful politics America was desperate for a Ronald Reagan to lead a renaissance.

Perhaps 2024 will be 1980. That would be fine. We'll need it after weathering this '70s show Biden is putting on.

The things that don't work in America are the way they are because they're corrupted and obsolete. But America isn't corrupted and obsolete. America is still around, and America is still the beacon of freedom, innovation, and prosperity the world turns to.

As terrible as we think things are, there is still a line waiting to get in. It's unquestionably a policy failure that two million people immigrated illegally to this country in 2021—but the fact that two million people were willing to break the law to get into the USA still puts us far ahead of anywhere else as a place worth living in. There is no line to get into Russia or Venezuela or Iran. More people want out of China than in.

America isn't over. America doesn't need any kind of "fundamental transformation," as Obama preened about and Biden mumbles in echo.

America simply needs a revival. A big one. Not just a 1980-style rout of an election. We need a sea change in how we operate, and current realities indicate that's exactly what's coming.

We need to rediscover our spirit and our civil society. We need a revival of Main Street at the expense of the multinational corporations that have clawed too much of our economy into their orbits. We need the revival of our justice system our juries have consistently demanded from suspect prosecutors and judges. We need a cultural revival, one in which the arts—performing, visual, recording, and otherwise—validate us as a society rather than turn on us.

And yes, we need a spiritual revival as well.

In these pages you'll see a rather stark assessment of modern-day America, though in the context of a broader historical framework. You'll see a discussion of both the Left and the Right, especially from the standpoint of why neither one seems capable of governing effectively anymore. And then you'll see a vision of an America that is both not very far away and quintessentially different from what Team Biden has wrought so far in its transformationally awful term.

Hopefully this book will spark ideas and start a conversation about that vision and how to bring it about.

CHAPTER 2

James Piereson and the Fourth Revolution

Perhaps it isn't often that a book will recommend the reader pick up another book, but for those who are concerned that America's precipitous decline over the past decade or so might signal a permanent state of crisis from which we can't recover, I would suggest some additional research.

In 2015, a couple of months before Donald Trump descended that escalator and changed American politics in ways our political establishment has still not sufficiently processed, a historian named James Piereson penned *Shattered Consensus: The Rise and Decline of America's Postwar Political Order*. It's a very underrated piece and an excellent read, and what it details is something all patriots should understand about where we are as a country.

Namely, that we've been through most of the things that terrify us before, and we've come through them quite well. American society is flexible. It adapts. It flows past problems and makes them irrelevant.

America moves on.

Piereson's book divides American history into three distinct periods, the last of which is coming to an end and causing the dislocation and rancor of the past several years. The eras he describes were born of major societal upheavals—Jefferson's "Revolution of 1800," the Civil War, the Great Depression—which concluded with lasting institutional and cultural adjustments that set the stage for new phases of political and economic development.

Each of the eras Piereson describes was formed by the creation of a national consensus around a set of policies and cultural imperatives that informed the times, a consensus both major political parties generally wedded themselves to.

Piereson says, in fact, that it's more accurate to say America has operated on the basis of a one-and-a-half-party system rather than a two-party system through most of its history, because the dominant party will set the agenda for a given era, and the opposition then has no choice but to adapt to the times and take on a "me, too" approach to its search for political power.

Another way to describe this would be to refer to the Overton Window, the political model first proposed by policy analyst Joseph P. Overton of the Mackinac Center for Public Policy. Overton's core concept is that politicians are limited in what policy ideas they can support, as they can generally only pursue policies that are widely accepted throughout society as legitimate policy options. When a consensus around public policy forms, as has happened periodically in our history, the Overton Window is thus created. And the Overton Window doesn't just apply to politics; some version of it or other is present in business, culture, sports...you name it. It's only the really exceptional, or fabulously incompetent, figures in a given field of endeavor who'll do something truly outside of the main, and while some of those departures shake the ground, the majority of them are fizzles.

From a political perspective, when you have a period of upheaval that makes new ideas and practices acceptable to a receptive electorate, that Overton Window shifts and then settles. All the players then calibrate their plays based on the new reality. Any departures from it usually have to be subtle and gradual.

Consider the attempts during the George W. Bush administration to add some sort of private sector investment option for younger people within the Social Security system, and you'll understand how difficult it is to change the political consensus.

In the first historical era Piereson describes, which was set in place with President Thomas Jefferson's "Revolution of 1800," the Democratic Party assumed dominance in national politics as the Federalists collapsed. America was mostly a rural nation then, with some lightly industrialized urban areas in the northern states, and we governed ourselves according to the needs of rural and agricultural interests. The international cotton trade, which was at the time centered in the American South and depended on large plantations employing sizable slave labor forces, was perhaps the single most powerful economic reality of the time.

The Democrats were, by current standards, anti-capitalist, in the sense that national policy was not formulated to incentivize capital growth. They were expansionist; America engaged in diplomatic activity and military expeditions on several occasions for the purpose of adding territory from France, Spain, Mexico, and other nations.

And of course, they were pro-slavery. It was the coming apart of that national consensus on slavery which brought a bloody end to that first American era in the Civil War.

Looking back on that era one might have concluded that the Civil War could have been avoided were some grand bargain struck to buy out the Southern plantation owners. But no such bargain was available within the Overton Window at the time. When the war came, that window was obliterated along with the political and social consensus of the antebellum era.

And after a decade and change of war and reconstruction, a new era and a new consensus emerged. And there were major changes from the America of Jefferson and Jackson to that of Lincoln and Grant.

This remained an expansionist nation; in fact, with the question of slavery having been removed from the table with the Union victory in the war and the passage of the Thirteenth Amendment, there were no longer impediments to Americans settling the full length and breadth of what became the continental forty-eight states.

But while the pre-Civil War national economic policy had been pro-rural and anti-capitalist, what came next was pro-industrial, heavily pro-capitalist, and radically pro-growth.

The federal government became a main driver of national infrastructure, particularly with the building of the transcontinental railroad in the 1870s, and business interests played an unprecedented role in the formation of national policy. American culture and politics moved strongly toward a homogenous character; Southern states were encouraged, if not dictated, to adopt policies mimicking those of the North, and the new states and territories being added in the West were likewise influenced to copy the Union states.

As technology and commerce created America as an interconnected nation, and as America's cities rapidly grew to service the needs of the burgeoning industrial revolution, inevitably the political and cultural post-Civil War/Gilded Age consensus became frayed.

Ultimately, between the international balance of payments problem arising out of World War I, the inequalities between capital and labor made into crisis following the stock market crash of 1929, and the rise of socialist movements in Russia, Germany, Italy, and other European countries amid a global economic depression, the second era of American history fell apart.

What came next began with Franklin Delano Roosevelt's New Deal and continued through American victory in World War II to generate the current American era. Namely, the creation of the modern welfare and regulatory state, together with the development of the military-industrial-intelligence complex and the attendant overseas adventurism to fuel it.

We're living in the era of the biggest government in the history of mankind, and strangely enough given that the most successful presidents of the age—Eisenhower, Nixon, and Reagan, defined by their key accomplishments on the economic and geopolitical stages—were Republicans, this is most certainly a Democrat era. That was established some ninety years ago, when FDR and Harry Truman won five straight presidential elections from 1932 to 1948, and the policy agenda created and cured in those years amid the Great Depression and World War II, when Democrats dominated both the White House and Capitol Hill, was hardened to the point that it couldn't be broken by Republican administrations who came later. Most of those GOP administrations didn't even try.

Just as previous eras were similarly built by party dominance, Democrats won six elections between 1800 and 1820 as the first era of American political consensus was established, and Republicans won six straight between 1860 and 1880 to construct the second era. It's Piereson's theory, which this book shares, that one of the two parties is about to go on a similar run and establish a new political consensus.

All of the key consensus items in American national policy originated on the Left: Social Security. Medicare. Medicaid and other entitlement programs for the poor. The massive crush of federal agencies governing every aspect of American life. Foreign aid directed toward furthering American progressive aims across the world, and the creation of a utopian globalist world-government entity in the United Nations. An activist, politicized judicial branch. And finally, the recent flowering of the woke movement out of decades of marinating critical theory in the universities the Left has controlled.

The first era in American history was a Democrat era. The second was clearly Republican. This era, which is ending now, has belonged to the Democrats.

It's reasonable to believe the fourth era will be a Republican one. But only if Republicans are worthy to set the next consensus. And that's why a revivalist movement is necessary.

With a few exceptions, every facet of the Republican Party's conduct since the birth of the New Deal is inadequate to the kind of political leadership necessary for setting the tone for the fourth era of American history.

And yet it has to be the Republican Party which assumes that leadership, because the Democrats are a spent political force.

It might seem strange to say that, given the leftward lurch you can see everywhere in America—mostly among the culture and chiefly among our monolithic ruling elite class. Corporate America, Big Tech, Hollywood, the Washington establishment, Wall Street—each of them have been increasingly friendlier to an agenda the Democrat Party set decades ago and is attempting to expand. And the Democrat presidential candidate has won the popular vote in every election since 1992, save for George W. Bush's victory over the hapless, French-looking John Kerry in 2004.

But that agenda is out of gas. The Democrats can't run on it much anymore. And attempts by people within that party to install new ideas have gone exactly nowhere.

What are the political initiatives animating the Democrat Party today? They've all got whiskers on them. Every one of their big projects are leftovers from an era rapidly becoming bygone.

Medicare for all? Essentially, that's a copycat plan to install the British National Health Service, or its counterpart in Canada, here in America. But the American public continues resisting full-on socialized medicine, and the passage of Obamacare, the most aggressive attempt at socializing health care they've been successful in enacting, was one of the most Pyrrhic victories in the annals of American politics.

In fact, Obamacare ended up greatly fueling the growth of the Tea Party movement, which had begun in 2009 as a result of a famous Rick Santelli CNBC rant and wiped out the Democrats' majority in the House. The Tea Party faded away as a coherent political force, but it came back a few years later as the Make America Great Again phenomenon upon Trump's political rise in 2015 and 2016. This book will make the case that it'll resurge once again in

2022 and 2024 as revivalism, and finally become an unstoppable force that changes American politics.

But the common threads that run through all three iterations of pushback against Democrat rule are unmistakable.

First, all three were and are truly organic, grassroots-driven movements. Unlike Black Lives Matter, for example, which is the recipient of billions of dollars in corporate guilt money and has made multimillionaires of its leaders like Patrisse Cullors, nobody created the Tea Party movement. Nobody created the MAGA movement either. Trump may have branded it, but his rallies and the huge crowds at, for example, Trump boat parades are without a doubt bottom-up phenomena.

And the polls showing a likely Republican wipeout in the fall of 2022 certainly aren't a reflection of the popularity of, say, Mitch McConnell or Kevin McCarthy. There isn't a galvanizing figure driving the GOP's midterm hopes.

In other words, the Democrat Party that branded itself so long ago as the party of the little guy and the masses now seems to have a nasty habit of generating a popular revolt every time it attempts to use political power to push its agenda.

That, friends, is a spent political force.

As a quick historical aside, each of our previous political eras has come following a highly tumultuous and spectacularly unsuccessful presidency. Jefferson took office following the four-year term of John Adams, a great patriot whose presidency was nonetheless chaotic and quite unpopular given controversies like the civil unrest in response to the Direct Tax of 1798, which led to the Alien and Sedition Acts; the XYZ Affair and the "Quasi-War" between America and France; and the intraparty rivalry between Adams and

Alexander Hamilton. Adams's presidency, in retrospect, was a reasonably successful one, but as to his popularity it was an unmitigated disaster.

But Adams's performance holds up exceptionally well in comparison to that of James Buchanan, who held office from 1857–61 and whose administration heralded the collapse of the first era of American political consensus. Generally regarded as the worst president in the nation's history, Buchanan presided over a sharp economic recession and the centrifugal forces surrounding slavery that ultimately tore America apart. His robust endorsement of the ridiculous Dred Scott decision greatly hastened Northern passions for abolition and, consequently, Southern disillusionment with remaining in the union.

And then there was Herbert Hoover, who was in office when the Great Depression began. Virtually everything Hoover did after the 1929 stock market crash was a mistake, most notably signing the 1930 Smoot-Hawley tariff bill, which crashed international trade at a time when economic activity was spiraling downward, and the Revenue Act of 1932, which raised taxes in the middle of an economic recession. Hoover was a great American in many respects, but as a president he was disastrous in ways that had the effect of ushering in a whole new era of American politics.

You're welcome to consider these examples in light of the current occupant of the White House.

The Democrats embraced the idea of the Green New Deal, which is one of the most top-down political initiatives ever invented. Essentially, the Green New Deal is about electric cars, renewable energy, and massive government regulation of industry. None of those things poll particularly well, and there is certainly no grass-roots movement to support them.

They're for "antiracism," which essentially amounts to an embrace of Critical Race Theory (CRT). How does that play? In Virginia, which had been trending blue for more than a decade, voters abruptly turned against former Governor Terry McAuliffe and instead elected a political newcomer in Glenn Youngkin with Critical Race Theory as the chief issue driving the 2021 gubernatorial race there. Republicans captured Virginia's other two statewide elections, for lieutenant governor and attorney general, and stole the majority in Virginia's House of Delegates from the Democrats—all as a reaction to woke CRT and transgender policies, mostly in the state's public schools.

And then there's the question of immigration. The Democrats, since Ted Kennedy spearheaded the 1965 immigration bill, have vigorously pushed an open borders immigration policy with the most cynical motivation possible: importing a new electorate that they believe will embrace policies a majority of native-born Americans will not.

In this, the Democrats got a gigantic free pass from the Republican Party—until the waves of populist conservative movements began. The Tea Party had as one of its motivating factors the limitation on illegal immigration, though the Republicans who came to power as a result of their activism didn't listen very much. Then Trump came along and prioritized securing the border and slowing down immigration as a whole, and the issue was a winner for him.

Then came Joe Biden and two million illegal immigrants coming across the border in 2021. Is that a political asset to his party?

Not according to Rasmussen Reports. At the height of the border mess Biden's policies set loose, in September 2021 a Rasmussen survey asked likely voters to rate Biden on the border and illegal immigration. The numbers? Thirteen percent rated Biden as excellent. Another 17 percent rated the president as good, and 15 percent said Biden was doing a fair job on immigration.

And 52 percent rated Biden's handling of immigration issues as poor.

Worse, a CBS News poll in January 2022 found Biden upside down by a 36–64 count on his handling of immigration.

It's obvious the open border is a long-term play. When New York and California and other Democrat-run jurisdictions began acting to give the vote to non-citizens, that was a clear signal that importing a new electorate was what this was all about.

But the importation only works if it doesn't cost the Democrats current voters. And there is an unmistakable trend indicating that, particularly among Hispanics, they're bleeding citizens in order to secure the allegiance of non-citizens.

That isn't a particularly good trade. And when word came out that a plurality of new arrivals over the border in 2021 were Venezuelans, it raised questions. Venezuelans are, after all, refugees from the kind of socialism the Hard Left in this country has been spoiling for since Barack Obama beat Hillary Clinton in the 2008 Democrat primaries.

The New Deal and Great Society, which were the policy agenda highlights of what Piereson calls the Third Era for the Democrats, were big political hits. But the positive policy effects of those agendas have largely petered out at this point.

The war on poverty hasn't eliminated poverty. It just redefined it. When it's more lucrative to draw government assistance than work a minimum wage job in more states than not, and of course when obesity is a larger national problem than malnutrition, the real question of poverty is whether it should be defined by values and behavior rather than dollars and cents.

We've had a solid decade in which the American people have been expressing more and more loudly our displeasure at the status quo our mostly Democrat ruling elite have been giving us, and the active ingredient among the Democrats promises more and more of the same.

Given that, it's really just been a matter of when Republicans would catch up to them and pass them by.

In January of 2022, Gallup released the results of their quarterly party-identification survey. The results were eye-opening. Whereas the quarterly survey released in January 2021 showed Democrats with a 49–40 party-ID advantage, one year later, after the public had endured a year of mostly unfettered Democrat political control, the number had flipped almost completely. Republicans had a 47–42 advantage in the January 2022 survey.

Since Gallup began quarterly polling for party identification in 1991, in only five of those quarterly surveys have Republicans held a five-point lead. GOP political consultant Josh Jordan put the result in an electoral context. "If that were to hold into the 2022 midterms it would be a seismic victory on election night—this is the biggest advantage for Republicans since the 1994 'Republican Revolution,'" he said in a tweet.

Then there was the January 2022 POLITICO/Morning Consult poll that delivered a fairly broad-based rejection of Democrats on policy grounds. On the economy, the poll's respondents favored the GOP by a 47–34 count. On jobs, 45–35. On immigration, 45–37. On national security, 49–32. On gun policy, 45–36. There were items where Democrats fared slightly better, like COVID policy and climate change, but the poll's respondents clearly indicated those questions named above were more important.

Polling results, which are certainly fleeting and reflect a mere snapshot of public opinion at best, shouldn't be used as predictive of long-term trends. But in this case there is a pattern going back to the performance of the Obama administration, or even the early years of the Clinton administration before the 1994 elections Jordan references. The American public recoils from Democrat governance everywhere it's in evidence.

That pattern, plus the manifest fact that our entitlement/welfare state is fiscally unsustainable as is, much less expandable in any way, indicates that all assumptions about this current era and its long-held basket of policies and programs are invalid. In *Shattered Consensus*, Piereson makes this point with erudition:

> "Some people may find it difficult to imagine that our present system of social programs and entitlements might be undone because it is widely assumed that the welfare state is a historical destination with no further political possibilities beyond it—that we have at length reached the 'end of history,' where the future is simply a gradually improving extension of the present. This is the conventional view, and for many of us it is a comforting expectation. When systems have been in

place for a long time, there is a tendency to believe that they are natural or permanent, even as their foundations may be crumbling underfoot. We should bear in mind that something similar was believed not so long ago about other deeply rooted institutions, such as slavery, the gold standard, and the British Empire. An uprooting of long-established institutions may be rare, but that is not the same as impossible.

"Rare events of low probability, moreover, have disproportionate effects on our lives, as Nassim Nicholas Taleb writes in *The Black Swan*: 'Almost everything in social life is produced by rare but consequential shocks and jumps, while almost everything studied about social life focuses on the "normal,"....' We have been fortunate to live in a time when most change happens in gradual and incremental steps. But not always: many wise heads have gone wrong by making projections from current trends, as when Norman Angell wrote in 1910 that a war among the European powers was inconceivable, or when the economist Irving Fisher said in 1929 that stocks had reached a permanently high plateau, or when John Kenneth Galbraith said in the 1980s that the Soviet Union was as stable as the United States.

"A 'fourth revolution' in the American political system is not inconceivable; neither does it have to mean a decline of civilization or the end

> of America. Quite the opposite—it could launch a new phase of growth and dynamism in the American experiment."

The problem is, we don't particularly embrace Republican governance either, at least not at the national level. Republican governors in red states like Florida, Texas, South Carolina, Arizona, and Tennessee seem to do just fine in both attracting support of the population and pulling economic migrants from other states.

And that Gallup survey showing the major shift from D to R has been too long in coming. Just as, historically, we're overdue for the fourth revolution Piereson discusses in his book. It's been ninety years since the current political era began with the 1932 election; the first American era only lasted sixty years, and the second lasted seventy-two years.

The current burgeoning disapproval of Team Biden isn't even reflective of anything the GOP is doing correctly at present. It's a pure public rejection of a leftist Democrat political regime that has attempted to press the residue of its agenda into reality over the objections of the majority of the American people. All Republicans have to do is oppose crazy policies like Build Back Better, the Green New Deal, institutionalizing the irregularities of the 2020 elections into federal law, and cementing Critical Race Theory as the basis of governmental administration, and of course they're going to become the majority party.

The problem is, over the majority of this New Deal-postwar era, Republican politicians have only really been successful when rejecting the aggressions of the Democrats. Actual Republican policy offensives that have broad public support and move the country forward have been few and far between. In particular the eight wasted years of George W. Bush's presidency, which were defined by de facto open borders immigration policy, expansion of entitlements, and poorly planned, nonstrategic foreign wars, cemented the GOP in the public eye as the Stupid Party. And that failure to seize the initiative as the Democrats have run out of philosophical gas especially accounts for America's poor performance and geopolitical decline over the past decade.

The American people don't take well to decline. There will be political consequences to it; those are overdue. We can see the beginnings of them all around us. But if the GOP is to take up the mantle of reforming America and creating a new governing consensus that lasts a lifetime, it will need to up its game and abandon the ways of its political establishment. It's time for visionaries and opportunists, ruthless operatives and independent thinkers.

CHAPTER 3

The Era of Consensus Politics Is Over

One of the primary characteristics of the New Deal/post-WWII era that is now ending has been the prevalence of consensus between Republicans and Democrats on many or most of the great issues facing the country. Obamacare's passage in March 2010 was a watershed moment in that it was the first major piece of legislation in almost a century passed solely along party lines, and the Biden administration hardly even bothers to seek consensus even with paper-thin legislative majorities. But the falling away of consensus didn't begin with Obamacare. It really began with Democrat governance of America's cities in the latter years of the 20th century.

In a speech he gave at the University of Colorado in March 2019, Piereson openly wondered about the formation of a new political consensus in a country where not only do Americans not agree with each other but openly dislike each other.

There is a great deal of contempt out there. Consider a survey done by Rasmussen Reports in conjunction with the Heartland Institute in the first week of January 2022, which found that:

- 45 percent of Democrats would favor governments requiring citizens to temporarily live in designated facilities or locations if they refuse to get a COVID-19 vaccine.
- 29 percent of Democratic voters would support temporarily removing parents' custody of their children if parents refuse to take the COVID-19 vaccine.
- 59 percent of Democratic voters would favor a government policy requiring that citizens remain confined to their homes at all times, except for emergencies, if they refuse to get a COVID-19 vaccine.
- Nearly half (48 percent) of Democratic voters think federal and state governments should be able to fine or imprison individuals who publicly question the efficacy of the existing COVID-19 vaccines.

It's pretty clear that a country in which members of one political party are fairly enthusiastic about the idea of imprisoning people for refusing an experimental vaccine of questionable effectiveness is a country with some problems in national unity.

We grew up expecting, as Americans, that there were basic values and assumptions we could all share. The major items for debate between Left and Right, Democrats and Republicans were over how the social goods we all wanted would be achieved.

But if Democrats want to put the unvaccinated in concentration camps until they take the jab, and if Democrats are for destroying bipartisan institutions like the Senate filibuster, packing the Supreme Court, giving statehood to Puerto Rico and the District of Columbia, and imposing socialist programs like "Medicare for all" and the Green New Deal, it's clear we don't share the same values and assumptions anymore.

You can't operate on the basis of consensus politics when there is no consensus. And very rapidly, it's abundantly clear we don't have a consensus.

"The far left hates everyone, themselves included!" tweeted Elon Musk in April 2022, after a week-long national panic among Democrats ensued following his purchase of the social media company. Musk was not wrong.

We're going to have to have a spirited fight for the future of the country, and it's going to be rough sailing for a while. What's needed are leaders with the stomach for that fight.

But before we talk about the effect of our loss of cohesion, let's talk about how we got here. To do this, we'll start with a story that took place in February of 2020—just before the COVID epidemic got rolling.

The end of winter in New Orleans coincides with a festival for which the city is best known and that serves as the primary fuel for its tourism-dependent economy. Fat Tuesday, or in the local vernacular, Mardi Gras, is a two-week drinking party manifesting itself in the consumption of sugary, oval baked products and the sublime mindless entertainment of standing streetside as masked revelers throw plastic beads from elaborately decorated trailers pulled by tractors interspersed among high school marching bands as parades make their way along venerable tree-lined boulevards.

The Mardi Gras carnival season is so much fun it hurts. Most people who participate in full have made themselves more or less catatonic and in need of recuperation well in advance of the actual Mardi Gras date. By Ash Wednesday, the somber religiosity of having one's forehead marked with ash in the Catholic tradition is usually made so by a colossal, debilitating hangover on the part of those who fully invest in the carnival.

And few who annually do Mardi Gras would trade the experience for anything. It's spring break without the spring. And without Mardi Gras, New Orleans—a declining port city with extreme demographic issues, a virtually nonexistent manufacturing base, and an economy so stunted that downtown office buildings are being redeveloped as high-rise condominiums for rich out-of-towners to turn over as Airbnb properties—would be Baltimore.

The public-sector dysfunction of New Orleans is legendary.

As much of the city is reclaimed swampland lying in a bowl between the banks of the Mississippi River to the south and the shore of Lake Pontchartrain to the north, New Orleans depends on a massive pump-and-drain infrastructure which, more than a century ago, was a miracle of modern engineering. But despite millions—billions—of your tax dollars poured into New Orleans following the failure of federally built levees after Hurricane Katrina to reinforce that drainage system, the pumps are mostly the same ones that have been around since before the New Deal.

All that money poured on the Big Easy, and a big chunk of the drainage system still runs on an obsolete power system that only laboriously connects to the city's power grid. One of the turbines powering the pumps spent six years offline from 2012 to 2018 as the system's managers lazily pondered its future.

Late in 2021, the FBI conducted raids on New Orleans's Sewerage and Water Board, the public agency in charge of that drainage system, as part of a corruption investigation. The raids weren't even much of a campaign issue for the mayor, Compton transplant and leftist community organizer LaToya Cantrell, despite her billet as the agency's president (which is part of the mayor's portfolio). Cantrell won reelection in a jungle primary with well more than 60 percent of the vote.

Something else that doesn't work in New Orleans is its police. Crime has always been rampant in the Big Easy, but since Cantrell's predecessor, Mitch Landrieu, conspired with former Obama Attorney General Eric Holder for a 2011 consent decree that all but neutered the New Orleans Police Department, the lawlessness has become endemic. Things are so bad that random gunshots routinely impact car windshields while motorists speed past the worst parts of the city on I-10, and carjackings barely make the news anymore, save for when, in one day in January 2022, there were no less than *nine* such episodes.

NOPD now unofficially stands for Not Our Problem, Dude, and the morale of the force reflects that spirit. So does recruitment. It isn't that New Orleans defunded the police, the cops themselves did the job by simply leaving for better-run and better-supported suburban forces like the Jefferson Parish Sheriff's Office next door. Cantrell and her predecessors have sent signals for years that the NOPD wasn't a priority or even an asset to their way of thinking, and nobody chooses to be an orphan.

But in February of 2020 the dwindling number of police officers in New Orleans began to impact the city's signature festival event in a way no one expected, though they probably should have.

Cantrell imposed several rules on the krewes—a krewe (pronounced "crew") is a club that puts on a parade, or ball, or both during the Mardi Gras carnival—in advance of the 2020 Mardi Gras. One of them was a time restriction on parades because the city didn't want to budget for police overtime, and that restriction meant the parades would be motoring past the crowds just a little faster than normal.

Or even a lot faster.

Another restriction, which wasn't new, was a maximum of forty-five floats per parade. A float is defined by the number of "pull-units"—usually tractors, but in the more lowbrow parades a semitruck is used as a pull-unit—and one means of expanding the number of krewe members in a parade while still staying within the forty-five-float limit is the use of a "tandem float." Simply, that means attaching a tractor to two trailers rather than one.

Nobody really thought of tandem floats as unsafe, but then somebody who inexplicably tried to cross the street in the middle of the Krewe of Nyx parade by ducking under the connection of a tandem float didn't manage to survive the experience. A few nights later, someone else also fell under a tandem float during the Krewe of Endymion parade.

Cantrell then banned tandem floats while castigating not the irresponsibility of the drunks and stoners along the parade routes who don't bother staying behind the barricades, but that of the krewes putting on the parades.

Without a word, of course, about her own responsibility for having imposed the time restriction that incentivized the high rates of speed at which the Nyx and Endymion floats were traveling.

Because she didn't have enough cops to work those parades.

There was no Mardi Gras in 2021. Its absence was blamed on COVID. But the future of the carnival in the city is very much in doubt due to New Orleans's crumbling public services. In December 2021, the city announced a fresh round of parade-route limitations and restrictions.

"Every parade will be asked to make some accommodations," Cantrell said. "No one is being singled out; no one is being given special treatment."

She shortened the parade routes so as to better reflect the ability of the police to staff them. The parades were shaved by a third—which was a number reflective of the one in three hotel rooms in the city that sat empty during the 2022 carnival.

Will the krewes agree to share the pain of parading through a declining, dying city? Not forever. It's really a matter of time before most of the bigger parades finally join the population in decamping for the suburbs.

You could see this as a tragedy, and in one sense it is. But consider something else that happened in New Orleans within recent vintage; namely, that a number of works of public art that had been bedrocks of the city's cultural landscape for well more than a century were bowdlerized.

One of them was a massive, iconic statue of Confederate General Robert E. Lee, which stood atop a gigantic pedestal in the middle of a traffic circle named for the general. Another was a beautiful equestrian statue of a local figure, Confederate General P. G. T. Beauregard. Landrieu, engaged at the time in an interracial extramarital affair and supposedly seeking the approval of his paramour, spent virtually the entirety of his second term seeking to remove those statues.

Landrieu pontificated at length about the woke necessity to fight racism, going so far as to say that the Confederacy only lasted four years and therefore it was the *preservation* of history rather than the elimination of it to take those statues down. A fringe communist group, Take 'Em Down NOLA, funded by East Coast white money and fronted by a dashiki-wearing, self-described Maoist black professor at Southern University's New Orleans campus named Malcolm Suber, spurred what turned out to be an exceedingly small grassroots movement agitating for the bowdlerization.

Three years of agitation went by before Landrieu finally dragooned the city's fire department and police into toppling the Lee and Beauregard statues, plus another of Confederate President Jefferson Davis, and leaving defaced empty pedestals in their wake.

All the while, those not living in the city and thus having no voice in the proceedings (while leftist money from outside New Orleans fueled the expurgation campaign) were perplexed. Polls indicated more than two-thirds of Louisianans opposed the removal of the monuments. Even in the city itself the polls were split. No clear consensus on the subject was present despite a sustained, determined effort by the local legacy media to support Landrieu's folly.

If you think that's evidence of the continuing racism of the ignorant rubes of the Bayou State, understand the context behind which the Lee and Beauregard statues were erected in the first place.

Lee had been venerated in the post-Civil War period not just for his military acumen during the war, after all, but for his postwar efforts at stitching the country back together. He voiced his support for the end of slavery in terms that must have been shocking to the average Southerner. "So far from engaging in a war to perpetuate slavery, I am rejoiced that slavery is abolished," he said. "I believe it will be greatly for the interests of the South. So fully am I satisfied of this, as regards Virginia especially, that I would cheerfully have lost all I have lost by the war, and have suffered all I have suffered, to have this object attained."

He spent his final years as present of then-Washington College, later renamed Washington & Lee, promoting the training of a new generation of Southerners to be loyal citizens of a free America.

Some racist figure, this. There's a reason why, before Critical Race Theory and other woke aggressions came to the fore, Robert E. Lee was universally acknowledged as one of the greatest American figures of the 19th century, and statues of him could be found even in Union states.

As for Beauregard, who was born and raised in the town of Chalmette just east of New Orleans and who settled in the city after the war as a local celebrity and hero, his expurgation was even more puzzling. Beauregard was such a profoundly "racist" figure that in 1872 he helped form the Reform Party of Louisiana, which had as its central philosophical precept the promotion of equal civil and political rights for blacks. At a symposium put on to promote the party's agenda of equal political rights, the sharing of political offices equally among the races, black land ownership, antidiscrimination, and antisegregation, Beauregard said this:

> "I am persuaded that the natural relation between the white and colored people is that of friendship, I am persuaded that their interests are identical; that their destinies in this state, where the two races are equally divided are linked together, and that there is no prosperity in Louisiana that must

> not be the result of their cooperation. I am equally convinced that the evils anticipated by some men from the practical enforcement of equal rights are mostly imaginary, and that the relation of the races in the exercise of these rights will speedily adjust themselves to the satisfaction of all."

These were two of the men the elimination of whose statues Mitch Landrieu tore the city of New Orleans apart over.

Meanwhile the potholes in the streets grew so large that the public took to decorating them with floral arrangements and Mardi Gras beads, and even gave them the names of Confederate generals in hopes that it would motivate Landrieu's administration to finally address them.

And the carjackings, murders, graft, and corruption continued unabated.

Eventually the city would flood in June 2020 due to a simple three-hour rainstorm, whereupon the executive director of the Sewerage and Water Board would use global warming as an excuse. This while SWB's computerized system of billing for water customers broke down to such an extent that people with one-bedroom apartments were receiving $1,000 monthly water bills with zero explanation of why, and outraged customers were lining up at its offices to be sneered at and dismissed when they arrived to protest.

We tell the New Orleans story as an example. We can use any number of others. Detroit, Newark, St. Louis, Chicago and its nearly one thousand murders in 2021, New York, Los Angeles, and San Francisco and their hordes of homeless. They've all got something key in common.

Let's call it Weaponized Governmental Failure. It's the single most explicative factor in the breakdown of American political consensus in the 21st century, even though it's been around since the latter part of the 20th century.

The simple definition of Weaponized Governmental Failure is this: it's the deliberate refusal to perform the basic tasks of urban governance for a specific political purpose.

The crime and the graft and the potholes and the bad drainage, not to mention the spotty trash collection or nonexistent snow shoveling, aren't incompetence. In fact, none of what you see in the American public sector is incompetence. The people responsible for it are quite highly educated and well-trained in their craft. You just need to understand what their craft is.

It's a *choice* to do a poor job with the more mundane tasks of running a city, and an educated and purposeful choice at that. If you do those things effectively, after all, what you will get is middle-class voters moving in. Middle-class voters tend to choose to live in places where they can expect to get actual value out of their tax dollars—good roads, safe streets, functional drainage, decent schools, a friendly business climate, and a growing economy, among other things—and those things are hard to produce when you govern the way the Left does.

Put a different way, middle-class voters are a pain in the ass.

They want lots of things that make for unrewarding grunt work for a mayor, and a Democrat blowhard like a Mitch Landrieu or Ted Wheeler of Portland would rather spend his time on vacuous cultural aggressions like "social change" and offering wealth redistribution and excuses for the bad personal habits that cause so many people to be poor.

Not to mention tilting at bronze statues of better men long dead and nearly forgotten as a means of "making a difference."

For a Landrieu, or a Kwame Kilpatrick, Marion Barry, Bill de Blasio, or Lori Lightfoot, it is no great loss if those middle-class voters declare themselves fed up and decamp to the suburbs. Their exodus simply makes for an electorate that is a lot less demanding and easier to control.

That "white flight" is a feature. It's not a bug. And it isn't all that white either. Those suburbs the folks are leaving for? Their minority population share usually increases as their population does. Why do you think that is? Simple: the black middle class has no more use for these woke urban Democrats than the white middle class does.

And it's quite a mutual sentiment, to be sure.

The urban socialist Left wants a manageably small core of rich residents and a teeming mass of poor ones, and nothing in between. That's what Weaponized Governmental Failure produces, and it's a wide-scale success. New Orleans votes 90 percent Democrat. Philadelphia is 80 percent Democrat. Chicago is 85 percent. Los Angeles? Seventy-one percent. None of those cities will have a Republican mayor or city council again, or at least not in the foreseeable future.

Because there are very few middle-class voters left in the cities.

Rich voters don't really ask for anything, because they can generally pay for whatever they need out of pocket (for example, their kids go to private schools, and they've got private security in their neighborhoods). All they require is that the WGF politicians give them access and the occasional favor, and they'll not only vote for them but write campaign checks.

Poor voters? Please. They're generally unsophisticated and susceptible to government dependency, and thus manipulating them is no great task. Give them the occasional crumbs from the table, and keep them busy with stupidities like bowdlerizing old monuments, or midnight basketball, or Black Lives Matter "defund the police" pandering, and you can get them to vote however you want without ever lifting a finger to provide real opportunity for social and economic advancement.

Or even by vigorously promoting policies and outcomes that actively hold back the social mobility of the urban poor.

You don't really think the public schools in those cities spend $15,000 or $20,000 per student per year to turn out functional illiterates because the people involved in making all that money disappear are all idiots, do you?

Louis Miriani was the last Republican mayor of Detroit. He left office on January 2, 1962. When Miriani gave up the mayor's gavel to Jerome Cavanagh following a major upset in the 1961 elections, Detroit was the richest, most productive city in the world with a population of nearly two million. It had the richest black community in the world and an industrial output that dwarfed the vast majority of nations on earth.

By 1967 Detroit was in flames thanks to the 12th Street Riots. Coleman Young, elected as the city's first black mayor in 1973 and the third in a string of Democrat mayors, which as of this writing appears impossible to break, would oversee such an economic rout that a peculiar tradition called "Devil's Night" was born. Arsonists would descend upon the city and burn large swaths of its dead industrial base the night before Halloween, with little response from the fire department. This went on for years.

Today, Detroit's population stands at 639,000, less than a third of what it was when Miriani said his farewell. It's one of the poorest cities in America; the poverty rate in Detroit in 2019 was 31 percent, compared to 13 percent in Michigan as a whole and 10.5 percent nationally. Detroit's public schools spend some $14,750 per student per year, ranking among the top ten most expensive in America, and yet in 2018 just 5 percent of fourth graders were proficient in reading and 4 percent proficient in math, the worst scores in the nation.

The more middle-class voters you drive out of the city, and the fewer middle-class voters your public school system creates, the more pliable the electorate becomes.

A pliable electorate is one you can rule forever without successfully governing.

They rule over a ruin, *but they rule.*

And the Democrat Party barely exists outside of the ruins those urban machines produce. Check out any county-by-country or congressional district-by-congressional district electoral map from the 2016 or 2020 presidential elections, and what you'll see is a few islands of blue in a sea of red. Even in blue states like Washington, Oregon, Illinois, and Minnesota most of the territory is solidly Republican; it's the dense population of Seattle, Portland, Los Angeles, Philadelphia, Chicago, Minneapolis, and the other big cities that always, or at least often, overwhelms Republican votes in the suburbs, exurbs, and small towns.

We don't have political consensus because, increasingly, we're two countries living side by side. And migration patterns, which are quickly accelerating as Americans evacuate states run by Democrats like Illinois, New Jersey, California, and New York in favor of Texas, Florida, Tennessee, and other red states, are fast sorting America into two countries.

This is, of course, a fantastic argument for federalism. A country polarizing into two very different models of governance can still have a reasonably happy coexistence if we just accept that New York is going to handle its business a whole lot differently than Arkansas or South Dakota will, and that it's OK if that happens. There is a reason why states are called "laboratories of democracy" after all. You can experiment with policies at the state level, and if they don't work, two things are true. First, the damage a policy failure in Montana will do isn't likely to affect Kentucky. And second, the competition within the states will tend to mitigate the duration of those policy failures.

That argument should be a persuasive one. But it isn't. Why?

Well, why was the Berlin Wall built?

Following World War II, when that devastated German city was split into American, British, French, and Soviet sectors and governed according to the values of the occupiers, the results became progressively differential. Berlin initially consisted of countless piles of rubble in 1945, but within a few years it began to be rebuilt, and life there began to normalize.

The Western sectors of the city coalesced into what became West Berlin, and it rapidly developed into a free, prosperous, and stimulating place. But East Berlin, the Soviet sector, was repressive, poor, bureaucratic, and awful.

Which meant East Berliners were busy getting the hell out of there and making their way to the west.

Between October 1945 and June 1946 some 10 percent of the Soviet sector's population made their way to West Berlin. And by 1952, an additional 5 percent of the whole East German population had emigrated to West Germany.

And then it got worse, as between 1952 and 1961 one-fifth of the East German population bugged out for West Germany. Berlin was the primary conduit for that migration, and the communist Soviet puppet government of East Germany finally had enough and put up the Berlin Wall.

It didn't stop the migration, but it definitely slowed it down. From 1962–88 that east-west migration was one-sixth of what it was from 1949–61. And when the wall finally came down, East Germany collapsed altogether and was soon swallowed up by West Germany.

You might think the Berlin Wall example doesn't have anything to do with New Yorkers decamping for Florida, but you'd be wrong. The fact is that people always, on net, leave high-tax, low-freedom jurisdictions for low-tax, high-freedom jurisdictions. History proves it, and what's happening now in America was completely predictable.

New York and California can't build walls to keep their people in. The wall has to be built in Washington, DC, through public policy. Put another way, federalism doesn't work for the urban socialist Left any better than open borders worked for the East Germans, and so their policies have to be put in place nationwide.

California has to impose itself on Texas, or else Texas will clean out California's population, jobs, and capital.

This is why Chuck Schumer is willing to attempt to destroy the filibuster in an effort to pass a bill federalizing American elections behind a series of "reforms" most people don't want and most states won't accept.

The fact that the urban left fears losing the competition is one reason we're not allowed to have a federalist America. Another is spiritual and cultural.

It may have been the liberal writer Andrew Sullivan who best identified the issue. "[W]e have the cult of social justice on the left," Sullivan wrote in *New York Magazine* in December 2018, "a religion whose followers show the same zeal as any born-again Evangelical."

Wokeness has all the hallmarks of a religion. Except the world's major religions all contain some formulation of the Golden Rule—do unto others as you would have them do unto you. Wokeness doesn't have that. There is no admonition to act in a good faith manner among the social justice cult, because it's based in the concept of collective, rather than individual, salvation.

And among the sacraments of the woke religion is the attainment and possession of political power.

For the social justice left, all of the causes are messianic. The world will end in a dozen years if something isn't done about global warming (something they've been saying for more than a dozen years). Racism, the worst sin ever to plague mankind, must be stamped out at all costs. Gender is a social construct, and it must be redefined to accommodate those who don't fit the traditional binary. Meat is murder. Speech is violence, and violence is speech. And on, and on.

Critical theory, on which wokeness is based, rejects the concept of objective truth as a tool of the oppressive white patriarchy. Woke theory isn't about truth. It's about power. And power is everything.

For people who see power as everything, letting people alone to do and say "wrong" things is unthinkable. So there will be no federalism and no consensus unless it's the rest of America agreeing with the Left.

But the rest of America doesn't agree with the Left.

And we're going to have a very high-stakes fight over who gets to define what America is in the years to come.

CHAPTER 4

Oligopoly and the Ruling Class

In 2010, the great conservative philosopher and polemicist Angelo Codevilla penned perhaps the most important political treatise of the 21st century to date.

In a long piece at *The American Spectator*, which will be discussed in more detail later in this book, Codevilla described an America divided into two parts: the ruling class and the country class. Much of his formulation was driven by something Americans across the political spectrum recognized—that the 2008 financial collapse that led to the Great Recession carried zero consequences to those responsible for it, and that the business and political elite increasingly centered itself within a Democratic Party newly rebuilt to cater to it. The ruling class conceit and mentality is abetted by an economy structured around a small group of politically connected corporations that increasingly dominate their market sectors and a culture fueled by Hard Left-dominated universities and an equally oligarchical media. Not many Americans wanted this development, and the market has not responded well to it.

Our ruling class and country class are worlds apart in many ways, as Codevilla's treatise made clear, but it's the differing treatment of objective reality that seems to be the most notable of them.

Here's a scenario that, sadly, is a lot less implausible than it ought to be: let's say there are ninety-nine mathematicians who get together and agree that two plus two equals five.

And then let's say there's a guy from a construction crew who, in response, starts stacking bricks in little two-by-two piles.

Who has the better argument?

Perhaps it's always been true that common sense wins out over the collective expertise of the elites. It's probably never been more true than now.

America's elite—the world's elite, for that matter—is deeply corrupt. So much so that it's becoming difficult to understand what makes them elite anymore. This is true in many sectors of our national life, but it's incandescently so with respect to politics.

Consider the House Judiciary Committee, which met in summer 2020 for a session with Attorney General William Barr. To call that appearance a mess would be too kind.

You would be safe in calling the chairman of the House Judiciary Committee a member of the elite. But there is nothing—nothing—elite about Jerrold Nadler. He's a physically repellent, intellectually absent, morally repugnant individual who gets worse with every public exposition. Nadler amazingly contended during the Judiciary Committee hearing that the mayhem then happening in Portland was not rioting, that the "demonstrators" there were "peaceful."

Nadler called Antifa violence a "myth."

Barr attempted to counter Nadler's spit-take-inducing statements by outlining the litany of weapons those demonstrators had brought to their "mostly peaceful" protests and making the obvious observation that the federal agents engaged in a nightly melee with Antifa mobsters were defending federal property—specifically, as in the case of Portland, the federal courthouse.

"Since when is it okay to try and burn down a federal court?" Barr asked, in a moment that pointed out the complete absurdity of summer 2020.

And on January 6, 2021, when hundreds of thousands of Americans unconvinced that the chaotic presidential election two months earlier was conducted according to standard chose to demonstrate at the Capitol, a small percentage of them made their way inside the building during Congress's votes to certify the Electoral College. This was termed an "insurrection" by people like Jerry Nadler, despite the scarcity of the "insurrectionists," including hundreds of them who subsequently spent months in federal prisons without bail or trial, bringing any guns to their "insurrection."

There has never been a political elite in this country so utterly debauched and devoid of merit as there is now. Consider that the Democrat Party nominated a man with such diminished mental capacity that his handlers refused to send him out to campaign for fear of what would happen, and when that man nonetheless won in circumstances that set the country at odds with itself, he was so micromanaged that within months most Americans responded in polling surveys that they didn't believe he was actually running the country.

Joe Biden is an awfully good personification of the decrepit and corrupted character of our national ruling class.

He's not alone in that regard. After all, Nancy Pelosi is the Speaker of the House. Chuck Schumer is the Senate minority leader.

John Roberts is the Chief Justice of the United States Supreme Court, and a very significant portion of the public believes he is utterly compromised and subject to blackmail. His rulings quite commonly fuel that perception. Rumblings in various media organs that Roberts's name appears on the Jeffrey Epstein flight logs only harden the notion that Roberts has been corrupted.

Epstein is another perfect example of the corruption of our ruling elite, of course. For years, he essentially served as a conduit for rich investors and celebrities to have sex with underage girls, even flying them to a private island where such encounters could be had away from the prying eyes of law enforcement. This was fairly widely known in elite circles, but nobody did anything about it for a scandalously long time. And when the bell finally did toll for Epstein, what happened? He was found dead in a prison cell in circumstances almost no one believes was a suicide, and his clients were afforded undue privacy for their criminal acts. Epstein's pal Jean-Luc Brunel, the French modeling agent who helped him procure the victims of his scheme, was similarly found dead in a Paris jail.

A very reasonable interpretation, based on the circumstances and facts surrounding the Epstein saga, is this: Epstein, a mediocre financial planner, recognized that many of the richest and most powerful people in America were sexual perverts who fantasized about statutory (or even unquestionable) rape. So he recruited a bunch of at-risk teenaged girls from broken homes and groomed them into prostitution, then fed them to rich degenerates of his acquaintance. Epstein videotaped the resulting sexual encounters and used them to blackmail the johns into investing their money with him. It was a very clear carrot-and-stick offer: either put a chunk of your money with Epstein, who would make safe, nondescript investments with it, and be welcomed with a never-ending supply of underage girls he'd pimped out...or say no and be terrified of what would happen when those tapes surfaced.

That he was able to keep such a dastardly program in place for as long as he did indicates that Jeffrey Epstein knew the market exceptionally well. A ruling elite that shares the values of ordinary America would have spit out such a man right at the outset.

That's obviously not what we have.

Virtue is, in fact, an antidote to fame in current American society. No one earns accolades for living an upright life. Mike Pence makes a rule that he won't be seen alone with a female not his wife in order to quash any possible perception he might act in an untoward fashion or even be tempted to, and he's ridiculed and calumnied for it. When Drew Brees stands up for the American flag, he's forced to apologize. When Bari Weiss makes a stand for diversity of opinion within the pages of the *New York Times*, including running an op-ed from a popular US senator, she's hounded out of her job.

Our elites are venal and toxic. They're dishonest. They're stupid.

Our academic elites embrace outright idiocy on a regular basis. They teach our brightest young adults that to recognize two sexes isn't truth but bigotry. That America was founded on slavery and racism. That the world will end in twelve years because of cow farts. Employers rail against the character flaws and arrogant ignorance of their new hires straight out of the indoctrination factories. Parents are increasingly choosing trade schools for their kids rather than adding to the $1.6 trillion mountain of college debt academia has fleeced America into. Many of the richest men in America didn't even graduate from college. Bill Gates and Mark Zuckerberg certainly didn't.

Gates and Zuckerberg, and the rest of Big Tech, hardly conduct themselves in a manner one would term as elite. Gates engages in suspicious, if not nefarious, activity in the realm of vaccines; there are credible stories of his having corrupted the public health bureaucracies in this country and others. He openly talks of spreading chemicals into the stratosphere in order to block out the sun and stop global warming; were that ever implemented, it would surely cause massive crop failures and a global famine.

Zuckerberg and his cohorts in social media are busy attempting to censor the very free speech that made them billionaires. So much so that in the summer of 2020 a newly formed group of physicians called America's Frontline Doctors held a two-day summit in Washington to bring public attention to the efficacy of hydroxychloroquine (HCQ) as a treatment for COVID-19 and to call for an end to economic lockdowns and mask mandates, and by the afternoon of the summit's second day, social media and Big Internet was actively engaged in scrubbing any evidence they had bothered to speak.

The doctors speaking out on behalf of HCQ were calumnied and insulted. Dr. Stella Immanuel, a Houston urgent care doctor and an immigrant from Cameroon with thirty years' experience in pediatrics and emergency room care and whose testimony included some 350 COVID-19 patients she had successfully treated, was labeled a crank and a quack. Nothing Dr. Immanuel said about HCQ was any different from what Dr. Harvey Risch, the head of epidemiology at Yale School of Medicine, has stated in multiple scholarly and journalistic articles about the drug, which has been prescribed millions and millions of times over seven decades all over the world for various ailments.

Is Harvey Risch a quack? Is he insane? Is Risch lying when he notes that the use of HCQ in Pará, a state in northern Brazil, deflated a major COVID-19 outbreak, while in Switzerland, a ban on HCQ resulted in a spike in the COVID death rate? Are these stories not true?

Zuckerberg, Jack Dorsey at Twitter, and the faceless goons at YouTube spiked America's Frontline Doctors. Squarespace even took down their website. Practicing physicians are not allowed to discuss medicine because the non-doctors running Big Tech have decided to deplatform them.

Back to our political elite.

I'm friends with just about every one of the eight people who served as Louisiana's Trump electors following the 2016 election.

I mention this because in the wake of that election, and before the eight convened to cast their electoral vote, they were deluged with a cascade of emails, letters, and phone calls. It turned out that Hillary Clinton's camp, not satisfied with multiple public statements trashing our electoral process, opted to set loose an army of goons on Donald Trump electors across America.

Some of the entreaties toward the electors were polite, if pathetic. Others were hostile. Many were threatening. The demands were nonstop. More than one of my friends changed their phone numbers as a result. Not one had the slightest inclination toward changing his or her vote as a result of the harassment.

Democrats have attacked the sanctity of our electoral process every time they've lost a presidential election this century. At this point it's expected they'll do that. Following the 2016 election, they didn't just harass Trump electors, they rioted in Washington on Inauguration Day. Damage from the mayhem stretched into the seven figures before law enforcement regained control of the streets.

Was anybody prosecuted for organizing those riots? No. Did anyone spend months in DC jails without bail or trial for participating in them? No.

But were there calls to change the format of our electoral process? Oh, yes.

We're in the midst of a long-form campaign to pervert the electoral process by having states agree to unilaterally abandon it in favor of adhering to the "national popular vote," in which the people of, say, South Dakota are supposed to surrender their role in American elections based on the vote totals someone might run up by reaping a rich harvest of ballots in New York, Chicago, or Los Angeles. It's the kind of idea favored by the overeducated and undereducated alike, and it does direct violence to the spirit of our founding—namely, that we are the United *States* of America, and that what's sovereign here is Texas, Illinois, Utah, or South Carolina and not the District of Columbia. Paramount in that equation is that California doesn't get to tell Mississippi what to do.

It's important to remember that each state has a role to play in the governance of this nation. When that isn't remembered, the results are always less than our standard. The Left has no interest in that standard.

Also following the 2016 election, the Left did something else to our electoral process. They bragged about it later in the pages of *Time* magazine. A cabal of people with power and money got together and plotted out a perversion of the system—which they arrogantly termed a "fortification" of it—to break down election integrity in key states.

Laws were changed without the participation of state legislatures, in direct violation of the Constitution's prescription that those legislatures should have plenary power to dictate the manner of their conduct. The COVID "emergency" was used to justify things that are, or were, universally accepted as poor practice—most importantly, mail-in balloting, which a bipartisan commission on elections more than fifteen years before had castigated as the worst possible idea.

And then $400 million in Big Tech-generated "grant" money flowed to local elections offices in heavily Democrat jurisdictions, turning those offices into get-out-the-vote operations for the 2020 Biden-Harris ticket.

The meddling of oligarchs in the functions of local governments isn't limited to attempts to rig national elections. It goes far deeper.

Like in Milwaukee, San Francisco, St. Louis, New Orleans, and many others where high-profile mayhem has taken hold, Philadelphia's district attorney is a Marxist buffoon named Larry Krasner who is in office in large measure because he was backed by the left-wing financier and essentially perfect James Bond villain George Soros. The latter has made it a personal project, after corrupting America's elections through similar attempts to elect revolutionaries to secretary of state positions around the country a decade or so ago, to install pro-criminal district attorneys in major and mid-sized cities across America.

In 2017 when Krasner was elected, a Soros-affiliated PAC dumped an unprecedented $1.7 million into the race for his benefit.

Nobody had ever spent that kind of money in a Philly DA race before. But it was nothing for Soros.

For example, Soros a few years ago dropped nearly a million dollars into a district attorney race in Shreveport, Louisiana, something no one in that area was prepared for or could believe. The bottom has fallen out of law enforcement in that city since, and it is losing population faster than almost any municipality in America as a result.

In Milwaukee, a Soros-backed imbecile district attorney named John Chisholm championed little or no cash bail even for violent criminals, gleefully admitting that there would be blood on the streets as a result. He paid off that promise, and then some, when in suburban Waukesha a career criminal and open Black Lives Matter supporter named Darrell Brooks massacred six people by smacking his SUV into a 2021 Christmas parade. Brooks was out on $1,000 bail after running his girlfriend over just a few days earlier.

And then there is the bumbling moron Kim Foxx in Chicago, the recipient of a cool $2 million in Soros bucks. You saw Foxx's handiwork in the Jussie Smollett case, and you've seen the results of her performance: nearly one thousand murders in the Windy City in 2021.

Krasner's list of foibles as the DA in Philadelphia rival the worst of the Soros roster. When he took office he announced he would no longer prosecute marijuana possession, essentially decriminalizing weed without any legislative body—either in the city or the state—having a hand in that making of policy. Friends in Philadelphia inform this writer that the smell of cannabis has pervaded the streets since. Krasner also announced he was all but ending prosecution of prostitutes. He said the policy was not to prosecute any "sex workers" with less than three convictions—which means the young and pretty ones get off scot-free, apparently.

Then he instituted case reviews with an eye toward dramatic restructuring of sentences for Philadelphia's criminals, particularly the "non-violent" ones. "Fiscal responsibility is a justice issue, and it is an urgent justice issue," said Krasner. "A dollar spent on incarceration should be worth it. Otherwise, that dollar may be better spent on addiction treatment, on public education, on policing and on other types of activity that make us all safer."

He fought capital punishment. And in 2018 when Philly cop James O'Connor IV was killed by a drug dealer named Hassan Elliott, who was free thanks to Krasner's decision to drop drug charges against him, the Trump-appointed US attorney in Philadelphia directly blamed Krasner.

Three years later Philadelphia had shot past its previous murder record of five hundred, set back in 1990. There's a murder once every sixteen hours or so in Philadelphia.

How bad is it? Some Philly residents actually expect their loved ones—not the criminal ones, normal folks—will be murdered, and they turn out to be correct. From a *Philadelphia Inquirer* article in summer 2021:

> Pamela Owensby woke up every day for three years fearing her son would be shot.
>
> Her 23-year-old, Sircarr Johnson Jr., had opened a clothing store on West Philadelphia's 60th Street in 2018. Because of ongoing violence in the neighborhood, she became licensed to carry a gun and accompanied him at closing time. This

> spring, she even researched life insurance for each of her four sons—the youngest of whom is 9.
>
> But before she could fill out the paperwork, Johnson was killed in front of his store.
>
> In the middle of a July 4 cookout, gunmen jumped out of a car and pumped bullets into the crowd—a crime police believe was part of an ongoing conflict between rival neighborhood groups. Four people were struck, including Johnson, who was shot in the torso.
>
> He died within minutes.
>
> "I just knew they were gonna take my baby," Owensby said.

When the murders don't come, the rapes do. You probably heard about the October 2021 incident when a passel of thugs on a train in South Philadelphia thought it would be a good time to reenact scenes from *A Clockwork Orange*. The train wasn't empty, but they were perfectly safe in committing the gang rape against an unfortunate victim—no one came to her aid; they just took out their phones and recorded it.

SEPTA, the public transit authority on whose watch it happened, scolded the phone-wielding spectators for not calling 9-1-1. The correct response, of course, was "What for?" Everybody knows Larry Krasner is allied with the criminals and not the victims. Certainly the cops do. Why bother arresting anybody? That'll only make them angry, and then they'll just be right back out on the street looking to apply stitches to the snitches.

So what happens is the law-abiding citizens who are beset by rampaging, pillaging criminals decide that if the cops and Larry Krasner won't enforce the law and keep the peace, they'll do it themselves.

And fourteen-year-olds shoot would-be robbers in the face when said villains are choking their parents in pursuit of what's in the cash register. Which was exactly what happened in December 2021 as three thugs attempted to knock over a family-owned pizzeria on Spring Garden Street. And in late January 2022, a pizza delivery man blew away an attempted carjacker in Kensington. The public in Philadelphia is fighting back against the criminals with the same level of violence they've had visited on them.

This is Larry Krasner's fault, and it's George Soros's fault. This movement to put allies of criminals in charge of prosecuting crime, something that comes straight out of a Christopher Nolan Batman movie, is directly slaughtering what little quality of life remains in America's cities. That those cities have not yet devolved into American Baghdads in which private militias rule street corner by street corner is surprising. Were it not for the massive out-migration of middle-class citizens to the suburbs and exurbs, this would have already happened.

We've discussed that phenomenon—Weaponized Governmental Failure—in the previous chapter. A Soros DA is proving to be the H-bomb of Weaponized Governmental Failure. Philadelphia's nobody-cares governance exemplifies the phenomenon perfectly.

It's no longer plausible to blame this on incompetence. Larry Krasner is no liberal. He's a leftist, a Marxist. He isn't for civil rights. Pamela Owensby had a civil right to expect her son would not be shot dead before his 24th birthday. This is how you keep the Pamela

Owensbys impoverished, miserable, and dependent. It's how you keep beleaguered people under your thumb and begging for what little relief you might afford them.

Or worse, it's how you condition them to see crime as normal and acceptable to participate in. Then they've got criminal records, and they'll never escape the cycle.

And they'll never vote Republican no matter how bad it gets in Philadelphia. Or Milwaukee. Or New Orleans.

You can't get rid of Larry Krasner. Even if you did, he'll be replaced by somebody just as bad. Soros will make sure of it.

And Philadelphia can't be saved. Only the people who realize the oppression and evil that a criminally allied political class represents and are willing to move away can be saved.

And at some point, Soros has to be held accountable for the damage he's done over the years and the lives he's destroyed. It should have already happened.

But this isn't just a George Soros-Mark Zuckerberg issue. The elites running our cultural institutions and entertainment have installed an oligarchy that is directly hostile to the American people.

There are countless examples of this, the most famous of which probably involves podcast superstar Joe Rogan, who wasn't allowed to challenge the ruling elite's narratives about COVID. Once the cancel mob got started, Rogan was tagged as a racist because he'd used the "N-word" several times over the course of many years on his podcast in the context of repeating other people's words.

But two other examples, both from 2021, are instructive not only in the injustice of our cultural elite's jackbooted enforcement of its declared, and undemocratic, norms but the public's swift response to cancel culture that really began to flower.

Take, for example, country singer Morgan Wallen. And, while we're at it, actress Gina Carano.

In Wallen's case, the up-and-coming young star had just released a double album with some very interesting tracks marking him as more than just a "bro-country" singer with a reputation as a hard-drinking bad boy off stage. There is real depth to some of his lyrics, and the music is, at times, quite good.

But Wallen, who is known to have a problem with alcohol, as many twenty-somethings suddenly blessed with great fortune are prone to have, found his career and status in the music industry crashing down over something utterly ridiculous.

Wallen, out carousing with friends and deep into his cups, called one of them a "p***y a** n****r" while horsing around. The outburst was recorded by a stranger, who then sold the recording to the celebrity gossip site TMZ.

When the exchange went public, Wallen apologized. It wasn't enough. He was castigated and defenestrated in the entertainment media, his record company "suspended" him, and he was made persona non grata within country music while opinion-makers began pontificating about whether Wallen's outrageous racism isn't representative of the "problematic" nature of country music as a whole.

Carano, meanwhile, is a former female MMA champion who is one of the few actresses actually capable of pulling off the new Hollywood trope—the female action hero who routinely beats the hell out of men. She plays, or played, Cara Dune in the Star Wars-derivative Disney+ series *The Mandalorian*, and she earned strong reviews in that role.

But Gina Carano happens to be a conservative, and she lives up to her tough-girl image at that.

Mobs of cultural Marxists attacked her, seeking to cancel her and ruin her career. This went on for at least two years. She has been unfazed and unapologetic in the face of their attempts to beat her down.

Carano refused to cave to the cultural Left's demands that she "identify her pronouns" on her social media profile, and supposedly that makes her "transphobic." She expressed doubt, as perhaps most Americans have, that Jeffrey Epstein killed himself. Carano made fun of the wildly over-the-top COVID restrictions in California, a mainstream enough position that opposition to those restrictions fueled a recall election against that state's governor, Gavin Newsom. She expressed doubt over the integrity of the 2020 election.

And she posted that "Expecting everyone you encounter to agree with every belief or view you hold is f—ing wild."

And then Carano shared an Instagram post making the case that abusive governments run by psychopaths are capable of so otherizing disfavored people and poisoning the public against them that massive atrocities can result. The Instagram post contained a heartbreaking and disgusting image from Nazi persecution of Jews in Poland during World War II; it's a terrified woman in her underwear running from a mob of bloodthirsty animals attempting to beat her to death.

The point being that we should never allow ourselves to be manipulated in such awful ways by our political leaders that the Holocaust could happen again and that political disagreement can create such conditions just like racial or ethnic animus has.

After all, what the Nazis did to the Jews, while certainly an unacceptable stain on the human escutcheon that must never be repeated, was neither unprecedented nor even the bloodiest example of genocide in recent world history. Awful governments stoking public hatred in pursuit of genocidal aims is actually a common theme in the last century or so. It's what the Turks did to the Armenians, what the Soviets did to the kulaks and Ukrainians, what the Chinese Cultural Revolution signified, what happened in Rwanda and Cambodia. Political and economic hatred, the 20th century proved, can be just as deadly as the racial and ethnic variety.

But when Carano expressed that point, she was fired from the cast of *The Mandalorian*, while her co-star Pedro Pascal, who also posted Nazi Holocaust memes, only from the Left, has not been.

The Wallen and Carano fiascoes are hardly the worst examples of elite-driven cancel culture in an America badly off-kilter. But the reaction to them has been noteworthy.

Who was far and away the hottest recording artist in country music in the week after his cancellation? That would be Morgan Wallen. Within a few days after his defenestration, Wallen had eight of the top twenty songs on the iTunes country charts.

That alarmed the entertainment media, which used it as proof that country music fans, seeing as though they tend to be white and rural and from flyover country, are a bunch of mouth-breathing racists. Wallen himself was trotted out to implore them not to defend him, in one of the more obnoxious public relations hostage crises in recent memory. But of course when the rapper Lil Nas X got together with Billy Ray Cyrus to cut the crossover hit "Old Town Road" a couple of years ago, country fans couldn't get enough of it. And Wallen later released a collaboration with another rapper, Lil Durk, called "Broadway Girls." Within a month it had sixteen million views on YouTube.

The accusations of racism among Wallen's fans are exactly why there was so much enthusiasm for buying up his music right after his cancellation. For one thing, Wallen didn't use a racial slur when he said what he said to his white drinking buddy; he essentially quoted about 22.4 percent of Quentin Tarantino's movie dialogues. And everybody understood that.

Unwise? Of course. Worthy of a public apology? Naturally. Career-ending? Ridiculous. Evidence that Wallen harbors hatred for African Americans? Nobody really believes that.

The fans bought up Wallen's music because (1) there was a perception it would come off the market given the current idiocies, and (2) and this is the important bit, Americans are absolutely sick and tired of cancel culture. They're tired of seeing people otherized for stupid reasons and being told any sin against ever-changing leftist cultural pieties puts one's livelihood at risk. It's now a real threat not just to entertainers making millions; middle-class Americans are, as Daniel Greenfield correctly observed at *FrontPage Magazine*, being terrorized by our ruling elite on the basis of Critical Race Theory and cancel culture. Publishing houses are firing Christian employees for having a Gab account, for Pete's sake. At some point ordinary Americans would have had enough, and this is it.

And in the case of Carano, the public backlash against Lucasfilm and Disney, its parent company, was severe. Calls to cancel Disney+ appeared everywhere, and the attacks on the company were widespread.

And Gina Carano became a lot bigger name than she was before being fired, whether Hollywood will cast her again or not. Shortly after her firing from *The Mandalorian*, she landed a multipicture contract with Ben Shapiro's Daily Wire to act and direct;

the first product of that deal, a western titled *Terror on the Prairie* starring Carano, Samaire Armstrong, and Nick Searcy, was due out in June 2022.

And of course, you're aware of the flagging financial fortunes the wokesters in charge of entertainment giants like Disney and Netflix have imposed on those companies. Woke Hollywood is a loser, and there's no denying it.

Also, you already know that the mainstream media, with the sometime exception of Fox News and a few newspapers and websites, pushes out a conventional narrative daily which turns out to be...mistaken, shall we say. Every new sensational news item seems to be, substantially, a lie. No diversity from the official story is possible, until that can't be sustained—and then the narrative quietly shifts.

If you don't agree, then explain why it took so long for anybody in the mainstream media to credit the lab-leak origin story of COVID-19, when there was never any evidence presented of an organic transmission of the virus. Or how it took a whole week or more before anyone bothered to notice the Jussie Smollett story was a hoax. Or the multimillion-dollar payday Covington, Kentucky, teenager Nick Sandmann picked up from various news organizations who fraudulently reported he had provoked a Native American activist during a confrontation at the National Mall. Or the lies told about Kyle Rittenhouse after he shot three Antifa hoodlums during a riot in Kenosha, Wisconsin, in 2020.

And remember when Hunter Biden's laptop scandal was derided as "Russian disinformation"...until it wasn't.

Just consider how stock news is reported during the drive-by radio news reports. "The Dow fell on fears that..." is almost always followed by some explanation that furthers a media narrative. Talk to someone in that business the next time you hear one, and see what he or she says. You'll get guffaws and rolled eyes out of the experience.

Our news media is now mostly populated with millennials who went to journalism school, a wholly unnecessary academic pursuit that is dominated by all the worst professors. Students in J-schools now are trained to view global and local events through a social justice prism preferred by corporate media entities, and the training is rigid and doctrinaire. A politician of my acquaintance tells the story of a promising young intern in a district office in a college town who tearfully resigned. When asked why she was leaving a position she was quite good at and had a solid future in, she said a professor teaching a journalism class—she was majoring in mass communications—told her that he wouldn't pass anyone working in "racist" Republican politics.

The public isn't amused. Americans, according to surveys, afford our news media less credibility than any other nation on earth. That underlies the fact CNN drove away some 90 percent of its base audience during the 2021 calendar year, at the same time it was preparing to launch a paid streaming service called "CNN+." The network managed to pilfer *Fox News Sunday*'s Chris Wallace as one of CNN+'s headliners, while most of America yawned.

That led Greenfield to make a solid observation. "CNN's effort to launch CNN+, a paid streaming service, at a time when its core ratings are crashing is confusing observers who wonder why the news network thinks people will pay for CNN when they won't even watch it for free," he wrote.

Greenfield was right. CNN+ barely lasted a month before the bosses pulled the plug. It was generating only about 10,000 users a day, about what my Louisiana politics site The Hayride routinely does with no corporate backing.

Woke sensibilities are not bottom-up. They're top-down. And the public has begun to hate the top, setting the stage for a major cultural upheaval.

PART TWO

FROM PROGRESSIVISM TO NEOCOMMUNISM

CHAPTER 5

The Bad Idea That Won't Go Away

One of the enduring failures of capitalist America, which will someday, hopefully, be remedied at long last, is that the motion picture industry has never made the biopic of Karl Marx that man truly deserves.

I don't say this from a Marxist perspective, in case you misunderstand. What the modern public needs to see of Marx was what an utter, unmitigated oxygen thief he was. If some filmmaker of a conservative or non-Marxist bent were to give Marx the treatment Hollywood has given various conservative or Republican figures—Roy Cohn, Nixon, George W. Bush—there's a chance the public might get a sour taste in its mouth for a profoundly meritless, degenerate little man whose philosophy reflects his own lifestyle.

Namely, that Marx was a leech, and Marxism is a philosophy for leeches.

We know a good bit about Marxism, seeing as though it gets foisted on us so commonly in our culture, education, and politics, but not as much about Marx himself. So here's a quick nickel tour for you.

Karl Marx was born in Trier, Germany, in 1818, the son of a well-to-do lawyer from a rich family with extensive landholdings including several vineyards. The Marxes were a Jewish family, from which a long line of rabbis had come, but Heinrich Marx, Karl's father, was the first with a secular education, and he had converted to evangelical Christianity.

Karl was baptized Lutheran, but he converted to atheism. He was sent off to college at the University of Bonn, but amid a marination in radical politics, he drank his way out of that school, and his father made him transfer to the University of Berlin instead. There he found a bit of direction in life, marrying the daughter of an aristocrat and studying law and philosophy in hopes of finding a way to fuse the two. He dabbled in writing fiction and poetry while again finding society among political radicals and found himself lacking in means after his father died in 1838. By 1842 he was living in Cologne and working as a journalist for a radical left-wing newspaper, *Rheinische Zeitung* (the *Rhineland News*).

This wasn't the most popular place for the young Marx to ply his trade as a writer. The Prussian government was leaning on his employer quite heavily. As he wrote, "Our newspaper has to be presented to the police to be sniffed at, and if the police nose smells anything un-Christian or un-Prussian, the newspaper is not allowed to appear."

The next year, the Prussian monarchy shut down the *Rhineland News* following an international incident involving its sharp criticism of the tsar, and Marx was on the move again. This time he surfaced in Paris as the co-editor of *Deutsch-Französische Jahrbücher*, or *French-German Annals*. It was a fiery, left-wing radical newspaper, and it hardly lasted a year, especially after Bavarian authorities banned its importation for having issued forth some rather biting satire of King Ludwig. Marx was soon bouncing to another Parisian German-language paper, dead broke with a newborn daughter and a wife giving him the evil eye and frowning upon his life choices.

He spent most of his free time reading books and developing his philosophy, a dog's breakfast of Hegelian dialectics, French utopian socialism, and English market economics. Marx wrote a book titled *The Economic and Philosophic Manuscripts* in 1844, a boring tome that discussed philosophy at length despite ultimately rejecting the concept that ideas mattered—Marx held that it was physical action that ruled the world.

One is tempted to believe that came from his wife telling him he was a bum and that he needed to get a real job.

Then he met Friedrich Engels. That turned out to be an important moment in Marx's life, as the German-language paper he was editing at the time had been shut down by the French government at the request of the Prussian king, and the French had invited him to hit the road. Marx took the family to Brussels, where he was granted asylum on condition that he publish nothing about contemporary politics, and Engels, who was a German socialist writer in his own right, settled in that town as well.

Marx and Engels hit it off, and by the summer of 1845 they'd made their way to England at the invitation of a leftist group called the Chartists, for whose newspaper Engels had found employment writing and editing. With Engels's help, Marx wrote his second book, *The German Ideology*, the major thesis of which was that materialism was essentially the sole driver of human conduct and using that as the basis of "scientific" socialism.

It's all about them deutsche marks, y'all.

The German Ideology wasn't published until 1932 thanks to government censors in several European countries giving it a profound "Hell, no." And in 1847 Marx tried again, writing a book titled *The Poverty of Philosophy*, which was intended as broad appeal to the working class's best material interest as being the best way to mobilize the proletariat to make a revolution and change society.

Marx and Engels were then involved in a secret leftist society in Brussels called, self-indulgently enough, The League of the Just. They realized they weren't going to bring about the revolution of the workers in secret and that they'd have to openly form a political party if they were going to get anywhere. And in 1848 that's what they did, changing their name to the Communist League and publishing Marx and Engels's best-known work, *The Communist Manifesto*. Its aims were modest: just worldwide revolution to replace governments and bourgeois capitalist society with a socialist utopia.

At the time, though, in most of Europe there wasn't all that well-established a bourgeoisie. The real power in most of these countries was with the aristocracy, and the aristocrats treated the bourgeoisie like dirt when they weren't trying to borrow money from them. Marx didn't actually know what the hell he was talking about.

And to this end, Marx spent a third of an inheritance from his father, which his uncle had withheld for a decade, buying weapons for Belgian workers to kill government officials with. It being 1848, after all, and Europe being engulfed in revolutions and uprisings.

It wasn't long before the Belgian government found out about that. Consequently, Marx was moving again, this time to Cologne after a short stint in Paris where the Communist League's new international headquarters had been set up. In Cologne, he began distributing handbills titled *Demands of the Communist Party in Germany*, which called for the bourgeoisie to overthrow the nobility so as to allow the German proletariat to overthrow the bourgeoisie and therefore remedy the fact that his revolutionary prophecies were more or less nonsense as applied to his native country.

Strangely, the bourgeoisie wasn't roused by Communist Party demands that they kill the aristocrats and make it possible for the proles to kill them in turn.

He used the rest of his inheritance to start a newspaper in Cologne, the *Neue Rheinische Zeitung*, or *New Rhineland News*. This did a little better than the *Old Rhineland News*, but not much. Marx found himself beset with various police charges and spent a lot of time in court fighting off prosecution. Finally, a few months later, the paper he'd plowed his family's fortune into ran afoul of the new reactionary Prussian government, and the cops shut him down. As a special bonus, Marx was told he was welcome to leave the country at any time of his leisure so long as it was immediate.

So he went back to Paris, which was in the middle of a reactionary counterrevolution and a cholera epidemic, and it wasn't like anybody had much time for a newspaperman who kept pissing off the wrong people and getting canceled when he wasn't spending his family's money playing Santa Claus to the violent proletarian vanguard.

That's not an opinion. The local authorities informed him of that very assessment when they told him quite snootily to get the hell out.

London was next, and Marx's wife, Jenny, was now pregnant with their fourth child. One might imagine that Mrs. Marx had become a bit exasperated with her husband at this point, and evidence for such an assumption can be found in what happened next.

Which was that the Communist League had settled on London as its third international headquarters in less than a year. And no sooner had that happened then many of its members declared it was time to launch the international proletariat revolution Marx had been writing about for the better part of a decade.

Marx said no.

In one of the more lucid moments of his life, he assessed that a spontaneous revolution in which the workers of the world would unite to crush the capitalist bourgeoisie might actually be a disaster, and the revolutionaries would just get rounded up and imprisoned or shot. And that when this happened, it would be a good bet that the Communist League and all of its members probably would face more negative consequences than getting run out of yet another European capital.

Marx said that changes in society are not achieved overnight through the efforts and willpower of a handful of men, and that the magic formula was scientific analysis of economic conditions of society and moving toward revolution through different stages of social development.

I'll boil this down: Marx was now in London where you had to do more than make fun of German potentates and write boozy screeds attacking governments for screwing over the workin' man to get your publication shut down. And Marx noticed there were a whole lot of indolent sons of wealthy, productive men hanging around, all of whom could be marks for the big grift of raising money while talking about a revolution he had no intention of participating in. These circumstances meant that, probably to get his exhausted wife off his back, he wanted to lay low and chisel some change off the swells for a while.

He'd found the Big Rock Candy Mountain, and Marx wasn't coming down off it in the short run.

This attitude was not very well received within the organization, and particularly not by one of its leaders. Specifically, a military man named August Willich, who like Marx was German but unlike Marx was a bit more physically courageous in his lunatic socialism.

Willich had been a leader in the Baden-Palatinate uprising in 1848, where Engels had served as his aide de camp, and his personal motto seems to have been straight out of Graceland: he was for a little less conversation and a little more action, please. Willich smuggled himself to London when his revolution went to seed, and he joined the Communist League. When Marx rejected the demand for the revolution for which he'd publicly scribbled, Willich plotted to kill him and even challenged Marx to pistols at dawn.

Marx said no to that, too, instead rustling up a young proletarian named Konrad Schramm to challenge Willich to a duel, which was fought in Brussels. Willich won, Schramm survived his injuries, and by the time the authorities caught up to what was happening, Willich was on a boat to America where he later became a Union general in the Civil War.

So the Communist League ended up splitting in half, with the hard-core revolutionaries heading off to plan Marx's revolution without Marx. And Marx himself was now working on something called the German Workers' Educational Society. By September of 1850, though, the educated German workers were calling Marx a sellout for not putting his money where his mouth was and kicking off his revolution, and he resigned from that organization.

How was Marx making a living at this point? He wasn't. He was mooching off Engels, who was himself mooching off his wealthy industrialist father. Marx managed to get a few writing gigs here and there, and then in 1852 the *New-York Daily Tribune*, published by the famous newspaperman Horace Greeley, hired him as its European correspondent. All of a sudden Karl Marx's goofy revolutionary theories that he'd neglected to put into force when his followers had asked him to were appearing in the pages of the world's most widely circulated periodical. He wasn't getting rich, but at least he could tell Jenny that he was working at a job.

When that was plausible, that is, because Marx was known by all in his acquaintance as a quite impressive drunk whose liver was, let's say, problematic from his first stint in Paris onward.

In 1852 Marx published a theoretical work about the French revolution of 1848, which wasn't exactly a hot seller.

By this point it should have been somewhat clear that history wasn't really playing out the way Marx had theorized and that maybe his theories weren't the most accurate. But since he had a meal ticket in Engels making sure he had three hots, a cot, and a roof over his family's heads, there was no particular reason for Marx to endure that reckoning. And since the British government at the time didn't see much reason to regard Marx as any kind of existential threat, he was living a fat and happy life by his standards.

The severe economic consequences of the Civil War did some damage to the *Daily Tribune*'s finances, and the readers were not surprisingly less interested in European affairs, and Marx found himself laid off in 1862. Some of the contacts he'd made at the paper, however, including the impresario George Ripley, had begun an encyclopedia and hired Marx and Engels to contribute articles to it.

Engels contributed fifty-one, Marx sixteen. Marx managed a minor commercial success in 1859 when he published *A Contribution to the Critique of Political Economy,* which sold out and was appraised as a critical success. He intended it to be the first volume of *Das Kapital,* which was to be his masterpiece of economic theory.

In 1864 he got involved in another revolutionary cabal, this one called the International Workingmen's Association, which was later known as the First International. Shortly thereafter Marx found himself in another internal struggle, this one with the Russian communist Mikhail Bakunin, over how to produce the great proletarian revolution, which wasn't generating as much buzz as everybody had hoped. But his writing career took off at that point; in 1867 he published the first part of *Das Kapital,* and it was a sizable commercial success. People were actually beginning to listen to Karl Marx. It was almost as though capitalism was treating him pretty well, and maybe he could have been grateful.

And meanwhile in 1870, an actual communist revolution broke out in Paris. But the Paris Commune was a singular failure on basically every front, given the chaos and starvation it inflicted on the poor saps who were sucked into it. In only two months the French government had gotten its act together and lustily slaughtered the revolutionaries while returning Paris to market economics and regular order.

Marx wrote and distributed a pamphlet entitled *The Civil War in France,* essentially saying the Paris Commune was awesome, and it should have been given more of a chance.

What about the second and third volumes of *Das Kapital?* Yeah, about those: Marx tinkered with manuscripts of both until his death in 1883, but he didn't publish them. It was Engels who did that, publishing the second volume in 1893 and the third volume in 1894. Essentially, he was recouping the cash he spent propping up Marx for all those decades.

And in the last decade of Marx's life, when he was in his more lucid and sober moments, he spent a lot of time writing letters back and forth to other socialist revolutionaries, offering theories on how, for example, Russian farm communes could be the basis of a socialist revolution there. It's funny, because when the Russian communist revolution did come in 1917 and that very idea was tried, half the country nearly starved to death.

Nobody ever seemed to recognize that "Hey, this stuff we keep theorizing about doesn't really seem to work all that well." Well, that's not true—the vast majority of the proletariat in all these European countries got that, and an even larger share of the bourgeoisie did. At least, those of the bourgeoisie who, unlike Engels, didn't just have a bunch of family money they could live off of while supplying sinecures to their leech friends.

But admitting his theories were bullshit just wasn't who Marx was.

He didn't just boil all of humanity down to a stupid binary of bourgeois capitalists vs. lumpen proletariat, which is perhaps the most insultingly simplistic view of life imaginable. He demanded his audience believe that any deviation from his binary meant the dissenter failed the test of "class consciousness" and was therefore not fully awake. Then he demanded we accept the inevitability of the revolution of the proletariat according to his prescriptions.

That Marx offered a relatively thoughtful critique of the inequities of capitalist society in the early stages of the Industrial Revolution is hardly enough to justify the idiocy of his other arguments. Even amid that critique, Marx and his followers never did have a good answer for the question, "Compared to what?"

If working among the industrial proletariat was so terrible, after all, why did so many people leave their ancestral villages for the cities to join it?

The answer, of course, was that the capitalist society Marx said was so soul-crushingly awful was nonetheless richer, more active, and more fulfilling than anything that had come before. He didn't consider that because he hadn't actually experienced much of privation or suffering. Somebody was always there to bail him out.

Marxism is, and always has been, most popular with lazy rich dilettantes who don't anticipate the consequences of applied Marxism or even really understand the world around them. In America, there have always been an ample supply of those, as we have lots of families that can attain sizable fortunes.

So does Europe. But there's a difference. In Europe, most of the rich families, particularly prior to the destruction of the Ancien Régime in World War I, came as landed nobility and were essentially government-sanctioned elites. Whereas in America an interesting saying came to the fore: "Shirtsleeves to shirtsleeves in three generations."

We don't use that one much anymore, as it's less true than it used to be. But it's still valid. What it means is the first generation of an upwardly mobile family will achieve a fortune by hard work. The second generation, born to the privilege of the first's upward struggle, is a little softer and probably spends down some of that fortune.

And the third generation will piss away the rest and end up broke and working-class.

You can't take that literally, necessarily, but it does have something valid to say about social mobility in a free society—namely, that it's based on productivity and attitude. If you don't have those, it doesn't matter how much privilege you were born into; it isn't going to end well.

We've always understood that in America, and that insulated us from Marxism taking much hold here. In a society like ours, gobbledygook like this, from *Das Kapital*, generally gets laughed at:

> "The capitalist maintains his rights as a purchaser when he tries to make the working-day as long as possible, and to make, whenever possible, two working-days out of one.
>
> "On the other hand...the laborer maintains his right as seller when he wishes to reduce the working-day to one of definite normal duration.
>
> "There is here, therefore, an antinomy, right against right, both equally bearing the seal of the law of exchanges.
>
> "Between equal rights force decides. Hence is it that in the history of capitalist production, the determination of what is a working-day, presents itself as the result of a struggle, a struggle between collective capital, i.e., the class of capitalists, and collective labour, i.e., the working-class."

I discovered that passage back in 2012 when an Obama administration official named Rick Bookstaber, who served on something called the Financial Stability Oversight Council, had created a minor disturbance when he posted it on his personal blog.

And it's fundamentally idiotic, because it misses a crucial part of the economic equation. Namely, that *the laborer can most of the time find another job.* Marx thinks capitalism is slavery because there is some immutable binary between labor and management, but he totally disregards that an economy isn't linear; it's three-dimensional.

Marxists refuse to understand all this. Instead they gravitate toward institutions in which these dynamics don't come off as quite so stupid. In each of them—government bureaucracies, Hollywood, public schools, higher education and so on—there is a distinct hierarchy that looks a lot like a pyramid and fits a Marxist analytical model.

But the local construction industry doesn't work like that. If you're a roofer, you might well find yourself in demand from four different home builders, and you can play them off against each other and choose to work for the one who offers the best compensation and work conditions. The idea you're the proletariat and what's in your interest is to shoot the home builders dead and take over their businesses so you can run them as part of a committee and get a small, but equal, share of the proceeds....

Well, let's just say most roofers would react to such lofty, if bloodsoaked, utopianism by saying, "Why the hell would I want to do that?"

Marxism has universally failed for that very reason, and it's no surprise that every Marxist state ultimately resorts to lies and terror as a means of keeping control of the population.

Karl Marx was a loser and a leech in life, whose writings were generally regarded as a parlor curiosity among the rich and comfortable. Furthermore, he was an incurable asshole. As his biographer Werner Blumenberg wrote of his personality:

> "He argued cuttingly, his biting satire did not shrink at insults, and his expressions could be rude and cruel. Though in general Marx had blind faith in his closest friends, nevertheless he himself complained that he was sometimes too mistrustful and unjust even to them. His verdicts, not only about enemies but even about friends, were sometimes so harsh that even less sensitive people would take offence.... There must have been few whom he did not criticize like this...not even Engels was an exception."

His liver condition contributed to another affliction; namely, Marx was covered with boils, which were so bad that he could hardly sit down. He was a notoriously dirty, drunk, unkempt, hairy ogre who hung around the library at the British Museum smoking cheap cigars and biting people's heads off for speaking to him.

But after his death when others with an investment in making him into something he wasn't began promoting him, he went from the mid-19th century version of Paul Krugman to the spiritual founder of an ideology that has killed well more than one hundred million people and subjected literally billions of our fellow human beings to unfathomable suffering and misery under the thumb of the cruelest, most brutal murderous regimes the world has ever known. It's Karl Marx, or perhaps more to the point his propagandist followers, who brought us Venezuelan dumpster-divers and North Koreans executed in the streets for listening to K-Pop on the radio.

Someday, hopefully, that biopic will be made, and when it is, it ought to be utterly savage in its portrayal. If it does come out, buy tickets and take the whole family. Twice.

So why didn't this bad idea of Marxism just die out? Well, this book has a lot to say about that. But we'll start with this.

A 2009 article by the Hudson Institute's Herbert London explains how Marx's unworkable doctrine was transformed into something that wouldn't go away, thanks to an Italian commie named Antonio Gramsci:

> "Gramsci, while still in his twenties, organized the Italian Communist party in 1921 with his colleague Togliotti. Since this was four years after the Russian Revolution, Gramsci assumed Italians would welcome a Bolshevik convulsion of their own. But it didn't happen.
>
> "In reviewing the political landscape, Gramsci sought to explain why what seemed to him inevitable had not yet occurred. He found three explanations: Christianity, nationalism, and charity. As he explains in his writing, the way to set the stage for a Marxist revolution was in coming to grips with these three conditions.
>
> "As a consequence, Gramsci converted Marxist economic theory into a cultural battle—as he saw it, a march through conventional and normative institutions. The first stratagem was the assault on Christianity by arguing religion should not inform or be employed in public

> discourse. Gramsci realized that if religion were confined to private worship, its hold on Italians would dissipate. Hence his arguments relied on science (more accurately scientism) and material claims devoid of references to the Church and its historic antecedents.
>
> "Second, Italians took great pride in their newly constituted nation fifty years old in the 1920s. Gramsci contended Italians were part of a grand global mission, merely one story in the narrative of mankind. He therefore cleverly attempted to transform national loyalty into an abstract identification with human rights by describing patriotism as an anachronistic and childish fetish.
>
> "And last, Gramsci engaged in efforts to persuade Italians that the way, the only way, to express humanitarian concern for the poor or those left behind as the detritus of capitalism is through a government that can be benevolent and beneficent. For him, big government wasn't a temptation for tyranny but rather the adjudicator for life's unfairness."

Gramsci soon found himself on the wrong side of Italy's dictator at the time, a frowning brute by the name of Benito Mussolini, and in 1926 the fascist regime snapped him up, threw him in prison, and let him rot away to his death in 1937. Such is what Big Government can do for you.

We'll have a good bit more on Gramsci in the next chapter, because he's considerably more important to this history than you probably realize. But I wanted to mention him here nonetheless. Without Gramsci, Marx is quite unlikely to have mattered very much where modern America is concerned.

Because Gramsci's rejiggering of Marxism into a cultural engine is what allowed its influences to make a lasting impact on this side of the Atlantic.

At this point we should probably have a quick discussion of race in America, because the history of how the black vote ended up as it has is reflective of how bad ideas conjured up by unkempt Eurotrash drunks can enter the bloodstream and do a whole lot of damage.

No, we're not going to begin in 1619, as the ignorant fabulist Nikole Hannah-Jones, the originator of the awful 1619 Project the *New York Times* has sponsored and our leftist education cartel is busily inflicting on schoolchildren, would like. Instead, we're going to start in 1845, when *Narrative of the Life of Frederick Douglass, an American Slave*, the first book by the famous civil rights activist, was published and became an immediate bestseller.

People attach a lot of reverence to Douglass's name, and that's warranted. What's unfortunate is how little anybody seems to know about what he had to say.

Because Frederick Douglass was Clarence Thomas or Candace Owens, in a lot of respects.

Douglass said he didn't know exactly when he was born into slavery in Maryland, though it was later worked out that he'd entered this world in 1818, the same year as Marx did in entirely different circumstances. Douglass wrote that he was told his father was the slave owner on the plantation where he was born but couldn't prove it, though he was certainly of mixed race. He was separated from his mother as an infant and lived as a child with his grandmother, who was also a slave. But at six he was moved again, eventually ending up in Baltimore where he was a house slave to a man named Hugh Auld.

And at twelve, Auld's wife, Sophia, began teaching him the alphabet and how to read and write. Hugh Auld wasn't very pleased about that; as Douglass later wrote he delivered the "first decidedly antislavery lecture" he had ever heard. "'Very well, thought I,'" wrote Douglass. "'Knowledge unfits a child to be a slave.' I instinctively assented to the proposition, and from that moment I understood the direct pathway from slavery to freedom."

But that was the end of Sophia's interest in educating young Frederick, so he finished learning the language on the sly, taking instruction from neighborhood kids and wherever he could find it. By the time he was fifteen, though, Douglass had been shipped off back to the country. He'd been hired out to work for Edward Covey, a Simon Legree-style psychopath who had a reputation as a "slave-breaker." Covey whipped Douglass so frequently that his wounds would barely heal before fresh ones were laid on; Douglass later described the experience as breaking his body, soul, and spirit. Finally, the sixteen-year-old Douglass decided he'd had enough, and when Covey tried to beat him once again Douglass turned the tables and laid a solid drubbing on his abuser. Covey never tried to beat him again.

And as Douglass wrote, that was a key moment in his education. Telling the story in his autobiography, he prefaced it by writing,

"You have seen how a man was made a slave; you shall see how a slave was made a man."

By 1837, after a failed attempt at freedom, Douglass had fallen in love with Anna Murray, a free black woman living in Baltimore, and the two plotted his escape and a relocation to the free states. The next year, following a plan they'd concocted with the help of the Underground Railroad, Douglass used an actual railroad to travel with false papers on the Philadelphia, Wilmington and Baltimore Railroad to Wilmington, Delaware, then from there to Philadelphia on the railroad's steam ferry up the Susquehanna River. From Philadelphia he traveled again by rail to New York, now a free man.

He then sent for Anna, and the two were married, just eleven days after his arrival in New York. He was twenty years old.

"I prayed for freedom for twenty years, but received no answer until I prayed with my legs," he wrote.

Douglass's life progressed quickly. He joined a church, became an ordained minister, lived in a number of places in Massachusetts and New York before ending up in Washington, DC, wrote three autobiographies, became a world-famous orator, traveled to Ireland, Scotland, and England, and ultimately published several abolitionist newspapers. There has never been a more impressive American story than that of Frederick Douglass, and he truly was the conscience of 19th century America.

Douglass's political and moral philosophy did undergo refinement throughout his travels, but fundamentally he was known for making blisteringly righteous indictments of the "peculiar institution" of slavery.

But what of America's treatment of blacks once freed? Douglass had an answer, and it might surprise you.

> "Everybody has asked the question. . .'What shall we do with the Negro?' I have had but one answer from the beginning. Do nothing with us! Your doing with us has already played the mischief with us. Do nothing with us! If the apples will not remain on the tree of their own strength, if they are wormeaten at the core, if they are early ripe and disposed to fall, let them fall! I am not for tying or fastening them on the tree in any way, except by nature's plan, and if they will not stay there, let them fall. And if the Negro cannot stand on his own legs, let him fall also. All I ask is, give him a chance to stand on his own legs! Let him alone!"

Douglass was a great believer in education and a civil rights leader in the truest sense of the word; when slavery was abolished as a function of the North's victory in the Civil War, he adopted the cause of women's suffrage as part of his repertoire. But at his core, what Frederick Douglass preached was the liberty and equality of opportunity of each individual.

And in this, Frederick Douglass was one of the staunchest defenders of the founding documents of America who ever lived.

Among a host of others who followed Douglass in pressing the cause of black Americans came another great figure whose message has largely been lost to modernity.

Booker T. Washington was, like Douglass, born a slave, in Virginia in 1856. After the Civil War he grew up in West Virginia, then attended college at what is now Hampton University. He was only twenty-five when he began performing what can only be described as a miracle.

Washington was named the leader of a startup teachers' college in Alabama known as Tuskegee Institute. The college began in one room of an AME church. That was plenty enough for Washington to build from though.

One year in, Washington had scraped together enough money to buy an old plantation to serve as a campus. He simply enlisted its students in construction of its buildings, from classrooms to dormitories—going so far as taking clay from the riverbank on the campus property to make bricks. Tuskegee maintained a large farm on the property to be essentially self-supporting, rearing animals and cultivating needed produce. Before long Tuskegee had the look of an institution of higher learning which would rival that of smaller white colleges.

> "I have begun everything with the idea that I could succeed," he said, "and I never had much patience with the multitudes of people who are always ready to explain why one cannot succeed."

In 1895, as he had become something of a national figure for his work building the college, Washington gave what became known as the Atlanta Address. An excerpt that deserves a full examination:

> "...the opportunity here afforded will awaken among us a new era of industrial progress. Ignorant and inexperienced, it is not strange that in the first years of our new life we began at the top instead of at the bottom; that a seat in Congress or the

state legislature was more sought than real estate or Industrial skill; that the political convention or stump speaking had more attractions than starting a dairy farm or truck garden.

"A ship lost at sea for many days suddenly sighted a friendly vessel. From the mast of the unfortunate vessel was seen a signal, 'Water, water; we die of thirst!' The answer from the friendly vessel at once came back, 'Cast down your bucket where you are.' A second time the signal, 'Water, water; send us water!' ran up from the distressed vessel, and was answered, 'Cast down your bucket where you are.' And a third and fourth signal for water was answered, 'Cast down your bucket where you are.' The Captain of the distressed vessel, at last heeding the injunction, cast down his bucket, and it came up full of fresh, sparkling water from the mouth of the Amazon River. To those of my race who depend on bettering their condition in a foreign land or who underestimate the importance of cultivating friendly relations with the Southern white man, who is their next door neighbor, I would say cast down your bucket where you are, cast it down in making friends in every manly way of the people of all races by whom we are surrounded.

"Cast it down in agriculture, mechanics, in commerce, in domestic service, and in the professions. And in this connection it is well to bear in mind that whatever other sins the South may be called to bear, when it comes to business, pure and simple, it is in the South that the Negro is given a man's chance in the commercial world, and in nothing is this exposition more eloquent than in emphasizing this chance. Our greatest danger is that in the great leap from slavery to freedom we may overlook the fact that the masses of us are to live by the productions of our hands, and fail to keep in mind that we shall prosper in proportions we learn to dignify and glorify common labor and put brains and skill into the common occupations of life; shall prosper in proportion as we learn to draw the line between the superficial and the substantial, the ornamental gewgaws of life and the useful. No race can prosper till it learns that there is as much dignity in tilling a field as in writing a poem. It is at the bottom of life we must begin, and not at the top. Nor should we permit our grievances to overshadow our opportunities."

And Washington continued:

"To those of the white race who look to the incoming of those of foreign birth and strange tongue and habits for the prosperity of the South, were I permitted I would repeat what I say to my own race, 'Cast down your bucket where you are.' Cast it down among the eight million Negroes whose habits you know, whose fidelity and love you have tested in days when to have proved treacherous meant the ruin of your firesides. Cast down your bucket among these people who have, without strikes and labor wars, tilled your fields, cleared your forests, builded your railroads and cities, and brought forth treasures from the bowels of the earth, and helped make possible this magnificent representation of the progress of the South. Casting down your bucket among my people, helping and encouraging them as you are doing on these grounds, and to education of head, hand, and heart, you will find that they will buy your surplus land, make blossom the waste places in your fields, and run your factories. While doing this, you can be sure in the future, as in the past, that you and your families will be surrounded by the most patient, faithful, law-abiding, and unresentful people that the world has seen. As we have proved our loyalty to you in the past, in nursing your children, watching by the sickbed of your mothers and fathers, and often following them with tear-dimmed eyes to their graves, so in the future, in our humble way, we shall stand by you with a devotion that no foreigner can approach, ready to lay down our lives, if need be, in defense of yours, interlacing our industrial, commercial, civil, and religious life with yours in a way that shall make the interest of both races one. In all things that are purely social we can be as separate as the

> fingers, yet one as the hand in all things essential
> to mutual progress."

The "cast down your bucket where you are" metaphor is one so powerful that it's a shame it hasn't endured a century later. Washington's philosophy, which he outlined in his famous book *Up from Slavery*, was that while many black leaders were busily demanding to be mayors and congressmen and to gain acceptance as bigwigs in white society, the real progress that community simply had to make was in developing and demonstrating marketable skills in the productive trades of the time.

To Washington, when the economy recognized that it needed black people because they were the mechanics, carpenters, factory workers, and skilled agricultural workers, the political disadvantages affecting the former slaves in the post-Civil War period would begin melting away.

That's a profoundly different perspective than the one you see in the modern civil rights movement. Washington wasn't all that interested in the opinion of white people, even though he was criticized as forgiving black disfranchisement and other abuses; what he was essentially saying is that the best revenge is living well. When racist whites realized they needed black people for the skills they possessed, that would give blacks true freedom. As he put it, the surest way for blacks to gain equal social rights was to demonstrate "industry, thrift, intelligence and property."

This philosophy had worked for thousands of years for Jews, after all. Spread out across the world in a vast diaspora where they suffered as a hated minority, Jews nonetheless prospered because they placed a high priority on education and the acquisition of skills, and everywhere there were Jews there were doctors, merchants, bankers, and other practitioners in high-value professions who had liquid savings and could escape with enough to re-establish themselves elsewhere whenever the locals turned sinister.

To Washington, that was what had to happen for his people, and it didn't depend on the achievement of political power—though Washington had plenty of that, as in the 1890s and the first decade of the 20th century he was the most influential figure in black politics.

He put his money, or more accurately his time and effort, where his mouth was as well. Washington sought out and impressed national leaders in politics, philanthropy, and education and embarked on yet another miracle. With funds supplied by Julius Rosenwald, the owner of the vast Sears Roebuck department store empire, Washington commenced construction on what ultimately was nearly five thousand schools for black children across the South. He knew that the state and local governments in those places wouldn't commit to integrating the schools or giving blacks equal resources, so he went out and found them himself. Among the other titans of industry from whom Washington was able to secure commitments for his various projects were George Eastman, of Eastman Kodak fame, and Standard Oil magnate Henry Huttleston Rogers. They were self-made men as Washington was.

But you don't know as much about Booker T. Washington as you should, other than that there are high schools in lots of inner cities named for him. Why is that, when he's such an amazing figure?

Because in 1909, Washington began to take fire from his own community. And before it was over he'd been derided as, in today's ugly vernacular, an Uncle Tom.

That came courtesy of a man named W. E. B. Du Bois, who unlike Washington was not born a slave. Both of Du Bois's parents were free black people who had come from free families. Though his father left his mother when W. E. B. was very young, he was brought up reasonably comfortably in the home of his maternal grandparents. Du Bois graduated from an integrated high school in Great Barrington, Massachusetts, in 1885 and then attended Fisk University, a black institution in Nashville, partly on funds raised by the community of Great Barrington.

After three years at Fisk, where he saw true racism for the first time, Du Bois came home to Massachusetts and was admitted to Harvard, where he managed to pay tuition from working summer jobs and through a small family inheritance. Du Bois earned a scholarship to cover his graduate education at Harvard.

There were very few "privileged" black Americans at the time. W. E. B. Du Bois was about as close as one might expect. So much so that after Harvard, he was off to the University of Berlin, where he studied under a fellowship and traveled throughout Europe, meeting many of the prominent philosophers of the day.

And naturally discovered Marxism, before he came home to Massachusetts.

Du Bois became the first black man to earn a PhD from Harvard in 1895, the same year Washington was giving his Atlanta Address. Initially, Du Bois claimed to be a fan of the speech, but in 1899, while living and working in Atlanta, he was greatly affected by the lynching of a black man named Sam Hose. Upon seeing Hose's burned knuckles in a grotesque storefront display, Du Bois said, "One could not be a calm, cool, and detached scientist while Negroes were lynched, murdered, and starved." Du Bois realized that "the cure wasn't simply telling people the truth, it was inducing them to act on the truth."

And in 1901 he issued a sharp rebuke to Washington's approach, calling the speech the "Atlanta Compromise" because it suggested that African Americans should work for, and submit to, white political rule. Du Bois would settle for nothing less than full civil rights, due process of law, and increased political representation for African Americans.

Nobody can fault him for that, of course. But here's the suspect part. Du Bois insisted this great racial awakening in America was only possible through political activism by blacks as a community. And to get that he insisted on the development of "the talented Tenth"—an educated elite that would lead the race through agitation. Du Bois said Washington was "the Great Accommodator" for neglecting political activism to raise the black community.

Washington's answer was that this was madness given the racial animus of the white power structure in the South of the time, that blacks in the South were outnumbered, and where it applied, outgunned. To Washington it was a recipe for disaster to provoke a bunch of people still sore over the Civil War before the people who'd bear the brunt of the backlash had skills and money with which to survive or pick up and leave for friendlier environs if all hell broke loose.

But there was more to Washington than just trying to be friendly with the Southern oppressors. While promoting moderation, he was secretly funding efforts to mount legal challenges to disfranchisement and segregation in the South. But that was one thing; the conciliatory public presentation enabled him to bring resources from those Northern robber barons and put them to work elevating his people.

Du Bois in 1906 got together with some of his "talented Tenth" colleagues at Niagara Falls, on the Canadian side, and produced a statement of what they called the "Niagara movement" trashing Washington.

> "The Negro race in America stolen, ravished and degraded, struggling up through difficulties and oppression, needs sympathy and receives criticism, needs help and is given hindrance, needs protection and is given mob-violence, needs justice and is given charity, needs leadership and is given cowardice and apology, needs bread and is given a stone. This nation will never stand justified before God until these things are changed."

The implication being it would be the elite leftists of Du Bois's clique who would be doing the changing.

For his part, Washington understood very clearly what was going on here. A timeless quote ensued:

> "There is another class of coloured people who make a business of keeping the troubles, the wrongs, and the hardships of the Negro race before the public. Having learned that they are able to make a living out of their troubles, they have grown into the settled habit of advertising their wrongs—partly because they want sympathy and partly because it pays. Some of these people

> do not want the Negro to lose his grievances, because they do not want to lose their jobs."

Washington wasn't directing that at Du Bois in particular; despite their disagreements the two were not acrimonious, though their supporters definitely became so. But he recognized that there was a terrific grift available to people who'd focus on the problems of black America without any real plans or desire to remedy them as he was trying to do with the tireless, ground-level work of building up the community.

After a 1906 riot in Atlanta, caused by white displeasure that blacks were taking jobs away amid a recession, killed twenty-five people and injured hundreds more, Du Bois won the argument. He had the shinier objects, and it was too easy to suck in the influencers of the black community with the flattery that they were the "talented Tenth" and to blame the racism of white America—which absolutely, without a doubt, existed—for black America's inability to advance.

Washington was selling vegetables, and Du Bois was giving away ice cream. It was a mismatch.

By 1910 Du Bois had helped to found the National Association for the Advancement of Colored People, and the NAACP embarked on its program of agitating for civil rights for blacks, often through confrontation.

And as Theodore Roosevelt was president at the time of the Atlanta riot, Du Bois advocated that blacks abandon the Republican Party because it was indifferent to their interests. This worked out so well that a decade later when the virulent racist Democrat Woodrow Wilson occupied the presidency, he held a showing of the pro-Ku Klux Klan motion picture *The Birth of a Nation* at the White House.

By this point Du Bois was touting socialism as a better vehicle for black progress than capitalism, as though the white racists who ran the states most blacks were living in at the time would be willing to use the power of a socialist system to elevate blacks vis-à-vis their own people.

But while Washington and his style of raising up the black community fell from fashion, his legacy had nonetheless taken hold. As he said, "Success always leaves footprints," and the era from 1900 to 1930 was the "golden age of black business" in the words of historian Juliet E. K. Walker. Black entrepreneurship, something prioritized by Washington as he had created the National Negro Business League, a national business-to-business network, which was highly successful, had exploded. And black per capita income, even in the South, had risen measurably, though not enough to be world-changing.

But the political condition of the black community was unchanged. Perhaps that's an indictment of both approaches; more likely it's a factor of the utter backwardness of the Jim Crow South where most of America's black people were still living even amid the substantial migration to Northern cities, which was only accelerating.

The onset of World War II and the massive labor shortage that brought on is what gave black America the integration it desperately needed. Blacks were suddenly being hired en masse in the huge factories springing up to fuel the war effort, and the migration to big cities was breathtaking—as many as a third of black residents of Southern states had left by 1960.

By then the black community had a new leader. The story of the Reverend Martin Luther King Junior is very well known, but what's most importantly said about King is that he was a bit more Douglass and Washington than he was Du Bois. King's message to America was much like that of Douglass—he wanted a colorblind country in which it was the content of one's character that mattered. And it was a lot like Washington's—"If a man is called to be a street sweeper," said King, "he should sweep streets even as a Michelangelo painted, or Beethoven composed music or Shakespeare wrote poetry. He should sweep streets so well that all the hosts of heaven and earth will pause to say, 'Here lived a great street sweeper who did his job well.'"

King captured the fascination and hearts of Americans because he was notably imbued with the spirit of the nation's founders. His message was quintessential America at our best, and while there was obviously great resistance to it—only an idiot would fail to mention his assassination by a racist white Democrat at an Atlanta motel in 1968—its impact was unmistakable. He won, and he achieved at law a remedy to the discrimination and disfranchisement Du Bois had demanded, but he did it not by rejecting the system as Du Bois did but by challenging it to meet its ideals.

The problem was that when the black community got what it came for in the civil rights legislation of the 1960s, that wasn't all it received. Lyndon Johnson's government married that civil rights legislation to a massive raft of giveaway programs that did away with the necessity of preserving families and motivating people to seize the opportunities presented to them. When LBJ did that, he cut the legs out from under an entire race of people in this country. Black America needed obstacles taken out of its way, and what it got was a shell game.

The famous quote attributed to Johnson on the eve of his Great Society package passing was, "I'll have those n****rs voting Democrat for the next two hundred years."

Washington saw some of this in his day and had his own thoughts:

> "Among a large class, there seemed to be a dependence upon the government for every conceivable thing. The members of this class had little ambition to create a position for themselves, but wanted the federal officials to create one for them. How many times I wished then and have often wished since, that by some power of magic, I might remove the great bulk of these people into the country districts and plant them upon the soil—upon the solid and never deceptive foundation of Mother Nature, where all nations and races that have ever succeeded have gotten their start—a start that at first may be slow and toilsome, but one that nevertheless is real."

One of the worst injustices in American history is what grifters and exploiters, people Booker T. Washington warned about, have done to black people when slavery should have been put to pasture long ago.

And the awful theories of Karl Marx and his successors have played a terrible role in that.

Our next chapter will attempt to explain why these bad ideas persist and have, in too much of our national life, even expanded.

CHAPTER 6

The March through the Institutions

Among the non-brain-dead on the Left there's a growing, but totally insufficient, recognition that the neocommunist crowd is poison for its chances of holding the mainstream.

In January 2022, the liberal political analyst Thomas Byrne Edsall wrote in the *New York Times* that the massive amounts of cash dumped into the political process by corporate philanthropic entities were driving the Democrats away from the center. Edsall used an organization called Candid to assess the spending by those foundations on identity politics initiatives like Black Lives Matter and others. What he found was striking:

> "Before Floyd's death, Candid found that philanthropies provided '$3.3 billion in racial equity funding' for the nine years from 2011 to 2019. Since then, Candid calculations revealed much higher totals for both 2020 and 2021: '50,887

grants valued at $12.7 billion' and '177 pledges valued at $11.6 billion.'

"Among the top funders, according to Candid's calculations, are the Ford Foundation, at $3 billion; Mackenzie Scott, at $2.9 billion; JPMorgan Chase & Co. Contributions Program, at $2.1 billion; W. K. Kellogg Foundation, $1.2 billion; Bill & Melinda Gates Foundation, $1.1 billion; Silicon Valley Community Foundation, $1 billion; Walton Family Foundation, $689 million; The William and Flora Hewlett Foundation, $438 million; and the Foundation to Promote Open Society, $350.5 million."

Edsall went on:

"There are Democratic strategists who worry about unintended political consequences that could flow from this surge in philanthropic giving. Rob Stein, one of the founders of the Democracy Alliance, an organization of major donors on the left, argued in a phone interview that while most foundation spending is on programs that have widespread support, 'when progressive philanthropists fund groups that promote extreme views like "defunding the police" or that sanction "cancel culture," they are exacerbating intraparty conflict and stoking interparty backlash.' The danger, according to Stein, is that 'some progressive

> politicians and funders are contributing to divisiveness within their ranks and giving fodder to the right.'...
>
> "Darren Walker, president of the Ford Foundation, argued in a phone interview that no consideration is—or can be—given to partisan political consequences:
>
> 'We make no calculations about how our grantees give credibility or not to the Democratic Party. That is of no concern to the Ford Foundation, or to me personally.'
>
> "Walker continued: 'We support organizations that are working toward more justice and more inclusion in America, but we have no interest in the Democratic Party's strengths or weaknesses.'
>
> "I asked Walker about the concerns raised by Stein and [Matt] Bennett (senior vice president of the left-wing Third Way). 'We support issues that are about progress and inclusion and justice, but the chips fall where they fall,' Walker said."

The starting year of the Candid analysis Edsall used is a fortunate one, because 2011 was the first year we began to see the troubling trend of corporate backing to promote outright racism under the woke banner. And that timing itself was quite suspicious.

What happened in 2011? Why, Occupy Wall Street, of course.

It was September 17 of that year when Occupy protesters staged a takeover of Zuccotti Park in lower Manhattan not far from the trading desk, in order to rail against corporate influence in government, wealth inequality, and most importantly the fact that nobody had ever been held criminally responsible for the irresponsible behavior that led to the 2008 economic crash.

The Occupy protest was a public relations triumph. As a means of getting national attention for the movement, it was a grand slam. Though the protesters were generally an unruly, slovenly bunch whose personal practices during their conquest of Zuccotti Park invalidated most of their criticisms of the one percent, they nonetheless shook corporate America in ways that made the fat cats quite uncomfortable.

And nobody could be surprised that as soon as the Occupy gang had gone home, there was a new narrative in America. Namely, that this is a fundamentally racist country where a black or brown man can't get a fair shake.

Who was pushing that narrative? Well, who was funding it?

It didn't take long before those same corporate suits whose charitable foundations were bankrolling Black Lives Matter and its predecessors were backing those "philanthropic" efforts with their own marketing dollars. Wokeness was born.

And Wall Street itself got in on the game by creating something called "DEI"—Diversity, Equity, and Inclusion—as a metric for investing. Companies willing to jump through the woke hoops laid out by DEI inquisitors would see their stock prices mount regardless of whether their profit margins justified such investments.

They created the game and rigged it. And it was easy.

Kentucky State University professor, black conservative, and Twitter gadfly Wilfred Reilly, in a November 2020 op-ed at *USA Today*, recounted his own experiences as part of the Occupy movement:

> "I have seen the effects of this fracturing myself. Not always a be-spectacled center-rightist friendly with both the Brooks Brothers, I was active with the 2011 Occupy movement early in graduate school.
>
> "Occupy Chicago, possibly the largest gathering of Guy Fawkes-mask wearing radicals outside Manhattan's Zucotti [sic] Park, fell apart largely because of the endless bifurcation of members' agendas. Whenever a task force of leading members was proposed to discuss some almost-consensus working-class issue like support for an increased minimum wage, the call would immediately come for a women's task force. Then, what about a Black women's task force? A Black gay women's task force?
>
> "Very often, 37 quarreling proposals about what to do would eventually be made, and nothing would ever get done. By the end, there actually existed a separate all-Black and minority version of Occupy, called 'Occupy the Hood.'"

There's another book you'll want to read in order to get a full understanding of how the woke Left managed to occupy—and be occupied by—corporate America. *Woke, Inc.: Inside Corporate America's Social Justice Scam,* by investor and entrepreneur Vivek Ramaswamy, came out in the summer of 2021. It's a fantastic takedown of how the corporate world began to embrace the identity politics, critical theory, and cancel culture of the Hard Left, and at its heart lies an understanding very similar to the one Reilly learned in his days back in Chicago.

Namely, Ramaswamy says the Occupy movement was all about opposing "disproportionate economic power." But no sooner did that energy burst on the scene than it devolved into arguments about race, gender, and ethnicity. Reilly saw that tear apart Occupy Chicago, and as Ramaswamy notes, corporate America saw it tear apart the rest of the movement. As he says, "Woke culture eroded [Occupy] from within."

Intersectionalism doesn't move the needle, as much fun as it might be for the victims to compare their sob stories. And if you're corporate America, and you're scared to death that the public might turn on you over the bailouts and destruction of 2008, while at the same time you're engaged in a host of other activities the American public ought to be perturbed about, like offshoring your manufacturing to a hostile foreign country bent on world domination at our expense, you desperately want to find a way to co-opt and neuter your most effective critics.

So it became very easy to just get woke.

As Ramaswamy tells it, the sales pitch to the Left went like this: the real problem was not corporate power per se, but rather the fact that it was old white guys in charge of that corporate power that was doing all the damage. Giving the reins to black or brown people, or women, or even just young people would create the heaven on earth that the Occupy gang was looking for.

Which of course was never actually going to happen. Put a few women or blacks on the board, hire a Sri Lankan or Moroccan CEO, who cares? The same people were going to run those companies and control the stock no matter who sat in the c-suite.

But the optics would change, he says, and that would be enough to placate the Occupy mob while corporate America went on with business as usual.

Except it isn't really business as usual, because now we have something called "stakeholder capitalism," in which left-wing interest groups now get to collect tolls from legitimate business under the ambit of social justice. You see it with the environmentalists, the race-hustlers, feminists, and lots of others.

It's bad enough that corporations are screwing their shareholders out of dividend money being spent to purchase quietude from neocommunist extortion mobs. It's even worse when, having paid tribute to the wokes, those same corporations then loudly proclaim their activism in marketing offensives. You're not only being stolen from as a consumer and shareholder, now you're being proselytized with messaging traditional Americans generally find offensive.

We've gone from Michael Jordan, who admonished his critics by noting that "Republicans buy sneakers, too," to Colin Kaepernick. We've gone from Mary Lou Retton to Megan Rapinoe. Nobody appreciates the change.

But this entire woke project has nonetheless worked, at least so far, because large corporations have a greater share of the market, at the expense of small and mid-sized companies women and minorities have a far greater chance of owning, than ever before. Corporate profits are off the charts. And we're under the thumb of a woke oligopoly that tyrannizes the middle class.

Daniel Greenfield, writing at *FrontPage Magazine* last year, identified this phenomenon perfectly:

> "The Left bet that if it could radicalize the children of the wealthy that Corporate America would bend the knee. And that's exactly what happened. The radicals used their leverage over academia and

the entertainment industry to create radical generations. But that radicalism was heavily concentrated among the Ivy League and the children of the elites who would become the corporate leaders and also be the consumers with the most disposable income.

"Economics, like politics, proved to be downstream of the culture. Capturing the ecosystem at its base allowed the Left to take over the economy and turn some of the country's biggest brands into megaphones for its propaganda. But these are corporate brands that have all the qualities of the ossified elites that have always been an easy target for the revolutions of the radicals."

Greenfield continues:

"'Wokening' is a social disease of stale companies with stale brands whose products are overpriced and have fallen out of touch with the needs of many consumers. And the country's consumer marketplace is dominated by these collapsing giants whose leaders are just marking time and cashing big checks while trying to co-opt the revolution threatening to destroy them.

"European monarchs tried to co-opt leftist revolutions because they no longer had confidence in their own roles and had no idea what to do next. Coca Cola and the woke corporate giants share the same decadent sense of decline and their urban

> elites are selling out their rural base to appeal to the young radical generation to which their children and their social circle belong.
>
> "Wokeness is the consequence of a moral and economic brokenness among the nation's elites. The Left conquered the corrupt infrastructure of a decaying political and economic system. Now it's using that infrastructure to brainwash and suppress the country's middle and working classes by lecturing them on their racism, and redefining them as domestic terrorists."

It's been one of the most identifiable and unsettling aspects of America's recent cultural decline to see so many of America's iconic corporations taken over by people who have no particular use for America or most of the people in it. Much of that can be explained by the fact that the top management of many of those companies is not American, of course—Coca-Cola's CEO is British, Gillette's head of North American operations is Indian—but nationality doesn't explain the problem away.

Because no corporation is as woke as the elite universities that are disproportionately counted on to staff their upper management rosters. In fact, the capture of Corporate America is an end-stage development in the Left's war of conquest over the nation's cultural institutions.

Why are traditional Americans such strangers in our own land? Why is this suddenly a country whose elite citizens don't just fail to uphold and promote its core cultural and moral values but pride themselves on tearing them down?

America in the 21st century is a unique society. It has the most privileged revolutionaries and pampered radicals in human history.

But once you understand the origin of wokeness and the collection of toxic cultural viruses it's composed of, things become much less confusing. While the change in our national narrative seems sudden—it came upon us with the election of Barack Obama in 2008 and rapidly metastasized in politics and business from there—it's been coming for a whole lot longer than that.

We're back to Karl Marx here, obviously.

As noted in our last chapter, in the decades that followed his arrival on the intellectual scene, Marx collected many followers among the parasitical and indolent monied classes in Europe and North America, so much so that when World War I broke out in 1914, the international Marxist Left was certain that its carnage would be the spark that touched off the global revolution of the proletariat they'd been waiting for.

But just like the Heaven's Gate cult was disappointed when the world didn't end when the Hale-Bopp comet whizzed by, World War I was a big fizzle for the Marxists.

After all, of all the major participants in that war, the only one that experienced that revolution was Russia—the weakest, most backward, and most dysfunctional society in Europe. And Russia fell largely because Germany bankrolled the rise of Vladimir Lenin as a means of knocking their enemy out of the war.

For a movement that had convinced itself it would soon be in charge of France, Germany, Italy, the United Kingdom, and lots of other countries worth having, this was a bitter disappointment.

But Marxists don't give up. They never admit defeat. Their response to disappointment is to redouble their efforts.

And their response to the disappointment when the poor and working classes in so many European countries were willing to march into the maelstrom for king and country in World War I was to turn to Gramsci, who had said the key to bringing on the revolution was cultural, not economic.

Gramsci's prescription for the inevitable Marxist victory had it that cadres of fellow travelers would have to take over the intellectual life of society. They had to control the newspapers, the arts, the educational institutions, broadcast media, everywhere that ideas were the product.

Kind of like Du Bois's "talented Tenth"—that the socialist vanguard would be the super-smart intellectuals who'd obviously get to run things when the revolution of the proletariat finally got here was always part of the equation. Because there has to be something, y'know, for the effort.

Gramsci held that Marxists would have to stage a march through the institutions, and in so doing break down the hold a nation's traditional culture would have on the populace.

Thus was born cultural Marxism, and in the period between the world wars an enormous amount of energy was expended in building up structures and ideas to win the march through the institutions in all of the civilized world. One such structure was the Institute for Social Research (*Institut für Sozialforschung*), an attached institute at the Goethe University in Frankfurt, Germany. We know it as the Frankfurt School.

Founded in 1923 with a donation by Felix Weil, the parasitical twenty-five-year-old son of a wealthy grain merchant, the Institute for Social Research set its aim to developing Marxist studies in Germany. It soon attracted a cast of characters similar to Weil—rich from family money, Marxist, and Jewish. That last fact became an existential problem given what ultimately became the politics of post-World War I Germany; in 1933 the Nazis shut the Frankfurt School down. But the institute didn't die. It simply moved to the United States where it found hospitality at Columbia University in New York City.

What the Frankfurt School specialized in was something Gramsci also chewed on called critical theory. Aptly named, because literally all critical theory does is criticize. It's wholly destructive; it creates and protects nothing. According to critical theory there is no objective or natural truth; man isn't capable of finding that in any event, because we're blinded by the social hierarchies into which we're born. Oppressors don't even know they're oppressing, and the oppressed have no idea they're even being oppressed.

It's a self-licking ice cream cone of a philosophy if ever there was one, and it fails the first rule of rational discourse in that it isn't falsifiable. There is no way to prove critical theory wrong. There's no "if this happens, the theory necessarily fails."

But very few people in this country ever gave critical theory much of a hearing. For decades the Frankfurt School scribblers remained on the fringes of politics and culture.

At least, until the 1960s. That's when one of their number, a thoroughly obnoxious loon named Herbert Marcuse, published a pair of somewhat well-read books: *Eros and Civilization* (1955) and *One-Dimensional Man* (1964), and a 1965 essay titled *Repressive Tolerance*. A taste of his philosophy, taken from the third abovementioned work:

> "Liberating tolerance, then, would mean intolerance against movements from the Right and

> toleration of movements from the Left. Surely, no government can be expected to foster its own subversion, but in a democracy such a right is vested in the people (i.e. in the majority of the people). This means that the ways should not be blocked on which a subversive majority could develop, and if they are blocked by organized repression and indoctrination, their reopening may require apparently undemocratic means. They would include the withdrawal of toleration of speech and assembly from groups and movements that promote aggressive policies, armament, chauvinism, discrimination on the grounds of race and religion, or that oppose the extension of public services, social security, medical care, etc."

On a first reading, that would seem highly unconvincing: What's the value of tolerance that shortly devolves into repression?

And yet directly from Marcuse's writing comes modern cancel culture.

The Left became enamored with cultural Marxism and critical theory, but it took a very long time for this line of thinking to gain any real notice in the general population.

But once critical theory was married to race in the early 1990s, at a time Americans were experiencing mounting frustration over the suspect results of the 1960s civil rights reforms in solving racial inequalities, everything changed.

Nothing the cultural Marxists offer today carries the force of a Frederick Douglass or Martin Luther King. Today's radicals might purport to stand on their shoulders, but their arguments are unrecognizable to a Douglass or a King—because Douglass and King were builders, not wreckers.

And the woke radicals of today are wreckers.

They've wrecked the universities, which are no longer centers of progress or mass education but rather indoctrination factories for the cults of climate change, intersectional feminism, transgender theory and LGBTQ activism, racial grievance, and anti-Christianity. That wreckage is rapidly filtering down into K-12 education, as teachers indoctrinated in college are spreading critical theory into every subject through radical pedagogy learned in the education departments at those colleges.

They've wrecked our entertainment media. Netflix's *Bridgerton* would have you believe half of the English nobility in the Regency period, to include Queen Charlotte, was black. To get through the first season of *Ozark*, one of the better shows on that streaming service, you've got to endure a lengthy treatment of gay sex. Ditto for the first season of *Game of Thrones*. It's hard to remember the last HBO series that didn't promote exotic sexuality or black struggle, or both. There are barely any action movies made anymore that don't subject the viewer to the proposition that 105-pound women can beat up men twice their size or more.

That last bit is not good, by the way. It's actually a real problem. Teach girls that violence against men (or other women, for that matter) is a legitimate way to solve problems, and they'll act on that lesson. It will go badly for them. What's worse, if they grow up thinking they can get what they want by pretending they're Scarlett Johansson or Charlize Theron, they'll miss out on the traditional ways females have successfully interacted with others—ways society desperately needs from them.

Women have always been our best peacemakers. If our stupid woke culture robs us of that, there will be no peace and society will collapse.

Our news media has been similarly wrecked. The news networks and major newspapers no longer seek to inform but to indoctrinate. Narrative is everything, and the dissemination of wokeism is so insidious that it filters down all the way to style.

Formerly, there were black people and white people. You'll notice that now there are Black people, though not necessarily White people.

Our woke overlords even attempted to force upon us a nonsense word to describe Hispanics. But Latinx hasn't taken off for the simple reason that it's offensive to the people it attempts to describe. Why? Because the general form of the word is Latino, not Latinx. Spanish, which is a fully formed language in no need of woke perfecting, ascribes male and female characteristics to its words, and in Spanish the male form describes the general population.

Hispanic women are perfectly comfortable being included in "Latino." They don't need "Latinx" nonsense.

And left-wing Hispanic pressure groups have already given up on "Latinx." Who hasn't? White leftists.

Having made their march through the institutions Gramsci prescribed, the woke communists naturally would have invaded corporate America. But there's a problem.

As President Trump said, everything woke turns to shit.

Woke can't run anything. Woke can't make anything but propaganda and narrative. Woke isn't self-aware and it isn't empathetic, though it demands you accept it as such. Woke celebrates mediocrity and failure. Woke is emotional, not rational.

And woke eschews beauty and truth. Woke actually says truth is racist.

Woke is about power and coercion. It isn't about worth or grace.

Meet an example of who the woke priests are. His name is Mark Bray, a lecturer at Dartmouth and former organizer of the Occupy Wall Street movement whose credits include items published by the *Washington Post* and *Foreign Policy Magazine*, not to mention a book entitled *Antifa: The Anti-Fascist Handbook*. Bray has been fully embraced by the so-called "mainstream" media since he helped to found the Occupy Wall Street movement.

Here's what kind of guy Mark Bray is:

> "Our goal should be that in twenty years those who voted for Trump are too uncomfortable to share that fact in public. We may not always be able to change someone's beliefs, but we sure as hell can make it politically, socially, economically and sometimes physically costly to articulate them."

An institution that would employ such a thug is no institution of higher learning. And yet Dartmouth employs Mark Bray, just like woke psychotics, almost all of them privileged white people who rank far to the left of most Democrats, much less most Americans, have infiltrated and overpopulated our cultural institutions to a disturbing degree.

What's the effect of having our institutions captured by these woke cultists? Let's go to Tempe, Arizona, and we'll see.

Kyrsten Sinema is by no means a conservative, but she represents a traditionally red state in which Democrats generally require special circumstances to win statewide elections.

Sinema is in the US Senate because she managed a feat repeated just two years later—namely, beating the hapless Martha McSally. One could say McSally is single-handedly responsible for the Democrats' majority in the Senate, having lost not just to Sinema but to the DNC sock puppet Mark Kelly as well.

Democrats in Washington think those two elections are an indication of Arizona's bluish tint. Sinema, who spends time among her constituents, isn't so sure.

And so when Team D decided, amid an inflationary economy brought on by Branch Covidian lunatic public policy launched amid the panic over the China virus outbreak, to push a go-for-broke $5 trillion legislative spending orgy agenda, Sinema turned into a stumbling block for its passage.

Because she knows she's up for reelection in 2024, and she's obviously not convinced she's going to catch another Martha McSally as an opponent.

Kyrsten Sinema's sartorial taste is a bit questionable, but she's not stupid. That can't necessarily be said of some of the Democrats, particularly in the House of Representatives and also in the Biden White House. Sinema isn't a Hard Left loon. Not like Alexandria Ocasio-Cortez or Pramila Jayapal or some of the other buffoons who began calling her their enemy. She's one of the few "moderate" Democrats left. In the Senate, it's really just her and Joe Manchin who balked at Biden's lunatic, economy-killing bacchanal. Barely more than their number exist in the House.

But given the Democrats' tiny majority in both houses of Congress, those moderates are the difference between passage and failure. And Manchin and Sinema knew their voters back home would have at them if they voted for the full $5 trillion insanity. Both were on board with $1.5 trillion of it, the colossally wasteful "bipartisan" infrastructure plan. The rest, a $3.5 trillion budget reconciliation package stocked up with every stupid-fantasy governmental abuse of constitutional limits and basic economic truth Bernie Sanders could think up, they weren't on board with.

Since Jayapal and the rest of the loons took the position that they wouldn't support the $1.5 trillion infrastructure package without the $3.5 trillion festival of idiocy passing first, Congress found itself in a bit of a quandary. And with Republicans on Capitol Hill finally recognizing the value of saying no and allowing the Democrats to hang themselves, it became socialists-vs-moderates for the big fat "L."

Sinema boarded a plane on a Friday and went home to Phoenix rather than stick around for the hotbox sessions the Democrat leadership had planned for her when the Build Back Better plan was up for a vote. Without her on Capitol Hill, the $3.5 trillion package was off the legislative table for a quick smashmouth session; only the $1.5 trillion could be passed. Which wasn't good enough for Pramila Jayapal and her collection of angry clowns.

And while Republicans laughed, the Left decided to scream at the sky.

And at Sinema.

In a public bathroom at Arizona State University, where she teaches a class.

While filming themselves doing it.

We'll skip the big-picture commentary about just how lousy the Left is at persuasion anymore. You already know all of that. It'll suffice to say that this was more likely to have the effect of hardening Sinema's position against the $3.5 trillion than it was to persuade her.

Losers threatening to beat her in the next election when she's clearly had her own internal polling done and knows she can only win by minimizing the amount of irritation she imposes on independents and soft Republican voters won't really move the needle. Nor will impassioned pleas by illegals looking for free swill from the public till.

Again, Kyrsten Sinema isn't stupid. Rather, she was perturbed. After the restroom incident, she put out a long, understandably grumpy statement:

> "Yesterday, several individuals disrupted my class at Arizona State University," Sinema said. "After deceptively entering a locked, secure building, these individuals filmed and publicly posted videos of my students without their permission—including footage of myself and my students using a restroom without consent."

That happens to be a violation of Arizona law, by the way, not that anybody expects these loons to suffer for it.

"In Arizona," Sinema continued, "we love the First Amendment. We know that it is vital to our democracy that constituents can freely petition, protest or criticize my policy positions or decisions. The activist group that engaged in yesterday's behavior is one that both my team and I have met with several times since I was elected to the Senate and I will continue engaging with Arizonans with diverse viewpoints to help inform my work for Arizona."

She kept going.

> "Yesterday's behavior was not legitimate protest. It is unacceptable for activist organizations to instruct their members to jeopardize themselves by engaging in unlawful activities such as gaining entry to closed university buildings, disrupting learning environments, and filming students in a restroom.
>
> "In the 19 years I have been teaching at ASU, I have been committed to creating a safe and intellectually challenging environment for my students. Yesterday, that environment was breached. My students were unfairly and unlawfully victimized. This is wholly inappropriate.
>
> **"It is the duty of elected leaders to avoid fostering an environment in which honestly-held policy disagreements serve as a basis for vitriol—raising the temperature in political rhetoric and creating a permission structure for unacceptable behavior."**

That last bit, emphasis mine, is the money shot. Sinema called out AOC, Jayapal, and the rest of the Lunatic Caucus as responsible for what happened in the restroom. And nobody can blame her, because it's been several years of this kind of behavior on the Left thanks to the rhetoric of people like Barack Obama, Sanders (who called for a "political revolution" and then acted surprised when one of his stooge followers attempted the political assassination of several Republican members of Congress), and Maxine Waters.

Sinema demanded they be held to account. Which was a fruitless demand, because while she might be closer to the American mainstream than her tormentors, the institutions where these decisions are made are controlled by people much more like Pramila Jayapal. And when Sinema's personal information, including her Social Security number, was dumped out onto the internet it was clear even a Democrat US Senator isn't prominent enough to escape the wrath of the Woke.

Meanwhile, Manchin stays on a houseboat he owns in DC. The loons found him as well and harassed him as he sipped a cocktail on the gunwale.

Asked about the harassment of fellow Democrats, "Circleback Girl" Psaki essentially shrugged.

Them's the breaks, was more or less the White House's reaction.

Telling a senator you're trying to convince of something "Them's the breaks" when she gets chased into a ladies' room while at her other job is, well....

This is Biden, so there's no floor. Even so, that's obviously not going to fly.

By the end of 2021 there were real Democrat fears that Manchin, who loudly signaled the end of the Build Back Better plan, might cut a deal with Republican Senate minority leader Mitch McConnell for a committee chairmanship in a GOP-led Senate or something (not to mention a cleared field for 2024), which McConnell would absolutely do in order to reclaim that gavel.

Of course, should that happen, it would truly be the end of any moderate Democrats on Capitol Hill.

But given the implicit and explicit threats being made by the AOCs of the world that the moderates are going to catch primary opponents in 2022, many of whom might very well win in the same way AOC did but will find themselves far less likely to survive in the 2022 general election in swing districts, that end of the moderates might be coming eventually anyway.

We can predict the outcome of the Democrat Civil War. It's going to end up exactly the same in politics as it did in other venues like academia, Hollywood, the arts, and journalism, where the Hard Left has chased ordinary liberals and moderates off and has begun imposing ruin on the institution. But unlike those, in politics there are still some conservatives around to benefit from the implosion.

The question is whether those institutions corrupted, wrecked, and made dysfunctional by the cultural Marxists who've infiltrated them will drag down the whole country before they're replaced with something that works. More on this subject in a later chapter.

CHAPTER 7

The China Problem

Everything you need to know about what America's relationship with China has evolved into is encapsulated in a viral video that circulated in November 2020. It's a public speech given by the head of a Chinese Communist Party think tank explaining the last several decades of that country's history with the United States and how it handled the disruptions of the Trump administration.

"Trump waged a trade war against us," the Chinese bigwig told his audience. "Why couldn't we handle him? Why is that between 1992 and 2016, we always resolved issues with the US? Because we had people up there. In America's core circle of power, we have some old friends.

"During the last three to four decades," he went on, as his audience giggled quietly, "we took advantage of America's core circle. As I said, Wall Street has a very profound influence.... We used to rely heavily on them. Problem is they have been declining since 2008. Most importantly after 2016 Wall Street couldn't control Trump....

In the US-China trade war they tried to help. My friends in the US told me that they tried to help, but they couldn't. Now with Biden winning the election, the traditional elites, political elites, the establishment, they have a very close relationship with Wall Street."

Our ruling establishment, or so much of it as to be described as a majority, is in bed with the Chinese Communist Party at a time when China is responsible for setting loose the most deadly pandemic in a century, and at a time when the Chinese military is bristling with new weaponry and making leering eyes at Taiwan. China has had a thirty-plus-year run of forced repression, environmental destruction, geopolitical aggression, intellectual property theft, and diplomatic/espionage shenanigans since the Tiananmen Square massacre, *and we have assisted them at nearly every stage along the way.*

In early February 2021, Lee Smith published an opus at *Tablet Magazine* titled "The Thirty Tyrants," an article that made the case that the American globalist ruling and professional elite more or less consciously chose the Communist Chinese model of organizing society rather than that of the United States, for the facile reason that it's easier to be a member of the elite in a system like the one the ChiComs have established.

If you can't beat 'em, join 'em, essentially.

> "The Thirty Tyrants" is a reference to the puppet regime in ancient Athens that victorious Sparta installed following their victory in the Peloponnesian War, a regime the formerly democratic Athenian elite was now happy to preside over, having decided democracy wasn't any longer to their liking.

"We have a lot more than thirty tyrants.

"The one-word motto they came to live by was *globalism*—that is, the freedom to structure commercial relationships and social enterprises without reference to the well-being of the particular society in which they happened to make their livings and raise their children.

"Undergirding the globalist enterprise was China's accession to the World Trade Organization in 2001. For decades, American policymakers and the corporate class said they saw China as a rival, but the elite that [Thomas] Friedman described saw enlightened Chinese autocracy as a friend and even as a model—which was not surprising, given that the Chinese Communist Party became their source of power, wealth, and prestige. Why did they trade with an authoritarian regime and send millions of American manufacturing jobs off to China thereby impoverish working Americans? Because it made them rich. They salved their consciences by telling themselves they had no choice but to deal with China: It was big, productive, and efficient and its rise was inevitable. And besides, the American workers hurt by the deal deserved to be punished—who could defend a class of reactionary and racist ideological naysayers standing in the way of what was best for progress?

"Returning those jobs to America, along with ending foreign wars and illegal immigration, was the core policy promise of Donald Trump's presidency, and the source of his surprise victory in 2016. Trump was hardly the first to make the case that the corporate and political establishment's trade relationship with China had sold out ordinary Americans. Former Democratic congressman and 1988 presidential candidate Richard Gephardt was the leading voice in an important but finally not very influential group of elected Democratic Party officials and policy experts who warned that trading with a state that employed slave labor would cost American jobs and sacrifice American honor. The only people who took Trump seriously were the more than 60 million American voters who believed him when he said he'd fight the elites to get those jobs back.

"What he called 'The Swamp' appeared at first just to be a random assortment of industries, institutions, and personalities that seemed to have nothing in common, outside of the fact they were excoriated by the newly elected president. But Trump's incessant attacks on that elite gave them collective self-awareness as well as a powerful motive for solidarity. Together, they saw that they represented a nexus of public and private sector interests that shared not only the same prejudices and hatreds, cultural tastes and consumer habits but also the same center of gravity—the

U.S.-China relationship. And so, the China Class was born.

"Connections that might have once seemed tenuous or nonexistent now became lucid under the light of Trump's scorn, and the reciprocal scorn of the elite that loathed him.

"A decade ago, no one would've put NBA superstar LeBron James and Apple CEO Tim Cook in the same family album, but here they are now, linked by their fantastic wealth owing to cheap Chinese manufacturing (Nike sneakers, iPhones, etc.) and a growing Chinese consumer market. The NBA's $1.5 billion contract with digital service provider Tencent made the Chinese firm the league's biggest partner outside America. In gratitude, these two-way ambassadors shared the wisdom of the Chinese Communist Party with their ignorant countrymen. After an NBA executive tweeted in defense of Hong Kong dissidents, social justice activist King LeBron told Americans to watch their tongues. 'Even though yes, we do have freedom of speech,' said James, 'it can be a lot of negative that comes with it.'

"Because of Trump's pressure on the Americans who benefited extravagantly from the U.S.-China relationship, these strange bedfellows acquired what Marxists call class consciousness—and joined together to fight back, further cementing their relationships with their Chinese patrons.

> United now, these disparate American institutions lost any sense of circumspection or shame about cashing checks from the Chinese Communist Party, no matter what horrors the CCP visited on the prisoners of its slave labor camps and no matter what threat China's spy services and the People's Liberation Army might pose to national security. Think tanks and research institutions like the Atlantic Council, the Center for American Progress, the EastWest Institute, the Carter Center, the Carnegie Endowment for International Peace, Johns Hopkins School of Advanced International Studies, and others gorged themselves on Chinese money. The world-famous Brookings Institution had no scruples about publishing a report funded by Chinese telecom company Huawei that praised Huawei technology."

Smith's piece is one of the most important on the subject of China, a country that represents the most direct and pressing threat to America's future.

To take stock of the economic changes and resulting geopolitical implications between 1988, when protesters in the Chinese capital of Beijing filled Tiananmen Square demanding to participate in the flowering of liberty that had broken out over most of the rest of the then-communist world and were consequently crushed under People's Liberation Army tanks, and today, it's almost impossible to understand how our leaders could have been so generous. We didn't just refuse to punish the ChiComs for the brutalization of their own people who simply asked for what the rest of the world was embracing, we actively rewarded the butchers by first opening trade, then treating them as an equal, then giving them concessions that impoverished our own people.

Our policy toward China with respect to trade is either an exercise in naivete or corruption, or both. Nothing else can describe the idiocy of trading out American jobs for Chinese slave labor under the justification that economic ties with a totalitarian regime will eventually turn the Chinese into Jeffersonian democrats and lead to a mass breakout of Western civilization.

Nixon's opening to China in the early 1970s was made possible by the Soviet denunciation of Stalin, after all. The Chinese weren't interested in communism with a human face; they saw that as weakness and were willing to sit down with the Americans because to them, the Soviets were doomed.

Tiananmen Square was highly predictable. The USSR and its Eastern European vassals were collapsing by then, the communist enterprise's rotted core becoming exposed by Mikhail Gorbachev's embrace of *glasnost* and *perestroika,* and the aging tyrants of the Chinese politburo were resolute that they'd kill as many of their countrymen as necessary to ensure nothing like that could happen to them.

Melt their hearts with Cabbage Patch dolls and Ford F-150s and Dell PCs? No.

The Chinese changed, all right. They switched from communism to fascism in order to get rich off the Americans. It wouldn't work for the Chinese state to be doing all the business with their new interlocutors, so they just had the state create companies for that purpose.

But everything was still owned by the Communist Party or the PLA, or high officials therein.

As Mussolini said, fascism at its heart is corporatism. China built a whole series of corporations to serve as facades for state-controlled commerce, and American business interests bought the ruse hook, line, and sinker. They didn't even worry when the ChiComs insisted, as the price of doing business in Shanghai or Guangzhou, that our firms surrender their intellectual property. The size of that market was worth it, we heard.

Besides, eventually the ChiComs would give way and trading in Ningbo would be the same experience as in Vancouver. What's a little sacrifice in the short term against such a future?

Especially when so many Americans so quickly became so bought off.

One wonders whether any of the "globalist" crowd in the 1990s and following decades ever stopped to consider that the Chinese, inheritors of one of the oldest societies on the planet and long believers in the concept of their country as the Middle Kingdom, the civilizational center of the world, might seek to make America their cultural, economic, and political colony rather than the reverse. Clearly, the answer is no.

It should have been otherwise. China, after all, has lots of experience with respect to colonization and the West. The Chinese remember well that European nations spent most of the 19th century and the first three decades or so of the 20th exercising their influence over Chinese port cities like Hong Kong, Shanghai, and Macao, and the means the white man used to do so.

Under that context you might not be so surprised at the volume of Chinese-made fentanyl that is smuggled across our southern border on its way to ruin the lives of miserable, at-risk Americans.

It isn't like this history was a secret or that we didn't have lots of experts on Chinese history and culture to draw from in understanding the people we were dealing with. But nobody in a position of influence cared.

A quick timeline outlining our relations with the ChiComs since the Nixon opening in 1972:

1979: Then-President Jimmy Carter grants China full diplomatic recognition. Carter goes further, acknowledging the ChiComs's One China demands and thus severing normal ties with Taiwan, who had been our ally in the South China Sea. Later that year, Congress approves the Taiwan Relations Act, which maintains cultural and trade relations with the Taiwanese. The act requires Washington to provide Taipei with defensive arms, but it doesn't officially violate the US's One China policy.

1980: The city of San Francisco begins a "sister city" relationship with Shanghai. San Francisco's mayor? Dianne Feinstein.

1982: The Reagan administration issues the famous Six Assurances to Taiwan. Those include: 1. The United States would not set a date for termination of arms sales to Taiwan; 2. The United States would not alter the terms of the Taiwan Relations Act; 3. The United States would not consult with China in advance before making decisions about US arms sales to Taiwan; 4. The United States would not mediate between Taiwan and China; 5. The United

States would not alter its position about the sovereignty of Taiwan, which was that the question was one to be decided peacefully by the Chinese themselves, and would not pressure Taiwan to enter into negotiations with China; and 6. The United States would not formally recognize Chinese sovereignty over Taiwan. But later that year, Reagan visits China, and the two countries issue a Joint Communique that deals mainly with an agreement that the US wouldn't particularly take sides in the China-Taiwan sovereignty argument and an acknowledgement that while we would continue to sell weapons to the Taiwanese, we anticipated that one day we wouldn't.

But one section of the Joint Communique involves something quite interesting. It says, "Respect for each other's sovereignty and territorial integrity and non-interference in each other's internal affairs constitute the fundamental principles guiding United States-China relations."

Let's keep that in mind as we go forward.

1986: San Francisco mayor Feinstein and Shanghai mayor Jiang Zemin designate several corporate entities for fostering commercial relations. One of them is named Shanghai Pacific Partners. Feinstein's husband, Richard Blum, serves as a director.

1989: Following the Tiananmen Square massacre, the US halted weapons sales to China—yes, by then we were selling the ChiComs weapons—and froze relations. Not long after, though, reports surfaced that the George H. W.

Bush administration had sent two high-ranking officials, one of them National Security Advisor Brent Scowcroft, to Beijing on a conciliatory mission to prevent a true diplomatic split. Tiananmen Square was swept under the rug.

1992: During the presidential campaign that year, Democrat Bill Clinton attacks Bush for coddling the bloodthirsty Chinese regime. "I think our relationships with China are important and I don't want to isolate China, but I think it is a mistake for us to do what this administration did when all those kids went out there carrying the Statue of Liberty in Tiananmen Square," he says. "Mister Bush sent two people in secret to toast the Chinese leaders and basically tell them not to worry about it. They rewarded him by opening negotiations with Iran to transfer nuclear technology. That was their response to that sort of action."

1993: New American president Clinton announces a policy of "constructive engagement" with China. Amid broad public disconcert with that proclamation, coming as it did from a man who had excoriated the Bush thaw in relations with China, Clinton chooses to decouple human rights from the growing trade relationship. A brand-new senator from California named Dianne Feinstein takes to the Senate floor to express her strong support for continued trading with Beijing. Contemporaneously, Richard Blum is seeking $150 million in investment for a variety of Chinese enterprises in which he was participating. He succeeds. Later that year, Feinstein and her husband travel to China.

1994: A *Los Angeles Times* exposé outlines Blum's business ties and the potential conflict of interests they present: "Such encounters are fondly remembered when deals are clinched back in China, according to American experts in Chinese business practices. They said that Feinstein's consistent support for China's interests cannot help but benefit her husband's efforts to earn profits there."

1995: Feinstein is appointed to the Senate Foreign Relations Committee. Subsequently, she makes several visits to China, accompanied by her husband, where she meets with senior government officials.

1996: Feinstein pens an editorial in the *Los Angeles Times* calling for the United States to grant most-favored-nation trading status to China "on a permanent basis and get past the annual dance that is proving to be extraordinarily divisive and not at all helpful toward reaching the oft-stated goal: improvement in human rights." Also that year, Clinton wins reelection despite a rather peculiar scandal in which several individuals are indicted and convicted for laundering Chinese money into his campaign coffers. The corruption is so brazen that then-Vice President Al Gore presides over a Clinton fundraiser at the Hsi Lai Buddhist Temple in Hacienda Heights, California, at which hundreds of thousands of dollars are raised through straw donations purportedly made by the monks and nuns.

2000: After senior Democrats Dianne Feinstein and Joe Biden shepherd it through the Senate Foreign Relations Committee, Clinton signs the US-China Relations Act of 2000, granting Beijing permanent normal trade relations with the United States and paving the way for China to join the World Trade Organization in 2001. Between 1980 and 2004, US-China trade rises from $5 billion to $231 billion.

2006: China surpasses Mexico as the United States's second-biggest trade partner, after Canada.

2008: China surpasses Japan to become the largest holder of US debt—or treasuries—at around $600 billion. The growing interdependence between the US and Chinese economies becomes evident as a financial crisis threatens the global economy, fueling concerns over US-China economic imbalances.

2009: Hunter Biden co-founds Rosemont Seneca Partners, an investment fund, along with Christopher Heinz—the stepson of Obama's future Secretary of State John Kerry—and Devon Archer, a former Kerry adviser.

2010: China surpasses Japan as the world's second-largest economy after it is valued at $1.33 trillion for the second quarter, slightly above Japan's $1.28 trillion for that year. China is reported on track to overtake the United States as the world's number one economy by 2027, according to Goldman Sachs chief economist Jim O'Neill. At the start of 2011, China reports a total GDP of $5.88 trillion for 2010, compared to Japan's $5.47 trillion.

Also in 2010, Hunter Biden visits China as a Rosemont Seneca representative during the second year of his father's vice presidency. There he gains audiences with top officials of influential state-linked enterprises including the Postal Savings Bank, China Investment Corp., and Founder Group. He is joined on the trip by James Bulger, the politically connected co-founder of the Thornton

Group, an Asia-oriented financial services firm. Bulger is the son of famous Boston mobster "Whitey" Bulger.

2011: The US trade deficit with China rises from $273.1 billion in 2010 to an all-time high of $295.5 billion—just a decade after total trade with China was $231 billion. The increase accounts for three-quarters of the growth in the overall US trade deficit for 2011. The United States, the EU, and Japan file a "request for consultations" with China at the World Trade Organization over its restrictions on exporting rare earth metals. The United States and its allies contend China's quota violates international trade norms, forcing multinational firms that use the metals to relocate to China. China calls the move "rash and unfair," while vowing to defend its rights in trade disputes.

2012: Hunter Biden and Devon Archer make contact with Chinese financier Jonathan Li, who runs the private-equity fund Bohai Capital. The trio discuss a plan to become partners in a new operation that would invest Chinese cash in ventures outside the country. Eighty percent of the resulting company, Bohai Harvest, is controlled by Chinese state-owned interests.

2013: Vice President Joe Biden and his son Hunter fly on Air Force Two for an official trip to Beijing amid Chinese President Xi Jinping's military aggressions in the East China Sea. A few days following the trip, the Chinese business license for Bohai Harvest—the company that Hunter Biden and Devon Archer had been trying to launch for more than a year—is approved. Also that year, Chinese figures indicate it surpasses the United States as the world's largest trading nation with $4.16 trillion in goods exchanging hands.

2014: A US court indicts five Chinese hackers, allegedly with ties to China's People's Liberation Army, on charges of stealing trade technology from US companies. In response, Beijing suspends its cooperation in the US-China cybersecurity working group.

2015: US authorities signal that there is evidence that Chinese hackers are behind the major online breach of the Office of Personnel Management and the theft of data from twenty-two million current and former federal employees.

2016: China overtakes Canada as our largest trading partner.

That takes us up to the election and inauguration of Donald Trump.

Trump was the first national American political figure to openly question the spiraling nature of our relationship with China. The essence of his critique was the exportation of American jobs and economic activity to China, something that no one else in either party had bothered to address, for reasons Smith outlined in his *Tablet* piece.

And over the four years Trump was in office, he did what he could to realign our relationship with the Chinese, strongly intimating that decoupling our supply chain from China and bringing as much of it home as possible while diversifying the rest into countries like India and Brazil was America's new strategic aim. Smith wrote that Trump's anti-China agenda had the secondary benefit of breaking the rice bowl of the China-connected elite that enthusiastically opposed him from the beginning.

Sounds like a good plan. How did that work out?

Ask yourself that question. When you do, of course, consider the origins of COVID-19, and consider also that for weeks after the coronavirus had broken out in Wuhan, the Chinese government locked down domestic travel while leaving international travel from Wuhan wide open. By the time China admitted even a small portion of the truth about the virus, it had spread to the entire world and inflicted economic damage equal to or greater than that which had been done in China.

And without COVID-19 there would have been no real chance that Trump would have lost reelection.

Of course, official Washington and the legacy news media suppressed—vituperatively—the notion that COVID-19 originated in a lab at the Wuhan Institute of Virology, despite the fact that the president of the United States was asserting it, and our intelligence community considered it highly likely. To this day it's still a disputed idea despite the failure to credibly present any other cause or any evidence the virus might have migrated naturally from an animal.

And there is the question of the gain-of-function bat coronavirus research funded by the United States government through a nonprofit called the EcoHealth Alliance, which would certainly explain the reticence to admit a lab-leak origin. If you've paid attention to the contentious back-and-forth battles in Senate committee hearings between Sen. Rand Paul and National Institute of Allergy and Infectious Diseases director Dr. Anthony Fauci, that's not news to you.

This book is not about COVID, but it's obvious to any objective observer that China's behavior following the leak of that virus into the world was informed by whatever biowarfare playbook they had cooked up in advance. The information embargo, the wide-open international travel, the brazen falsehoods, and the vituperative blamecasting—they even accused the US Army of spreading the virus in China—were all obvious signs of organized obfuscation while the virus wrecked the global economy, and worse, governments across the world began treating their citizens with an eerie similarity to how China treats its own people.

We haven't influenced China. They've influenced us, and we are far worse for it.

Meanwhile, China's government has gone from brutalizing Tibet to violently repressing members of the Falun Gong sect, to cracking down on Hong Kong in violation of its promises, so much so that in a famous viral video one Hong Konger said as he and his fellow freedom-lovers took to the streets in an unfortunately futile protest, "Don't trust China. China is asshoe!"

Then-Houston Rockets general manager Daryl Morey, a Princeton graduate, openly criticized the iron Chinese fist in Hong Kong, and the response was swift and unforgiving. China outlawed the airing of Rockets games in the country, which was significant since the Rockets were the most popular NBA team in China, and threatened the dissolution of a billion-dollar relationship with the league.

"We believe any remarks that challenge national sovereignty and social stability do not belong to the category of free speech," CCTV Sports, the Chinese state TV version of ESPN that carries NBA games in that country, said in a statement.

Meanwhile Los Angeles Lakers star LeBron James, who attended no college and committed few acts of scholarship in high school, publicly chastised Morey as "uneducated."

NBA commissioner Adam Silver was put in a no-win position by the controversy, and he handled it the best way he could. Silver declared the league would never silence the opinions of players, coaches, or team management officials, while at the same time he sought to placate the Chinese by indicating the league had nothing to do with Hong Kong or its quest for freedom amid the People's Liberation Army tanks suddenly in its streets.

That controversy played out in October of 2019. The Wuhan virus was already infecting people at a cascading rate, and the government was readying welding torches to barricade citizens of that city in their apartments to stop the domestic spread while the airport remained open to international travel.

And of course there is Xinjiang, where the Chinese government is committing what can best be described as genocide, and was directly described as such by Trump administration Secretary of State Mike Pompeo, against the Muslim Uyghur minority by use of tactics like forced abortions, birth control, mass detentions, and imprisonment in reeducation and forced labor camps.

According to a 2020 report by the Australian Strategic Policy Institute, Uyghurs are used for slave labor in factories contracted to supply American companies like Abercrombie & Fitch, Adidas, Gap, Calvin Klein, H&M, L.L.Bean, Lacoste, Nike, The North Face, Polo Ralph Lauren, Puma, Skechers, Tommy Hilfiger, Zara, Victoria's Secret, and General Motors, among others. When, in response to that report, the Uyghur Forced Labor Prevention Act came up in the House of Representatives that year, Coca-Cola, Nike, Apple, and other companies lobbied to water it down according to a *New York Times* report. All three companies denied those reports and also denied they sourced any products from Uyghur slave labor.

Nobody believed them. This has gone on for decades.

The Chinese corruption of American institutions isn't limited to the NBA or Nike. Take higher education. There are dozens of Confucius Institutes that have been established at American colleges and universities across the country by China's Ministry of Education, centers of Chinese culture and intellectual exchange according to the official narrative. What those Confucius Institutes really are, according to a 243-page 2017 report by the National Association of Scholars, is a massive influence operation against the United States. To wit:

Intellectual freedom. Chinese teachers—hired, paid by, and accountable to the Communist Chinese government—are pressured to avoid "sensitive" topics like the Tiananmen Square Massacre and the Cultural Revolution.

Transparency. Contracts between American universities and the Hanban, the division of the Ministry of Education that operates the Confucius Institutes, are rarely made public. One university went so far as to forbid NAS researchers working on that report from visiting their campus.

Entanglement. Confucius Institutes cover all the expenses of classes and also offer scholarships to American students to study abroad. With such financial incentives, universities find it difficult to criticize Chinese policies like its genocidal treatment of Muslim Uyghurs in western China.

Soft power. Confucius Institutes avoid discussing China's widespread human-rights abuses and present Taiwan and Tibet as undisputed Chinese territories. As a result, the institutes "develop a generation of American students with

> selective knowledge of a major country"—and a major adversary. Confucius Institutes are a textbook example of soft power that causes universities in receipt of Chinese largesse to stay silent about controversial subjects like China's use of forced labor to pick cotton, a 21st century variation of the slavery of the antebellum South.

The NAS recommended the Confucius Institutes be shut down forthwith, but they haven't been. Many still exist. That's surprising given China's other campus activities. For example, in June 2020, a Harvard professor working on a $15 million US government research grant was indicted for lying about his $50,000 per month work on behalf of a ChiCom institution to "recruit, and cultivate high-level scientific talent in furtherance of China's scientific development, economic prosperity and national security." That case was not an isolated incident.

Chinese consulates across the country are espionage and subversion centers. The one in Houston was ordered closed by the Trump administration in July 2020, amid a rather bizarre and disconcerting scene. An article at *The Daily Wire* outlined the reason for the closure:

> "Top U.S. officials said in the hours following the revelation that the United States ordered the Chinese General Consulate in Houston to close that the move was carried out because the facility was a 'massive spy center' that was stealing information from Americans and running influence operations in the U.S.

"'The United States will not tolerate the PRC's (People Republic of China) violations of our sovereignty and intimidation of our people, just as we have not tolerated the PRC's unfair trade practices, theft of American jobs, and other egregious behavior,' the State Department said in a statement Tuesday. 'We have directed the closure of PRC Consulate General Houston, in order to protect American intellectual property and American's [sic] private information.'

"The State Department said Wednesday that China had been engaging 'for years in massive illegal spying and influence operations throughout the United States against U.S. government officials and American citizens.'

"Assistant Secretary of State David Stilwell said the move to close the facility was 'long overdue' and that the alleged criminal activity that the Chinese were committing at the facility had accelerated since the coronavirus pandemic, which originated in China.

"Videos surfaced this week that showed Chinese officials burning classified documents after receiving notice that they were being forced out of the country.

"'China's Houston consulate is a massive spy center, forcing it to close is long overdue,' Sen. Marco Rubio (R-FL) said in a tweet, later adding: 'China's consulate in Houston is not a diplomatic

> facility. It is the central node of the Communist Party's vast network of spies & influence operations in the United States. Now that building must close & the spies have 72 hours to leave or face arrest. This needed to happen.'"

Just before the FBI raid, employees at the consulate were burning documents in a pile in the facility's courtyard at such a rate that the blaze got out of control, and the fire department was called.

It was an almost comic scene, but in context it was nothing short of horrific. While the documents burned in Houston, buildings burned across America as George Floyd riots tore the country apart. And there is more than a little bit of evidence that Chinese money and organization helped to fuel the Marxist organizations behind the unrest. National Security Advisor Robert O'Brien made statements following the outbreak of Floyd-themed street violence that foreign action was suspected, and China was among the countries he mentioned.

And the Heritage Foundation's Mike Gonzalez dug down and found lots of disturbing connections between Black Lives Matter, the race-hustling left-wing outfit sponsoring the "mostly peaceful" protests that resulted in those riots, and an obscure Chinese political advocacy shop:

> "Go to the website for the Black Futures Lab, a venture of Black Lives Matter founder Alicia Garza, and click on the 'Donate' button. It will ask you to send your money to an obscure organization, the Chinese Progressive Association, explaining that

> 'Black Futures Lab is a fiscally sponsored project of the Chinese Progressive Association.'"

Gonzalez continues:

> "The CPA was founded in San Francisco in 1972 during the heady days of the Marxist-oriented Asian American Movement, and today it also has a very active chapter in Boston. From its start, it has been a promoter of the People's Republic of China.
>
> "According to an authoritative 2009 Stanford University paper tracing its early days to the present, and which can be found on Marxist.org, 'The CPA began as a Leftist, pro-People's Republic of China organization, promoting awareness of mainland China's revolutionary thought and workers' rights, and dedicated to self-determination, community control, and "serving the people."'
>
> "The CPA, continued the paper, 'worked with other pro-PRC groups within the U.S. and San Francisco Bay Area.... Support for the PRC was based on the inspiration the members drew from what they saw as a successful grassroots model that presented a viable alternative to Western capitalism.'
>
> "One of the ways it did this was by holding 'film screenings that were open to the public, sometimes showing Chinese films as well to facilitate understanding of the country's revolutionary ideas.... CPA also took the lead with groups

such as the U.S.-China People's Friendship Organization to celebrate China's National Day on Oct. 1.'

"To this day, CPA Boston continues to be a partner of the PRC in the United States. Three years ago, the Boston chapter teamed up with China's Consulate General in New York to offer Chinese nationals the opportunity to renew their passports, getting praise from China's official mouthpiece, China Daily.

"In 1997, CPA-Boston sponsored the raising of the PRC's flag for the first time ever over Boston's City Hall to honor the takeover of China by the Chinese Communist Party, just as the Stanford paper says has been CPA practice from the beginning. The event was organized, again, with the Chinese Consulate.

"These events now take place with some regularity. Chinese Consul General Sun Guoxiang, traveling from New York, was on hand at a similar event in Boston in 2014 to say: 'The common interests are far more important than differences between U.S. and China.'

"Suzanne Lee, a co-founder of CPA-Boston, also spoke at the 2014 event, noting her efforts to promote better U.S.-China relations.

"The Chinese flag-raising event in Boston in 2019, marking the 50th anniversary of the communist takeover of China, drew protests.

> "Another CPA co-founder, Lydia Lowe, said in a written 'personal statement' in 1997: 'McCarthyism is behind us. The Cold War is behind us.'
>
> "However, in an essay that she co-authored last year on the Marxist revolutionary site LeftRoots, Lowe sounded as though she wanted to start another Cold War, writing that Asians should play a role in creating a 'revolutionary strategy' that would achieve a 'fundamentally different society.'
>
> "And CPA-San Francisco drew praise from China's mouthpiece China Daily just a few weeks ago, for taking part again in Black Lives Matter demonstrations in San Francisco."

Is there definitive proof that China instigated those George Floyd riots from consulates like the one in Houston? Not exactly. Do US officials suspect that was the case? You bet. That Chinese officials unleashed a propaganda offensive blasting America for our "racism" and "intolerance" to coincide with the worst of the Floyd riots didn't go unnoticed, particularly given US opposition to the abuses in Xinjiang and the Hong Kong crackdown at the time.

And just after Biden's inauguration, at a diplomatic meeting in Anchorage, Alaska, Chinese diplomats berated new US Secretary of State Antony Blinken with "woke" rhetoric along those same lines. Blinken's response was silence.

A whole lot of politically connected Americans, from Dianne Feinstein and Richard Blum to Joe and Hunter Biden, to Henry

Kissinger and Neil Bush, have made a whole lot of money facilitating the economic, cultural, and geopolitical train wreck the Chinese relationship has become.

Neil Bush, you ask? Why, yes. The brother of the former president resides in Houston, where he's the founder and chair of the George H. W. Bush Foundation for US-China Relations. And what does the George H. W. Bush Foundation for US-China Relations do? Well, according to Bush himself it's "to get Americans to change their negative views" of China and recognize the country's "natural kindness and gift giving."

Neil was the Bush brother associated in numerous media reports with the savings and loan collapse, his having been pals and business partners with a few of the worst malefactors in that debacle. He resurrected his business career during the 1990s with China. Neil Bush has made more than 150 trips to the Middle Kingdom. One of those trips was a June 2019 Hong Kong conference put on by the China Center for International Economic Exchanges and an organization called the China-United States Exchange Foundation (CUSEF). The latter is registered as an "agent of a foreign principal," or more specifically a front for the Chinese Communist Party, run by an American—a former State Department official named David Firestein. CUSEF had attempted to establish an analog to a Confucius Institute at the University of Texas in Austin in 2018, only to be shut down when a faculty member blew the whistle on the endeavor's financial backing.

Neil Bush gave a speech at that conference that was more than a bit disconcerting. *The American Conservative's* John Meroney recounts the proceedings:

"The lectern wobbled as Neil stood behind it, and music continued over him as he started to deliver his keynote. Neil said that his foundation was 'gearing up to do great work' and that it was 'run so ably by a real China expert, David Firestein.' From the audience, Firestein nodded with approval.

"For the most part, Neil's speech was his usual patter—'Dad often stated that the U.S.-China relationship was the most important bilateral relationship in the world.... China has benefited consumers with lower cost, high-quality goods'—but about five minutes in, Neil's speech took a bizarre turn. He said he had just returned from a family trip to Croatia where he'd been 'in full vacation mode.' One evening, his 'quite astute' son-in-law asked about China. 'Fueled by some wine,' Neil said, the discussion during the family trip turned heated.

"Hard as it may be to believe, Neil then proceeded to describe the most damning criticisms of China, in the voice of his son-in-law. The treatment of ethnic minorities. Use of facial recognition techniques that keep tabs on citizens. The plan for big data to give individuals a social credit rating designed to control behavior. Use of intrusive Big Brother tactics, including monitoring social media to crack down on government critics.

"Neil said his son-in-law called China 'nefarious' and 'aggressive' and said the country sought to dominate the world. 'I still love the boy,' Neil remarked, 'but he even compared authoritarian rule of China to that of Saddam Hussein in Iraq and Hitler in Nazi Germany. I almost flew out of my seat at this point.'

"We don't know what Neil said to his son-in-law that night on the family vacation. But his words about him at the communist-funded conference aren't in doubt. He then proceeded to throw his son-in-law under the proverbial bus in front of the comrades.

"'Clearly the wine was speaking,' Neil said. 'My son-in-law has never been to China. His facts and assumptions are clearly flawed and based on half-truths or all-out fake news. His views show just how hysterical and challenging the times are. My son-in-law and many Americans only know what they hear.'

"He closed his speech by imploring, 'Those who believe the U.S. and China ought to work together need to find our voices.... I advise my American friends not to meddle too much in the internal affairs of China.' He urged the U.S. and China to 'collaborate.' He also said the U.S. and China 'must set parameters to address the proliferation of fake news and to control other aspects of the cloud and internet and many others.'"

Meroney passes along a damning quote about Neil Bush and his Chinese exploits from former Trump advisor and China expert Peter Navarro who said, "What I do know is that the Bush family, and that person [meaning Neil Bush], should be registered foreign agents for the Chinese Communist Party. He's the Republican equivalent of Hunter Biden who basically sold out the country and traded off their famous fathers' names.

"This happened because it's part of the Chinese Communist Party game plan, their strategy. It's either money pots or honey pots. With honey pots, it's like Eric Swalwell—he's sleeping with a Chinese spy and she gets information from him. With Neil Bush and Hunter Biden, it's the money pot. The Chinese Communist Party, that's what they do. They co-opt our politicians."

It surely appears they co-opted the Bushes and Clintons.

Not to mention the Bidens. And Richard Blum and Dianne Feinstein.

And Nixon's foreign-policy guru Henry Kissinger, who pocketed a fortune making introductions to Chinese poo-bahs for American businessmen.

And Clinton's defense secretary William Cohen, who helped shepherd China into permanent most-favored-nation trade status and World Trade Organization membership in 2000. Cohen now has offices around the world, two of which are in China, for his current company, which peddles influence between connected business elites and high-ranking government officials across the globe. Among its employees is former Trump defense secretary James Mattis.

You might remember that Mattis trashed Trump's hard-line approach to China in a November 2020 op-ed in *Foreign Affairs*. "The economic prosperity of U.S. allies and partners hinges on strong trade and investment relationships with Beijing," he wrote, while taking Chinese coin through the Cohen Group. He didn't disclose the conflict in the *Foreign Affairs* piece and was promptly scorched for it by Fox News and the *Washington Times*.

Senate minority leader Mitch McConnell belongs on the China list as well. McConnell's father-in-law is James Chao, a Taiwanese-American billionaire shipbuilder with extensive Chinese business connections who went to college with Jiang Zemin. Yes, that's the same Jiang Zemin whom Feinstein befriended when he was the mayor of Shanghai and went on to become China's president from 1999 to 2003. Chao has lavished millions on his daughter, former Transportation Secretary Elaine Chao, and her husband, and McConnell is one of the Senate's wealthiest members as a result.

Of course, for sheer brazenness, no one on the China list can top California congressman and failed 2020 presidential candidate Eric Swalwell. Swalwell, a member of the House Intelligence Committee, carried on a long-term extramarital sexual affair with a ChiCom spy named Fang Fang. And when this was discovered, not only was Swalwell not faced with legal issues, *he wasn't even removed from the Intelligence Committee!* Little wonder that Navarro's quote about co-opted American politicians would have flowed so easily—literally sleeping with the enemy is unremarkable in today's Washington, so often has figuratively sleeping with them been the case.

What's come from this? Perhaps it's just a coincidence that the Biden administration abruptly pulled out of Afghanistan just before Chinese interests cut deals to develop the vast rare earth mineral resources in that country. Afghanistan is the Saudi Arabia of lithium, an element crucial to batteries found in products like electric cars. For twenty years while we were there, nothing was done to access that resource and perhaps derive some economic benefit to offset the $2 trillion spent on that hopeless, backward hellhole, but as soon as we were gone, China bought off the Taliban and will be mining in no time flat.

In a 2021 post at the conservative blog Power Line, John Hinderaker donned a conspiratorial cap and mused about exactly what it is we as a nation are going through and who benefits from it all.

An excerpt:

> "If you ran the Chinese Communist Party, what would your number one strategic goal have been in late 2019? Undoubtedly, to get rid of China's nemesis, Donald Trump, and replace him with Beijing Joe Biden. How far would China's rulers have gone to achieve that goal? Look what they have done to get rid of the Uighurs, a minor annoyance.
>
> "Could the Chinese have deliberately arranged for the worldwide dissemination of the Wuhan virus? Yes, rather easily. They could have created the virus, too, but that isn't necessary. Once the virus escaped from a laboratory in Wuhan, by means unknown, the rest was probably inevitable.
>
> "Of course, the virus did some damage within China, but nowhere near enough to pose a threat to the regime. And to the extent that there was collateral damage in Europe and elsewhere around the world, such damage, from the CCP's point

of view, was a helpful distraction at a time when China is building up its armed forces and extending its military footprint across Asia.

"Does anyone think China's rulers are either too inept or too principled to unleash the Wuhan virus on purpose? If so, why? They have done worse. And here, they would have been playing for enormous stakes—restoration of the pro-China, globalist regime that preceded Trump's America First rebellion. Hardly any price would have been too much to pay.

"And, having watched the first three years of the Trump administration unfold, China's rulers could well have calculated that a pandemic originating in their homeland stood a good chance of reshaping America's electoral landscape. The desperate Democrats and their press would blame the president and his administration for the disease—something that has never occurred before in American history, but was sure to happen this time. If the Chinese did seek to influence our presidential race, they were successful. President Trump has gone from being a prohibitive favorite in January to an underdog today, and the reason is the Wuhan virus.

"Do I think China's leaders deliberately unleashed the Wuhan virus on the world? I don't know, but I no longer consider the idea outlandish. The virus's origins are shrouded in mystery, and

> investigation of those origins has been discouraged, to put it mildly. Indeed, even mentioning the disease's place of origin—Wuhan—has been denounced as 'racist.' The virus may bring about the Chinese Communist Party's number one goal. I don't see any reason for a conclusive presumption that this fact is a coincidence."

Are you allowed to believe the things Hinderaker suggests? A certain political party in America would undoubtedly say no. Pompeo was in front of the Senate Foreign Relations Committee after unleashing a spirited statement signaling a definitive change in America's attitude toward the Chinese Communist Party in the summer of 2020, and he was ambushed by the uber-corrupt Robert Menendez, whose rhetoric differs little from that of the ChiComs:

"Under your watch, the United States has faced setback after setback on the world stage, ceding leverage and influence to our stated adversaries," said Menendez, the committee's ranking Democrat.

Menendez's broadside was eerily similar to a propaganda video released by the Chinese government-owned China Global Television Network, which lambasted not just President Trump but British prime minister Boris Johnson and Brazilian president Jair Bolsonaro as "populists" incapable of meeting real challenges and therefore "inventing" fake ones like controversies with China. Creepily, the video termed COVID-19 as the "test case" for that incapability, almost in a way suggesting that the virus was intended to so serve.

As Hinderaker noted, you are certainly not allowed to believe that the virus was a bioweapon. We all know that. Even to remind others within earshot that it was of Chinese origin would make you a racist by the modern crackpot definition of the term.

Of course, it isn't necessary for the virus to have been a bioweapon per se. All that was required was for it to get out into the world.

Are you allowed to believe that once the virus was plaguing the city of Wuhan and escaping to other cities to build body counts and threaten an economic shutdown the ChiComs couldn't afford, that regime deliberately allowed it to spread to Europe and the United States? It isn't an over-the-top belief, after all. If China were to suffer economically from the virus, would the regime not wish to level the economic playing field?

Does China not benefit from economic carnage in America and Europe? Did China not swallow Hong Kong whole without so much as a peep from the US and UK as they did the deed? Pompeo announced a long list of consequences, none of which change the fact that Hong Kong's independence is over.

In his 2020 Yorba Linda speech outlining the change in approach to China, Pompeo said what you know is true though are not allowed to believe—that opening trade to China has been a disaster, not just for America, but for the rest of the world. The Chinese have cheated their way to a position of economic strength they do not deserve, and while American interests have been damaged along the way, it's other countries—Mexico, Brazil, India, Thailand, and countless more—who have lost the opportunity to supply the international market due to Chinese state mercantilism allowed and promoted by corrupt, fuzzy-thinking American globalist policies.

Is it possible that China played a role in the mask mandate debate roiling America? Until the spring of 2020 it seemed to be fairly commonly accepted science that cloth face masks did little or nothing to prevent the spread of viruses, going so far that in early June of that year the World Health Organization's technical lead on COVID-19 suggested masks are useless because asymptomatic spread of the virus is rare. Less than twenty-four hours later she was sidelined, the WHO jumped on board the mask train, and your civil rights have been practically forfeit since, at least in blue states where despotic Democrat officials toggle COVID restrictions on and off at their whim.

Who makes the vast majority of those masks you buy in stores? China. And anyone who's spent time in Chinese cities knows that even before COVID it was fairly common for Chinese people on streets, on trains, and elsewhere to wear masks in crowded places. Blue America now looks a good bit like China in that regard, and in another: in Democrat-run locales and institutions, respect for individuals and individual rights and thoughts is very much on the wane.

Incidentally, the mask hasn't performed so well in stopping the spread of the virus, in case you haven't noticed. When this soon became obvious, what was the excuse for the poor performance of the mandates in stopping the spread of the virus? People weren't sufficiently complying.

Is China promoting Antifa and Black Lives Matter? Wouldn't it be in the interest of that regime to foment unrest in our streets to balance its own internal issues? The world has been made aware, in technicolor, of Chinese abuse of the Uyghurs—from photographs of bound prisoners being loaded onto trains to NBA coaches admitting their training camps in western China were essentially concentration camps for Chinese minorities. And of course there's what has happened to the people of Hong Kong.

Why wouldn't China want to push Antifa and Black Lives Matter to build the narrative that America is a racist, unstable, morally unsound country? China seeks to take away America's position of world leadership, especially at a time when Trump was building relations with India, and the Anglosphere is reorienting itself to act as one. Didn't that leadership suffer from the violence in our streets?

Are you allowed to believe that China exercises significant influence over America's major media? Chinese investors and companies, all with ties to the Chinese Communist Party, hold relatively significant stock positions in all six of the media companies that control 90 percent of the television channels and film entertainment producers in America. We've seen the Chinese exert influence on various film and television productions—there's a reason the *Red Dawn* remake, in a classic example, had the wholly implausible North Koreans as the invading bad guys. Or that Tom Cruise's Taiwan patch on his flight jacket in the *Top Gun* sequel had to be scratched. Is it so hard to believe something similar is at work with respect to news? We've already seen it in the case of Bloomberg, where reporting of stories inconvenient to the ChiCom leadership have been repeatedly spiked.

What are you allowed to believe about China and what they're doing? Nothing? Anything? Are you allowed to believe the Chinese played a role in torpedoing Trump's reelection and thus saved their dominant role in the US supply chain and the torrent of wealth and power that has afforded them?

Because once you are allowed to believe the Chinese have motive, opportunity, and capability to do these things, you'll find a mountain of evidence, though admittedly much is circumstantial, that they're playing a lot larger role in our current woes than we give them credit for.

And that, much like the Beijing think tank president in that viral video said, "they have people" among our ruling elite profiteering while cheering them on.

CHAPTER 8

Globalism and Anti-Americanism

The second Monday in October is Columbus Day, a wonderful celebration not just of Italian-American heritage but of the historical joining together of two continents and the advancement of Christianity and Western civilization.

But you wouldn't know that by reading the press releases the Democratic National Committee churned out on Columbus Day 2021. It's quite clear the DNC, and the Hard Left who control it, have a very different view of Western civilization and American history than the party was built on.

You really have to be a masochistic killjoy not to recognize the achievement of Christopher Columbus in 1492. Columbus, by crossing the Atlantic for what was thought to be the first time (it's likely that Vikings had accomplished the feat beforehand, but no permanent written record of it existed), opened up the Americas to settlement, enlightenment, and commerce and fueled the greatest civilizational leap in the history of mankind.

But civilizational leaps are bugs, not features, in the eyes of the American Left. Guess who runs today's Democrats?

You don't get any points for that one. Too easy. Here's what the Democrats' press flacks said about Columbus Day, which they instead call Indigenous Peoples' Day:

> "DNC Statement on Indigenous Peoples' Day
>
> "To honor the contributions and heritage of America's Indigenous people, DNC Chair Jaime Harrison and DNC Native American Caucus Chair Rion Ramirez released the following statement:
>
> 'On this Indigenous Peoples' Day, we celebrate the contributions and resilience of America's Native communities, and the work they have done today and every day to bring this country closer to our ideals. Democrats are committed to carrying forward the important work necessary to ensure dignity, sovereignty, and opportunity for our nation's 574 Federally Recognized Tribes.
>
> 'The Biden-Harris administration has honored this commitment to uplift and support America's Native communities from its very first week, when President Biden issued a memo prioritizing federal agencies' consultation with Tribal Nations. The president also appointed Deb Haaland the first Native Cabinet secretary, and the American Rescue Plan includes the largest-ever investment of resources in Tribal

> communities in U.S. history. The administration is working to address the issues that matter to Tribal communities, from the new Federal Boarding School Initiative to uncover the truth and help heal affected communities, to restoring federal protections to land and waters such as Bears Ears National Monument, which is sacred to Tribal Nations.
>
> 'We will never forget the sacrifices, brutality, assimilation, and dislocation inflicted upon Native communities. Today, we honor the 574 Tribal Nations and the significant contributions they have made to our country, and commit ourselves toward building a future marked by justice, promise, and equal opportunity for all.'"

Deb Haaland's father's people came from Norway, which means she's only half oppressed, but she'll take it. She celebrated her Laguna Pueblo heritage on Indigenous Peoples' Day by doing one of the whitest things possible—running the Boston Marathon.

Everything about Indigenous People's Day is awful. For one thing, as the DNC's release notes, there are 574 different tribes. Why don't they each get their own celebrations? There isn't all that much similarity between the Iroquois and the Shawnee, or the Lakota Sioux and the Navajo.

And what specifically are the "contributions" the DNC is talking about? The first line of this insulting release talks about them, but then they disappear amid a deluge of self-congratulatory boasting about all the things Democrats are committed to doing in order to patronize indigenous Americans.

The DNC didn't even bother to offer a half-assed reference to Columbus, who accomplished more with less than any Democrat alive will ever do. They left that to the addled president they foisted on the American people; Joe Biden coughed up a half-sentence of praise before trashing Columbus as an oppressor of the aboriginal tribes he found during his voyages from Spain.

There was no mention of the Carib tribe, with whom Columbus had his most negative interactions, in these panderings. Why not? Do we have to wait for Cannibalistic Indigenous Peoples' Day for that one?

At this point, it's tough for any Italian American not named Anthony Fauci to consider membership in, or voting for, the Democrats as other than treason to his or her heritage. And it's similarly hard for members of those 574 tribes of "Indigenous Peoples" not to be disgusted at the rank patronizing.

Oh, but wait. The second Monday in October was something else as well, and the patronizing and pandering was just getting started—because there was also this:

> "DNC Statement on National Coming Out Day
>
> "In celebration of the courage and strength of the LGBTQ community, DNC Chair Jaime Harrison and LGBTQ Caucus Chair Earl Fowlkes released the following statement on National Coming Out Day.
>
> 'National Coming Out Day serves as a reminder of the importance, courage and strength

> that living authentically can require. As we recognize this critically important day, we must also remember those who have not yet come out and provide them with the support they need to live bravely, boldly and openly. In a world where LGBTQ people, particularly transgender and gender non-conforming people, live in fear of violence or discrimination, we must also reaffirm our dedication to creating a world where LGBTQ people feel safe and valued, not negatively targeted because of their gender identity or sexual orientation.
>
> 'From his first day in office, President Joe Biden has prioritized protecting the LGBTQ community and affirming the rights and protections the community deserves. From implementing the U.S. Supreme Court's Bostock ruling and providing dozens of critical protections to LGBTQ people, to reversing the transgender military ban and restoring health care protections for LGBTQ people, the Biden administration has already been hailed by advocates as the most pro-equality administration in history. Together, alongside our Democratic majorities in Congress, we will continue to ensure that LGBTQ individuals feel protected, seen, and free to live their authentic selves.'"

If the gay and trans folks are "living in fear of violence or discrimination," then the rest of us can honestly tell them to join the club. Of course, there isn't a whole lot of that seemingly going on, because what we see more of is Twitter outrage from certifiably insane people who happen to identify as gay or trans—and that outrage is bent on inflicting violence or discrimination against people who disagree with them.

Like the comedian Dave Chappelle, for example, whose Netflix special they've been demanding be taken off the air because he happens to talk about the foul treatment he's been subjected to for joking about gay and trans people along with every other group.

And the DNC is taking the side of the loons against Dave Chappelle, which is fairly instructive.

You can see these two press statements, fired off in the same day, as one-offs. You shouldn't. You should see them in context, and that context is that the Democrats, or more specifically, the people who run that party, hate America. They hate everything about our people, our institutions, our heritage. The people now in charge of that party, who decades ago were on its fringes or out of the political mainstream altogether, always have.

Ask your Democrat friends what they love about this country, and the response you'll get will likely have something to do with Social Security or Medicaid or Obamacare or the civil rights movement, or even that Obama got elected and/or Trump lost. Their answers will tell you very clearly that what they love about America is what they can do to it. Not what it is.

They don't love the Constitution, other than they think it's a "living" document that can mean anything they want. They don't love the idea of America as a melting pot; they want it to be a salad, otherwise they wouldn't be pandering to "oppressed" intersectional groups two at a time. They don't love our history, they don't love our culture (now Superman has to be bisexual, and James Bond has to be henpecked), they certainly don't love the classic concept of the American Dream. They really, really don't love our freedom, unless it's to burn the flag, riot over false narratives, or kill the unborn.

They don't love any of it. What they love is power. They love to divide and conquer.

Sure, a political party is built as a coalition of interest groups, and as such one can expect that a party will spend much of its time pandering to one or another of them when opportunities present.

But today's Democrats are more than just interest-group panderers. They're Balkanizers. That party is literally uninterested in Americans unless we fall into some intersectionally oppressed category that can be leveraged to indict our forebears—from Christopher Columbus to Charlton Heston.

You really can't get a more illuminating example of how contemptuous of ordinary Americans the Democrats are, and the scale of their rejection of us in favor of the influence-peddling globalist elite, than the Biden oil policy. No sooner did he take office but he shut down the Keystone XL pipeline and attempted to end oil drilling on federal lands. In so doing he crippled the domestic energy industry, and when the economy began to recover a bit from the COVID lockdowns that gutted our GDP in 2020, the increased demand for oil sent prices through the roof.

And Biden then began begging OPEC to sell us more oil rather than change his policies and spark an increase in domestic production.

It's even worse than that. In late January 2022 a federal judge in Washington, DC, threw out a massive offshore oil lease sale the Biden administration had issued to several oil companies on the basis that the environmental impact assessments behind the sale were improperly done. The judge, Raul Contreras, is a leftist Obama appointee, but his ruling is probably correct as a matter of law.

The thing to remember is that the Biden administration wasn't going to offer those Gulf of Mexico offshore oil leases. They wanted to kill off the domestic offshore oil industry. A bunch of state attorneys general, headed by Louisiana's Jeff Landry, took them to court and forced them to hold that auction in the fall of 2021.

And after Contreras's ruling, Louisiana Solicitor General Liz Murrill blasted the Biden administration for "sabotaging" the offshore oil industry, which was a spot-on characterization of their intentionally botching the carbon emissions paperwork.

Joe Biden has never spent a single day in his life working in the private sector. What he knows about "business" chiefly involves influence-peddling and shaking people down for bribes. That's more or less universally true of the Marxist junta who control him as well. So perhaps the concept of "market share" flies well over their heads—a thorough disqualifier in itself, to be sure.

But it goes like this. When there is a level of demand out there for a product, and that demand can be expected to increase over a period of time, and your own domestic suppliers of that product are fully capable of meeting that demand, if you do nothing, supply will match demand, and the price will remain more or less stable at the end of the day.

When you cripple your domestic suppliers, and the demand goes up, you will get not only price increases but money flowing to foreign suppliers as they capture more and more of your market. You bleed money, your domestic suppliers become less competitive in the marketplace, and the political effects of this are that the foreign suppliers get more leverage in your halls of power.

Which might not signify stupidity on Biden's part at all, but rather something else. To be charitable, it might just be that Team Biden likes the idea of doing business with state-owned foreign oil producers rather than unruly domestic oilmen who are intensely independent and have a private-sector mentality.

We don't have to use "treason" as the alternative description of Biden's energy policy. We can call it "anti-American" instead, because it's certainly "anti-the American people."

What's the effect of a series of actions that rob America of its energy independence and reintroduce the kind of influence that countries like Saudi Arabia and Kuwait used to be able to buy in Washington?

The Swamp benefits at the expense of the American people, doesn't it?

And if this is done deliberately, and not as a result of some moronic bungling, what do you call it?

Let's have a look at another example of this peculiar inability to govern in ways beneficial to the interests of ordinary Americans. We bring you the former mayor of South Bend, Indiana, who found his way to a job as the Secretary of Transportation despite no discernible qualification whatsoever.

That would be Pete Buttigieg, who more than anyone else in America is responsible for a debilitating months-long supply chain crisis that emptied store shelves, crushed consumer confidence, and crippled whole industries for large swaths of 2021 and beyond.

If you've noticed a distinct diminution of options on the bourbon shelf at your local liquor store of late, pay attention.

Buttigieg is a rather queer choice for Transportation Secretary. Not just because he's a member of the LGBTQ community, and obnoxiously so. Buttigieg ran for president in 2020 not on the strength of his accomplishments, of which there were none; he was the mayor of South Bend, Indiana, a college town of one hundred thousand people that exists more or less to service the University of Notre Dame and largely runs itself except for its peculiarly elevated murder rate during his time in office. Buttigieg ran on the fact that he is openly, and obnoxiously, gay—the central precept of his campaign being that Christians objecting to his lifestyle were bad at religion while he is not.

This interesting brew of queer sanctimony and absence of any demonstrable executive success was strangely attractive to the Democrat base electorate, so much so that Buttigieg fared far better than many of the more accomplished contenders in the 2020 primary field like Tom Steyer, Mike Bloomberg, Andrew Yang, or even Kamala Harris.

As such, Buttigieg was given the job of Transportation Secretary without any particular reason to think he could do it.

The results were predictable, though the optics around them have not been. We were always going to have supply chain challenges given the disruptions from COVID-19 and the bad public policy decisions arising from them. But naturally, the emanations and penumbras from the Green New Deal being put in place in places like California have all but destroyed the trucking industry, and COVID lockdowns haven't made things any better. While the supply chain situation was bad even before the Biden administration took office, every decision it made has failed to improve things.

By October, the Biden administration was cautiously admitting they'd ruined Christmas by cracking jokes about late delivery of Pelotons, the president was stumbling through speeches calling for the Port of Long Beach to be open 24/7, prices skyrocketed, and American retail began to take on a Venezuelan feel.

It was worse than all this, though, because Buttigieg wasn't even working his job. Not that he'd be any good at it if he *were* making an effort, but he was phoning it in while all this was going on.

Buttigieg released a photograph of himself and his husband lying side by side in a birthing bed holding their two adopted children.

That was in early September. Buttigieg had been lollygagging and canoodling with his husband and their two newborn adoptees for two weeks at that point. The administration put together a useless task force headed by a former Obama bureaucrat back in July, and they'd been hosting Zoom calls since then to talk aimlessly about the supply chain problem.

But actually working on the problem? Actually changing federal policies to, say, get truck drivers and stevedores back to work?

Hell, no.

By mid-October, Buttigieg was still on paid leave while one could practically walk to China on the decks of the ships lined up from Long Beach. Sen. Marsha Blackburn blew up over that subject when interviewed by Breitbart.

"We're in the middle of a transportation crisis, and Pete Buttigieg is sitting at home," she said. "Meanwhile, cargo boats are unable to dock and shelves are sitting empty. Pete needs to either get back to work or leave the Department of Transportation. It's time to put American families first."

Blackburn was actually too nice. In a sane world, Buttigieg wouldn't have a choice to get out of that birthing bed (which, really?) and go back to work. In a sane world he'd have been thrown out on his ear, and somebody with some actual qualifications in transportation and logistics would be put in charge of the DOT.

Then there are the things that don't reflect incompetence at all, but rather an offensive level of arrogance mixed in with the dripping anti-Americanism of our governing elite.

Remember in the summer of 2020 when a host of congressional Democrats, led by House Speaker Nancy Pelosi and Senate Majority Leader Chuck Schumer, donned African kente cloth scarves and knelt on the floor of Emancipation Hall for some eight minutes and change in some sort of morbid tribute to George Floyd?

If you missed that one, it was a bit of a drive-by news piece, and much of America groaned upon seeing such a blatant pandering to Black Lives Matter. But it was illuminating nonetheless given what it said about Washington's in-crowd.

You might not be aware of the origins of kente cloth. It comes from West Africa, and it was a signifier of the kings of the Asante empire. The Asante were actually the sales agents for the international slave trade coming out of that part of the world. They sold defeated enemies, neighboring tribesmen, and even their own people who ran afoul of the Powers That Be onto those slave ships headed for the New World.

By any objective moral standard you would say the Asante were probably the worst of the actors in that awful play. And yet the "anti-racist" tribute honoring George Floyd honored the Asante. It's comical how upside-down that spectacle was.

When this was pointed out by people on social media and elsewhere, *USA Today* trotted out a "Cultural Specialist" from the Smithsonian to declare that "it's complicated." We were told that maybe kente cloth is really just a signifier of the African world, or maybe it's just a signifier of the weavers of that cloth. It doesn't have to mean you're honoring the Asante slave dealers if you're wearing it.

"My way of thinking about it is that it honors the creativity, the ingenuity, the skill of the people who actually make the kente," she said.

So despite the connection of kente cloth to slave traders, what wearing kente cloth really means is you're supporting somebody who sewed it?

Tell that to Oklahoma State University football coach Mike Gundy, who was forced to humiliate himself and grovel for the sin of wearing a T-shirt with the One America News Network name printed on it after his star running back Chuba Hubbard, who is from Canada by the way, publicly chastised the T-shirt as unacceptable and declared he wouldn't play for a coach who watches news channels Hubbard doesn't like.

Gundy should have consulted with Diana Baird N'Diaye, the Smithsonian Cultural Specialist, before abasing himself. What he could have said was he was honoring the Guatemalans or Filipinos who stitched the shirt, and not the news anchors at OAN. Maybe then he wouldn't have been forced to take a pay cut to coach the 2020 season.

If kente cloth signifies African heritage, and that heritage includes the trading of fellow Africans into slavery—particularly when this particular signifier of African heritage comes from a historical entity that was directly involved in and profited from the slave trade—why isn't kente cloth an endorsement of African slavery? And why isn't California Congresswoman Karen Bass, who passionately defended the use of kente cloth in that moronic spectacle in Emancipation Hall, excoriated as a defender of the slave trade?

Bass, and the rest of the Kente Defense League, essentially said that it's OK for Africans to trade other Africans into slavery, but it's a bad thing for non-Africans to do it.

Why does this matter?

Because all over the country people who share the same ideological fetishes as Karen Bass, Nancy Pelosi, Chuck Schumer, and Joe Biden have been demanding the destruction of historical landmarks, monuments, and objects of public art on the basis that the figures depicted therein either owned slaves, traded slaves, facilitated slavery, or otherwise committed words or deeds mean or unfavorable to People of Color.

But kente is unobjectionable because the slave-trading empire also did other things.

You mean like Christopher Columbus did other things? Or like Robert E. Lee did other things? Or like Jefferson and Washington did other things?

Naturally.

Slavery is not the reason Columbus, Lee, Washington, Jefferson, or even Jefferson Davis had monuments made and dedicated to them. It was other things they did—things that were a whole hell of a lot more significant than the certainly laudable non-slave-trading accomplishments of the Asante kings, whatever those might have been.

The lesson? Don't ascribe too much intelligence, perspective, and good faith on the part of the cultural Marxist revolutionaries who are running around the country bowdlerizing historical landmarks and monuments of public art.

Those revolutionaries are not acting on a righteous desire not to honor slavery. If they were, they would have stopped at Lee and Stonewall Jackson and Beauregard and Forrest, and obviously they'd have laid off the kente cloth. But when this ISIS-style campaign of iconoclasm progressed not just to Washington and Jefferson but to such insane lengths as Lincoln, Grant, Miguel Cervantes, Junipero Serra, Teddy Roosevelt, and even Frederick Douglass, and when even such supposedly intelligent and mainstream publications as the *New York Times* and *Washington Post* followed the Democrat Party's Twitter account in joining the fringe effort to chisel away Mt. Rushmore, we are long past the point of true righteousness.

It's a cultural revolution—literally a 21st-century equivalent of Mao's Red Guards—disguised as the signaling of virtue. These are revolutionaries who want to wipe away American law, culture, and economics and replace them with new norms and institutions of their own making. Much of that work has already been done in the schools—American youth are the least patriotic and most ignorant of their cultural and intellectual patrimony of any generation in our nation's history, ironically at a time when more information about that patrimony is readily available for perusal than ever before.

The ignorance spread by our schools informs the current iconoclasm in a very specific way, however, and at the risk of being accused of defending the Peculiar Institution of slavery, there is a point that must be made.

Which is that slavery, in all of its forms, has been with us from the beginning of time. It has been a key part of the wretched condition of humanity since the dawn of civilization, and its general end is something of exceedingly recent vintage. Even now, there are millions of people consigned to some form of slavery or other around the world, including actual slave markets trading in black Africans being run by Muslims in the northern reaches of that continent—a phenomenon that the Black Lives Matter crowd seem peculiarly silent about as they wrap themselves around the axle over whether Washington and Jefferson owned slaves.

And judge Washington and Jefferson, and Lee and Davis, and all the rest of our 18th and 19th century national heroes, as bums.

There's a word for this. That word is presentism. It's an intellectual fallacy that insists on judging figures from the past by current standards. Presentism, which should have been shouted down in our schools and colleges but instead has been promoted by quack educators who themselves are revolutionaries, Marxists, and other deficient thinkers, is why people sitting in plush chairs in air-conditioned rooms sipping lattes and munching on avocado toast spend their time whining about the immorality of their forebears who lived an existence unimaginably hellish compared to what we see today.

And what bridged that gap, what moved us from that horrific life with its ugly moral dilemmas and brutality to where we are now, is capitalism, which rewards technological innovation and productivity.

It was capitalism that gave us the inventors and entrepreneurs who created and distributed the technological advances liberating people from the worst of the back-breaking, life-stealing work and moved humanity to the state of comfort it currently occupies. Capitalism promoted advances in every facet of human life that provide today's flaccid revolutionaries in suburban basements with creature comforts a Washington, Jefferson, Jackson, Lee, or Davis couldn't even conceive.

And these same confused revolutionaries who castigate and disrespect our forefathers, those men who lacked all the comforts of our modern life and yet set the philosophical underpinnings for the great technological changes we enjoy through great works like the Declaration of Independence and Constitution, also attack capitalism as "racist" and demand it end.

It's a stupidity we shouldn't tolerate.

And that's to be kind, because as said above, the defenestrators and iconoclasts actively assaulting our history aren't opposed to slavery. They're opposed to everything we stand for and stand on. But even taking their babblings at face value, they don't hold water. A P. G. T. Beauregard, Robert E. Lee, Thomas Jefferson, or even John C. Calhoun is a far better and more consequential man than is a Shaun King or Ayanna Pressley, a judgment history will surely validate.

Assuming the revolutionaries aren't the ones writing the history, which they earnestly, viciously aim to do.

Bowdlerizing works of public art and historical landmarks is hardly the extent of the effort at wrecking our society today's Left spends time on, of course. Care to converse about climate change for a time?

Poll after poll shows the American people don't give a fig about global warming, and yet it's like religious dogma to the Left—and not just in this country. Celebrities, British royals, bad American politicians, and others who ride around the world in private planes (like, for example, the one Jeffrey Epstein used to have) and luxury yachts have been telling us that we only have a dozen years before planetary cataclysm caused by global warming will make Earth uninhabitable.

They've been telling us this for more than a dozen years, you know. It's become fairly comical by now.

And ordinary people have never been convinced by any of this. Ordinary people are fine with the idea of reducing emissions, whether of carbon or whatever other chemicals, from factory smokestacks or car engines or whatever. But very few people are bought into the complete climate change narrative the international Left is selling.

So the sales pitch gets harder and harder.

A couple of years ago we might have reached the zenith of the shamelessness when Scoldilocks was unleashed upon us.

Who's Scoldilocks? She's a manufactured maven of programmatic, propagandistic proselytization, coming to international fame as a sixteen-year-old invited to address the United Nations on climate change. And not the ordinary version of climate change that normal people call "seasons."

We're of course talking about Greta Thunberg, a Swedish child with a developmental disability who was sent out to harangue and insult the leaders of the free world over the supposed "mass extinction" that is coming as a result of global warming.

Thunberg suffers from Asperger Syndrome, a condition on the autism spectrum. One wouldn't normally expect someone with Asperger's to be chosen as the spokesperson for a global movement, given that sufferers from that condition are characteristically lacking in nonverbal communication, struggle with empathy, are typically very uncomfortable around large crowds, obsess pathologically about subjects not under their control, and often engage in long rants without consideration for how they will be received. Thunberg appears to be a more serious case, suffering from depression so severe she once went two months without eating and had to be pulled out of school.

And yet that's precisely what the global warming cultists did, plucking this highly susceptible child, juicing her up with all of the bleak Malthusian auguries of an apocalypse less than two decades in the offing, and then featuring her at protest events across Europe before taking the Angry Cassandra Revue transatlantic in 2019.

Thunberg was both inappropriate and spot-on as a poster child for modern-day climate hysteria. A Rasmussen poll found that half of Americans under thirty-five believe the "mass extinction" she prattles on about is coming within ten or fifteen years, despite zero evidence anything like it is coming (and the long duration of those very same predictions). And what do you get when you're that successful in selling the (Earth's) sizzle?

Well, according to the National Institutes of Health, nearly one-third of all thirteen- to eighteen-year-olds will experience an anxiety disorder. The numbers continue to go up; between 2007 and 2012, anxiety in children and teens rose 20 percent.

The suicide rate for young Americans is now the highest ever recorded. Between 2000 and 2017, the number of suicides has doubled for females aged fifteen to twenty-four. Males between fifteen and nineteen killed themselves at a rate of 17.9 per 100,000, up from 13 per 100,000 in 2000. This was even before COVID.

Is that all from global warming hysteria? No, but it's part of an abusive environment created within education and pop culture—worse in Europe than here, to be sure—that is targeted, relentlessly, toward wearing down to the nub the people who should be grateful for the bounty a market economy has delivered, and thus making them, in the words of Ming the Merciless, "satisfied with less."

A generation or two before, these same people were offering up the same cataclysmic prophecies arising from global cooling and the coming of a new Ice Age and attempting to inflict them on schoolchildren. Now it's the global warming catastrophe which never seems to get close enough to satisfy the doomsaying. There are real villains out there—and they aren't oil companies.

Eventually, at least in America, Greta Thunberg ceased being a thing. Perhaps we simply aren't interested in global warming, or perhaps the kind of child exploitation her ascent to stardom represented doesn't sell as well here as it does in Europe.

But when Thunberg didn't move the needle, we got something else. In December 2021, Netflix debuted a "blockbuster" film starring Leonardo DiCaprio and Jennifer Lawrence titled *Don't Look Up*, which on the surface was about a couple of astronomers who identify a comet heading directly for Earth and sound the alarm, only to find an unserious Trumpy president (played by Meryl Streep) who first attempts to monetize and then politicize the impending end of the world. The plot turns so farcical that Streep's character embarks on a political tour exhorting her followers, "Don't look up," while she claims the comet is a hoax—until the comet becomes visible in the night sky.

Don't Look Up is about global warming. Its producer Adam McKay, who made his Hollywood career with goofy Will Ferrell movies, explicitly said so.

Critics fawned all over *Don't Look Up*. Its star power created a wave of initial streaming views that petered out fairly quickly. The movie's appeal can best be described as limited, mostly because people generally don't find entertainment in being ridiculed and harangued as morons by Hollywood. And this film hated ordinary Americans with a passion unusual even for our modern entertainment industry.

The climate change debate, which isn't a debate anymore, but rather a self-righteous fusillade of emotionalist demands, is the perfect embodiment of the Left. They invented something they could call a crisis as a means of arrogating political power to themselves and pushed every lever they could to cajole the public into going along. But when they couldn't make a majority for it, they stopped trying to persuade and began to threaten, insult, and attack.

And when people noticed, and objected, that's when the real contempt began.

Meanwhile, in the real world the Left refuses to acknowledge, climate change advocacy led to a war. Because in February of 2022 when Russia invaded Ukraine, stupid "climate" policies were among the most prominent causes.

When the Biden administration, pandering to the global warming hysterics, kneecapped America's domestic oil and gas industry by imposing harsh regulations, barring offshore drilling and hydraulic fracturing on federal lands and water bottoms, and killing the Keystone XL pipeline, America went from a net energy exporter to a net importer in the space of a year. European energy policies, particularly in the case of Germany, are even more unserious.

What did that mean? Well, oil prices skyrocketed from thirty-six dollars per barrel to over one hundred dollars, and countries whose economies depended largely on oil exports—like Russia's—saw a massive windfall in revenue.

Biden begged the Russians to produce more oil. Russia's president Vladimir Putin laughed and said no. Then he massed troops on the Ukrainian border and ultimately sent them in. Putin has always wanted to lash Ukraine back into the Russian empire, and with the world economy more dependent on his oil and gas than ever before, he gambled that he could finally do it.

For four years Donald Trump fought like hell to suppress the Nord Stream 2 pipeline, which runs along the Baltic Sea floor and is poised to put Russia in charge of the bulk of Germany's energy supply, particularly given the stupid decision by that country's longtime leader Angela Merkel to wipe out its coal and nuclear power industries. Biden removed all the sanctions against Nord Stream 2. And when Putin invaded Ukraine, the Germans panicked, initially refusing to allow other NATO nations to supply the Ukrainians with weapons.

The flip side of the Green New Deal scam Biden and his leftist allies want to impose on us is that we're supposed to believe we can run our cars on electricity, and the electric grid that powers them can run on wind and solar power.

But China is in the process of cornering the market on the lithium those car batteries run on, and China has already cornered the market on the rare earth minerals used in making solar panels and wind turbines.

As of this writing the Chinese haven't invaded Taiwan. The reader's experiences may differ.

Someday, politicians on the Right will stop trying to sidestep the doomsaying and mau-mauing of the climate change crowd and take them on. Eventually, there will be someone who's willing to actually win on this issue.

Draw them out with a statement that none of this global warming theory is proven. They'll lose their minds about that. It's OK. Let them start in with their demonization and call you a "denier" and so on. And then say something like this:

> "You people want to turn our economy upside down and deny millions of Americans freedom and money in pursuit of this global warming business. In order to be able to do that, you should be able to show four things, and frankly you've had twenty-five years to do it and you've failed.
>
> "First, you need to show that the planet is actually warming. The most reliable data on global temperature is the satellite data, and it shows the planet isn't any warmer over the last two decades. None of your computer models predicted that.
>
> "Second, you need to show that global warming is anthropogenic. You can't show that, because there is no particular connection between carbon dioxide concentration in the atmosphere and temperature. CO2 is actually a trace gas in the atmosphere, and it's exceedingly difficult to show that variations in the levels of a trace gas govern global temperature and the amount of solar activity doesn't.
>
> "Third, you need to show that global warming is a bad thing. You haven't done that because you can't show higher concentrations of severe weather other than just hyping hurricanes more

> than they were hyped fifty years ago or dishonestly attributing things like seismic activity to the climate. You also can't explain why, when the planet was warmer centuries ago, and they were growing grapes for wine in England and Greenland was green, Earth's temperatures reaching the levels they had then would be a disaster when it wasn't for the Romans or the Medieval English.
>
> "And fourth, you need to show that our turning our economy upside down would make a difference in global temperature, which you can't do because regardless of what we do with emissions, China and India aren't changing their energy or industrial policies."

A Republican candidate—a true American revivalist—who is courageous enough to take these people on with that four-point challenge will win the debate. Why none of the GOP candidates will forthrightly put that out there and demand the Democrats answer it point by point is beyond me.

GOP politicians ought to flatly call the Democrats' position on global warming nuts and say that its consequences are horrible. The 2024 presidential nominee needs to say that global warming is a microcosm of virtually all Democrat policy—creation of a false crisis through harmonized dishonest messaging and then presentation of failed socialist policy as the only possible solution to the false crisis. And when nothing improves, the prescription is always more failed socialist policy.

The reaction to such a position will be vituperation and bile, but vituperation and bile don't sell in political campaigns. And when you respond to vituperation and bile with calm, dry ridicule, the voters will find you far more interesting.

This is how you win. You certainly don't win by allowing yourself to be pressured into accepting the other side's narrative.

And pressure is really all they have. The globalist Left, to which the people who run the Democrat Party today have gleefully yoked themselves, are all about concentrated power. They're constantly looking for opportunities to apply it.

The Great Reset is the greatest example we have. They're not even hiding this stuff anymore.

If you're not aware of what the Great Reset is, it's a globalist idea, first put forth publicly by the socialist crowd at the World Economic Forum in June 2020, to shut down the world economy and then bring it back as a socialist venture with strict government controls on private enterprise that include, among other things, attention to climate change and giving workers a say in corporate governance.

Yes, you should be horrified at this. You should also be horrified over the fact that Team Biden's slogan "build back better," which resulted in a $2 trillion proposed spending orgy stopped only by Manchin's refusal to give it a 50th vote, is derived from this Great Reset idea.

And Canada's prime minister Justin "Fidelito" Trudeau has enthusiastically endorsed the Great Reset, so this is awfully close to home. Trudeau gave us a very good preview of what Great Reset governance looks like when Canada's truckers, fed up with onerous regulations and COVID restrictions, staged a loud protest in that country's capital. Before they knew it, they were demonized as terrorists, had their bank accounts frozen, and many were carted off to prison. Video of the trucker protest consisted mostly of people dancing to techno music in the February cold, at least until the local police trampled through them on horseback.

Given the reaction to the Jan. 6 protests in this country, nobody ought to have been surprised. There is little difference between Fidelito and Team Biden.

You would not be out of line in interpreting the bizarre statements of Biden adviser Dr. Michael Osterholm just after the 2020 presidential election suggesting a two-month shutdown of the economy to beat COVID-19, paid for with a flood of borrowed federal welfare money, as a stealth Great Reset proposal. There are still globalist kooks out there trying to push COVID shutdowns two years later, and it starts to look an awful lot like the shutdown is the end and COVID is the means, rather than vice versa.

Archbishop Carlo Viganò of Washington, DC, said that "people will take to the streets" rather than tolerate such a Great Reset. Talk to anyone in business, and they'll tell you a two-month national shutdown would completely destroy their livelihood.

I made the obvious comment that a Great Reset in this country holds the very serious possibility of the streets running red with blood, because you will absolutely run the risk of civil strife and violence. When you take away people's dreams and futures, and in doing so you're also taking away their freedom to move and socialize, and none of your justifications are even remotely persuasive, the reaction is likely to be ugly.

I made that comment in a Facebook thread, and shortly thereafter I was told that I was barred from posting or commenting on Facebook for seven days.

But Klaus Schwab, the Ernst Stavro Blofeld wannabe who runs the World Economic Forum, predicted that by 2030, "You'll own nothing, and you'll be happy about it." The idea of stealing all your property, which is a crime, didn't get *him* kicked off social media.

It seems criticizing the Great Reset, and the likely reaction to it in this country, is one of those things you are not allowed to say on Facebook.

The elite Left, the people who make their way to climate conferences and Davos and the other self-congratulatory get-togethers so as to rub jowls with Klaus Schwab, have no use for ordinary people. They'd love to bring back the old-school feudalism and get the serfs back in line. And they'll never stop coming up with ruses to convince the people to give them that power. Perhaps we're done with COVID-justified Reset attempts, but that hardly means the danger has passed.

Go look at Democrat-run cities and states, and you'll see that in spades. A 2020 case in Texas having to do with COVID-hysteria lockdown is a great example.

Shelley Luther owns a hair salon in Dallas, in which a local tin-pot clown of a judge named Eric Moyé, who has an immaculate academic resume to go with a history of personal violence and a virulently partisan Democrat bias, demanded that Luther not only close her business but bend the knee and apologize to the politicians she had defied in keeping it open. Luther politely but forcefully told Moyé that he was the one who could get bent, and he promptly slapped her with a contempt of court citation, a $7,000 fine, and a week's jail sentence.

All hell broke loose in Texas over the Luther case, and a day later the state Supreme Court had sprung Luther after Attorney

General Ken Paxton and Gov. Greg Abbott had separate conniption fits over Moyé's judicial dipsomania. A GoFundMe installed for Luther's legal fees and other needs topped the half-million-dollar mark as an outraged public voted with their PayPal accounts.

And Shelley Luther became "woke" to one of the world's great truths: you may not care about politics, but politics cares about you. Following the tender mercies of Judge Moyé, she jumped into a special election for the Texas state senate. She lost that race, but she's a candidate for the state House of Representatives in the 2022 regular elections.

In his 1937 book, *A History of Political Theory*, George Sabine collected the views of many political theorists on consent of the governed. Within those pages, Sabine quoted from an earlier work by French theologian Theodore Beza, *Vindiciae contra tyrannos*, which held that "The people lay down the conditions which the king is bound to fulfill. Hence they are bound to obedience only conditionally, namely, upon receiving the protection of just and lawful government...the power of the ruler is delegated by the people and continues only with their consent."

In short, abuse your power, and you won't like what happens.

We're starting to see the ground shake a little bit under the feet of the wannabe dictators in charge of too many federal, state, and local governments. That's only going to continue.

And the globalist project so many of these anti-American wannabe tyrants have attempted to impose on us is beginning to fade. It had better, or we will recognize nothing about our country by the end of this decade.

Greta Thunberg isn't the only one who can make dire predictions, you know.

PART THREE

CONSERVATISM'S WOBBLY STOOL

CHAPTER 9

Standing Athwart History Yelling "Stop!"

If you think American culture, politics, and media are homogeneously left-wing, in a manner that is irreversible and getting worse, here's an interesting quote from 1954 that might surprise you:

> "The few spasmodic victories conservatives are winning are aimless, uncoordinated, and inconclusive...because many years have gone by since the philosophy of freedom has been expounded systematically, brilliantly, and resourcefully."

Who said that? William F. Buckley, regarded by many as the father of the modern conservative movement.

At the time, there wasn't even really a single conservative movement to speak of. There were three. There were traditionalist Americans who saw with horror that secularists were pushing God and long-accepted moral values out of society. There were libertarians railing against the big-government New Deal juggernaut of the day. And there were the "neoconservatives" of the time, former liberals and even ex-communists who, given the onset of the Cold War, saw opposition to the aggressions of the Soviet Union as the central project of American policy both foreign and domestic.

The first two groups were best described as, at best, a confederation. Anti-communism was the glue holding together what existed of a conservative movement in the early to mid-1950s.

And the national media's leftist bias might even have been worse than it is now. In a 2010 essay, Heritage Foundation historian Lee Edwards sets the scene:

> "Intellectually, there was a near vacuum on the Right. There were only three opinion journals of import: the weekly Washington newsletter *Human Events*; the economic monthly *The Freeman*; and the once-influential *American Mercury*, now brimming with anti-Semitic diatribes. Aside from the *Chicago Tribune* and the *New York Daily News*, the major daily newspapers leaned left. Of the three weekly newsmagazines, only *U.S. News & World Report* was reliably right.
>
> "Commentators like syndicated columnist George Sokolsky and radio broadcaster Fulton Lewis Jr. had their national audiences, but liberals smoothly undermined their effectiveness by associating them with extremists. CBS's Mike Wallace invited television viewers one evening to

listen to his guest Fulton Lewis explain 'the attraction the far right has for crackpot fascist groups in America.'

"In contrast, liberals dominated every important part of American intellectual life from *The New York Times* and Harvard to the *New Republic* and the Council on Foreign Relations. So it was, so it had always been, so it will always be, asserted liberal intellectuals.

"In *The Liberal Imagination,* literary critic Lionel Trilling declared that 'liberalism is not only the dominant but even the sole intellectual tradition' in America. When conservatives did attempt to express themselves, he wrote almost regretfully, the result was at best 'irritable mental gestures which seem to resemble ideas.'

"Reviewing Russell Kirk's *The Conservative Mind,* Harvard professor Arthur Schlesinger Jr. remarked dismissively that Kirk's 'scurrying about' for intellectual respectability had produced only 'an odd and often contradictory collection of figures' that did not rise 'to the dignity of a conservative tradition.' Prize-winning liberal historian Clinton Rossiter stated that America was 'a progressive country with a Liberal tradition,' making conservatism, despite its contributions here and there, a 'thankless persuasion.'"

There was no fun in conservatism then. But Buckley, and a small cadre of other scrappy conservative thinkers, nevertheless set about building a movement out of the various dissidents from the dominant New Deal liberalism of the time.

It's important to remember, in Piereson's framing, that the Third Era of American history had begun, and the Democrat Party of FDR and Truman had already set, inexorably so, or at least it was thought, the policy agenda of the age. America was to be a social democracy with a broad safety net, high taxes among the top marginal brackets, heavy regulation of industry and commerce by an activist federal government, and a large standing army backed by a military-industrial-intelligence complex actively pursuing an anti-Soviet agenda across the globe.

Most of this agenda had been installed over the objection of the various elements of what ultimately became the conservative movement, though anti-communism has always been a core tenet of American conservative belief, and a Cold War with the Soviet Union was not only inevitable but proper according to conservatives of every stripe, not to mention the vast majority of Americans.

Why the cascade of failure as Roosevelt was elected four times and Truman once while creating ever-expanding welfare and regulatory states? Political scientist Willmoore Kendall, who was a mentor of Buckley's and an editor of his first book, the smash hit *God and Man at Yale*, noted that conservatives existed in an unconnected network of small outposts strung out across the country while liberals were concentrated and could attack those outposts one at a time with overwhelming effect.

Sounds familiar, doesn't it?

God and Man at Yale, published not long after Buckley's graduation (he had been the chairman, or chief editor, of the *Yale Daily News* while in college), put him on the map as a conservative thinker, and he was an interesting and unusual animal in those days in that he could claim membership in all three of the major conservative camps. Buckley was an admirer of Soviet spy-turned-hardcore-anti-Communist Whittaker Chambers and called himself "spellbound" by Chambers's famous anti-Soviet screed *Witness*. Buckley was also a devotee of the famous libertarian writer and philosopher Albert Jay Nock and a fan of Kirk, the foremost traditionalist conservative writer of the time.

It was no surprise, then, when Buckley assembled the pieces and produced the first issue of *National Review* in 1955 that all three perspectives were represented in its pages as part and parcel of one movement the publication would champion on the national stage. But while Buckley was known for his grandiosity, his Publisher's Statement in that first issue would set a far humbler tone:

> "The launching of a conservative weekly journal of opinion in a country widely assumed to be a bastion of conservatism at first glance looks like a work of supererogation, rather like publishing a royalist weekly within the walls of Buckingham Palace. It is not that, of course; if National Review is superfluous, it is so for very different reasons: It stands athwart history, yelling Stop, at a time when no one is inclined to do so, or to have much patience with those who so urge it."

Standing athwart history, yelling Stop, came to be seen as the mission of the modern conservative—and so much of the movement's underperformance traces back to that famous line.

And it's unfortunate, because due to the work of Buckley and his *National Review* colleagues, and others who joined them in carrying the conservative standard (as an example, the great R. Emmett Tyrrell Jr., who founded *The American Spectator* just a few years after *National Review*'s founding; your author is a regular columnist for that publication), the time was limited during which conservatism's capability consisted of standing and yelling.

Buckley's statement was combative and iconoclastic. "We offer, besides ourselves," it read, "a position that has not grown old under the weight of gigantic parasitic bureaucracy, a position untempered by the doctoral dissertations of a generation of Ph.D.'s in social architecture, unattenuated by a thousand vulgar promises to a thousand different pressure groups, uncorroded by a cynical contempt for human freedom. And that, ladies and gentlemen, leaves us just about the hottest thing in town."

Also in that first issue was a Credenda written by *National Review*'s editors that was even more strident—but important in its stitching together of the various factions of the conservative side.

National Review's editors declared they were "irrevocably" at war with "satanic" Communism, and their formulation of the Cold War as requiring victory would resonate later when Ronald Reagan summed up his view as, "We win, they lose." The editors said they were unapologetically "libertarian" in the battle against the growth of government. They took the position as "conservative" in fighting "the Social Engineers" who had used the New Deal to create the fake scientific utopia of the welfare state. The editors declared themselves aligned with "the disciples of Truth" defending the organic moral order.

Anti-communism. Libertarianism in opposition to the welfare and regulatory state. Social conservatism standing against secularization and political atheism. Thus was born the "three-legged stool" of modern conservatism in the pages of that maiden *National Review* issue.

Later, *NR* senior editor Frank Meyer, in his own right a pivotal figure in the formation of modern conservatism, coined a term to describe the "three-legged stool." He called it fusionism, and his writings were dedicated to binding together traditionalists and libertarians. Everyone within earshot of *National Review* was already an anti-communist; that, he could take largely for granted.

That first issue of *National Review* was immediately panned by what one would call the mainstream media of the time. For example, the editor of *Harper's* said of Buckley's magazine that it was not "an organ of conservatism, but of radicalism." And *Commentary*'s Dwight Macdonald said *National Review* appealed to "the half-educated, half-successful provincials...who responded to Huey Long, Father Coughlin and Senator McCarthy."

Not that Buckley, who famously delighted in knock-down, drag-out fights with the Left, cared much at all.

While he spent most of those early years following *NR*'s founding fighting for the survival of the magazine, Buckley also produced a masterful political book: *Up from Liberalism*, a rather insolent title knocked off from the famous tome *Up from Slavery* by Booker T. Washington. That alone was enough to drive the Left insane (though by then they'd long since abandoned any of the substance of Washington's writings), but Buckley had only just begun.

"I will not cede more power to the state," Buckley wrote in *Up from Liberalism*. "I will not willingly cede more power to anyone, not to the state, not to General Motors, not to the CIO. I will hoard my power like a miser, resisting every effort to drain it away from me."

It got better.

"I will use my power as I see fit. I mean to live my life an obedient man, but obedient to God, subservient to the wisdom of my ancestors; never to the authority of political truths arrived at yesterday at the voting booth."

Buckley said this would be enough "to keep conservatism busy, and Liberals at bay. And the nation free."

If that last bit strikes you as a bit too limited, you're paying attention. We'll come to that in a minute.

Nevertheless, *National Review* built quickly into a powerhouse for the conservative movement. When then-Senator Barry Goldwater of Arizona published his manifesto, *The Conscience of a Conservative*, in 1960, Meyer gave it a glowing review and issued his own declaration:

> "Conservatism, we are told, is out of date. The charge is preposterous, and we ought boldly to say no. The laws of God, and of nature, have no deadline. The principles on which the conservative political position is based...are derived from the nature of man, and from the truths that God has revealed about His creation."

Meyer's review, which was unsurprising given that Goldwater's book had been ghostwritten by another of *National Review*'s senior editors Brent Bozell, was an important moment in modern conservatism's early history, as he fully endorsed the senator's policy program thought far too radical for mainstream politics at the time.

But what a program! Included in *The Conscience of a Conservative* were: slashing federal spending by 10 percent; "the prompt and final termination of the farm subsidy program"; passing right-to-work laws in all the states; and a flat income tax. According to Bozell as Goldwater, "Government has a right to claim an equal percentage of each man's wealth, and no more."

Goldwater's political stock skyrocketed following the runaway success of *The Conscience of a Conservative*, so much so that he won the Republican presidential nomination in 1964. That turned out to be a booby prize, of course, as Goldwater was shellacked by the incumbent Democrat Lyndon Baines Johnson. But even in defeat, there was victory—the Goldwater campaign gave the conservative movement the infrastructure, in the form of mailing lists, an activist and donor network, and other assets for the election of future candidates.

At that point conservatism was no longer limited to standing athwart history, yelling Stop. Buckley had built *National Review* into a political-intellectual engine that could fuel a presidential nominee, and he was at the center of the movement he had helped to lead since the magazine's founding. The Goldwater defeat hadn't stopped or even slowed the movement down.

"How this movement, considering the contrary tug of history," said Buckley in an October 1964 speech, "has got as far as it has got, is something that surpasses the understanding of natural pessimists like myself."

Modern conservatism might be the only major political movement in world history founded and fronted by pessimists.

Buckley acted decisively to banish from the conservative tent a pair of aggressive groups who were attracting small but noisy followings.

Not long after *National Review*'s first issue, he dispatched Whittaker Chambers to write a review of Ayn Rand's *Atlas Shrugged*, which was so scathing as to make clear that Randian objectivists were not welcome within the fusionist tent. Their economic libertarianism certainly fit within one of the three legs of the stool, but as a traditionalist Catholic, the objectivist rejection both of charity and religion was beyond the pale in Buckley's view.

It's interesting that while objectivism has never really taken off as a mass intellectual movement, *National Review* later became a cheerleader of former House Speaker Paul Ryan, who credited his reading of Rand with shaping his political philosophy. Modern conservatives generally hail *Atlas Shrugged* as prescient in its prediction of Big Government-driven decline, and attempts were even made to commit it to film. Let's just say, though, that you have to be a very big Ayn Rand fan to sit through all three of the *Atlas Shrugged* movies made from 2011 to 2014.

Similarly, the anti-communist John Birch Society, founded in 1958 by a wealthy candymaker named Robert Welch, who had retired from the presidency of the National Association of Manufacturers to build a national political machine, had by the early 1960s turned into a problem for the movement Buckley sought to build.

"I have had more discussions about the John Birch Society in the past year," Buckley told a supporter of both his magazine and Welch's organization in 1961, "than I have about the existence of God or the financial difficulties of *National Review*."

Welch and Buckley started out as friends, and in fact in the 1950s they supported each other. But as setbacks during the early days of the Cold War multiplied—the Korea stalemate, the Soviet military occupation of Eastern Europe, the crushing of a democracy movement in Czechoslovakia in 1956, Soviet acquisition of nuclear weapons, the Communists' victory in China's civil war, and the success of Fidel Castro's Communist revolution in Cuba—Buckley saw those reversals as an indictment of feckless leadership by the establishment of the time.

Welch, on the other hand, was convinced the cause was Soviet infiltration and outright treason, reaching all the way to President Dwight D. Eisenhower, whom he called a "dedicated, conscious agent of the Communist conspiracy." The Birchers were adamant that he was correct. By 1961 Welch asserted that "50 to 70 percent" of America was "Communist-controlled."

Kirk was unimpressed. "Eisenhower isn't a Communist," he said. "He's a golfer."

Buckley didn't agree with the Eisenhower-as-secret-Red allegation, which earned him a scolding from Welch. And then things got worse. As Alvin S. Felzenberg wrote in his 2017 Buckley biography, *A Man and His Presidents: The Political Odyssey of William F. Buckley Jr.*, the Birchers took off for the fringes and soon became counterproductive to the cause:

> "Welch had JBS run 'stealth' campaigns to win seats on local government bodies, where it would work to counter 'communist domination.' Its members paid close attention to book acquisitions by local libraries and pressed for the banning of certain

titles. They organized boycotts of stores that carried goods imported from Communist countries. A merchant who stocked such items could find that Birchers had placed cards on counters and shelves bearing the words 'Always buy your communist goods at ——,' with the name of the store written in the blank space. Birchers pressed local governments to impose heavy taxes, fees, or regulations on such merchants.

"Of the various projects the JBS took on, its campaign to impeach Chief Justice Earl Warren drew the most attention from the mainstream media. Welch pointed to a litany of actions the Supreme Court had taken under Warren's leadership that facilitated a Communist takeover of the United States: its striking down loyalty oaths; its extension of First Amendment protections to Communists; its ban of school prayer in public schools; its imposition of the 'one man, one vote' principle in legislative apportionment; and, above all, its overturning of the 'separate but equal' doctrine, which put the nation on a path to desegregation. Welch turned his disagreement with the Warren Court and its decisions into a national crusade.

"*National Review* had editorialized against all the Supreme Court decisions to which Welch objected. It favored reversing them through congressional action, appointment of rightward-leaning

> Justices, and, where necessary, constitutional amendment. As a result of Buckley's opposition to the 'impeach Earl Warren' campaign, *National Review* received numerous complaints by mail, many of them Birch generated. "His sister Jane Buckley Smith, who had joined *National Review*'s staff, patiently explained to those writing in that a jurist's written opinions, however inflammatory, did not constitute 'treason, bribery, or other high crimes and misdemeanors,' the constitutional standard for impeachment. Buckley argued in print that Warren rose in public esteem in direct relation to the intensity of Welch's efforts against the Chief Justice. In a tongue-in-cheek parody of Welch's logic, Buckley suggested that the effort to remove Warren had failed because a Communist plot to discredit those opposed to Warren had succeeded."

But there were many Birchers with *National Review* subscriptions, so Buckley initially felt he had little choice but to seek an accommodation with Welch's followers. That became more and more difficult as Welch's attacks on Eisenhower as a Soviet mole percolated, and the president and his supporters grew increasingly irritated. Buckley and the *NR* staff began weighing a break from Welch and the John Birch society, a frightening prospect not just from a business perspective. Conservative syndicated columnist James J. Kilpatrick warned Buckley of the likely consequences of such a move.

"As you know, these idiots set off on a harebrained campaign to impeach Earl Warren," Kilpatrick wrote. "The word got back to Welch that I thought the idea preposterous, whereupon he commanded all his faithful members to write Mr. Kilpatrick a letter. By God, they all did. The first 20 or 30 I answered with individual letters. The next 100 we answered with a mimeographed reply. The next 400, we filed. I am not even sure my Girl Friday is opening the damned things now. This has been the most incredibly disciplined pressure group ever to come my way, and we are frankly a little stunned by it."

By the time the 1960s got really underway, the Birchers had become a liability Buckley felt he couldn't afford. The Kennedy administration, which had come to power in 1961, declared right-wing "extremism" a problem it pledged to conquer, and the Birchers in particular were a declared target. The attorney general, Robert Kennedy, said the Birchers were a "matter of concern" to the Justice Department.

In California, the governor, Pat Brown, directed his attorney general to investigate the John Birch Society, and the state senate scheduled hearings on JBS. Nixon published a two-page letter in the *Los Angeles Times* panning Welch's opinions and tactics. There were calls for congressional investigations and denunciations of Welch and JBS on the Senate floor.

Much of this sounds familiar, of course, and it's tempting given the abuses of more recent Democrat administrations in bootstrapping fears of "right-wing extremism" and the chaos of the January 6 protests into kangaroo court-style inquisitions of center and right critics to feel sympathy for Welch and his followers. History might not repeat itself, but it does tend to go for reboots in the same manner Hollywood insists on.

But there was a certain frenzy to Welch's activism that was clearly not going to end well. He'd begun spreading the theory, for example, that the introduction of fluoride to the water supply in American cities was part of a Communist plot. Among conservatives there was fear he'd drag down and discredit the entire enterprise.

By March 1961, Buckley had reached the end of cooperation with the John Birch Society. Felzenberg notes his opening salvo was intended to cleave the followers away from their leader:

> "Buckley ran the first of what would be several editorials on this subject. Entitled 'The Uproar,' it appeared at a time when Buckley still thought it possible to differentiate between Welch's observations and those issued in the name of the JBS. With the intention of unifying most conservatives behind the stand he was about to take, Buckley began with a strong attack upon the Left. The John Birch Society was in the news, he said, because 'liberals' and 'the Communists' felt 'threatened by revived [conservative] opposition' to their agenda. Given the widespread publicity the JBS was receiving, he noted with sarcasm that it could hardly operate in 'secret,' as was commonly reported.
>
> "He then speculated on the intentions of the organization's critics: 'Certain elements of the press are opportunizing on the mistaken conclusions of Robert Welch to anathematize the entire

American right wing. In professing themselves to be scandalized at the false imputation of pro-Communism to a few people, the critics do not hesitate to impute pro-fascism to a lot of people. In point of fact, the only thing many of these critics would like more than a conservative organization with vulnerabilities is a conservative organization without vulnerabilities.'

"Having set the stage, Buckley repeated in public what he had privately said about the main failing in Welch's logic: that he inferred 'subjective intention' from 'objective consequences.' He closed with the hope that the JBS would reject Welch's trajectory and thrive. Buckley was aware that once he had criticized Welch in this way, his target might suggest that Buckley had gone over to the Left or that he, like Eisenhower, had secretly been a Communist all along. He also knew that some would take advantage of the split within conservative ranks to discredit the entire conservative movement. 'I wish the hell I could attack them [the JBS] without pleasing people I cannot stand to please,' he mused in private."

Over the next couple of years, as the Goldwater presidential candidacy built, and with it the conservative movement, Buckley's derision of Welch—and the backlash from JBS members—grew. In an effort to give a glide path to the worsening relationship, Buckley wrote Welch in his typical style.

"You will no doubt be hearing from around the country that I have been criticizing you and the John Birch Society," wrote Buckley. "I want you to know that that is incorrect: I have been criticizing you, but not the Society. I am forced to criticize you because of your continued line (which as you know I believe defies reason) on the reaches of the Communist conspiracy within our own government.... We shall continue, then, to do much disagreeing about this and no doubt in vigorous language; but I hope we can maintain a pleasant personal relationship. I am prepared to, if you are."

But that produced no positive results. Thousands of Birchers canceled *NR* subscriptions with nasty letters, and some of the magazine's donors also departed. Buckley nonetheless continued his criticisms as Welch's castigations of his critics as Communist sympathizers grew louder. Ronald Reagan offered support to Buckley; so did others, including Texas Senator John Tower.

By 1965 Buckley was ready for a clean break. In the first of three columns on the subject, he finally began challenging Welch's followers and not just the JBS leader on its outlandish positions and statements.

Buckley picked ten policy matters he found in an issue of *American Opinion*, the John Birch Society's magazine. In every one of the positions, the magazine assumed Communist control of the federal government. Buckley asked how the Birchers could put up with "such paranoid and unpatriotic drivel."

Following those columns, the conventional history had it that Buckley had "excommunicated" the John Birch Society from the conservative movement. That isn't true, strictly speaking. JBS's membership didn't actually fall off until the 1970s, well past the point where Buckley was inveighing against them. Birchers claimed that they, not Buckley, were responsible for pushing Goldwater to the GOP nomination, and his famous "Extremism in defense of liberty is no vice" speech at the 1964 convention was seen as a dog-whistle in support of JBS.

But Goldwater was hounded by Johnson's supporters and the mainstream commentariat for his supposed connection to the John Birch Society, despite his having publicly criticized Welch.

Given the rather significant headaches in building the modern movement, the success of conservatism surprised Buckley. He marinated in a sea of liberalism dating from his formative years, after all, despite being the son of an oil man. The disconnect between the intellectual solons of the movement as reflected by Buckley's experience and that of so many of his social colleagues made for unnecessary limits to his perception of the movement's prospects.

In fact, after Buckley ran what can best be described as a vanity/protest campaign for mayor of New York in 1965, earning just less than 14 percent to come in third as liberal Republican John Lindsay won election, he claimed conservative victory "is beyond our reach."

Buckley then authored a book about his ill-fated mayoral campaign, in which his runaway pessimism blossomed to full flower. In *The Unmaking of a Mayor*, Buckley lamented the lack of conservatism's "mass appeal." He said conservatism was destined to be a "force" and not "a political movement." He predicted the Republican Party's days as "a major party" were waning, and he moaned that the future opposition to liberal Democrat control of America was to be a "congeries of third parties, adamantly doctrinaire, inadequately led, insufficiently thoughtful, improvidently angry, self-defeatingly sectarian."

This doom and gloom wasn't altogether unwarranted at the time, but if Buckley was to be the father of conservatism, he may have been the Great Santini or at least Willy Loman.

By the mid-1960s America was well on its way to becoming a social democratic facsimile of Western Europe, as Johnson's Great Society program steamrolled its way through Congress, and the ultimately fruitless War on Poverty was born. So, too, was born the active movement to desegregate the South, something Buckley was a critic of on the basis that the federal government's heavy hand in imposing anti-discrimination laws encroached too much upon the concept of federalism—something he believed, not without reason, would manifest itself elsewhere with negative consequences once the precedent for such action had been set.

Whatever philosophical justifications there may have been for standing against the feds imposing anti-discrimination laws upon reticent Southern states, politically, the opposition of the conservative movement to the 1960s civil rights push led to the ugly charge of racism against the movement.

Here again, Buckley was an imperfect champion. In the 1950s he had written, though he later recanted as wrong, that the Southern segregationists were in the right, using the defense of federalism as his primary stratagem. And Buckley had also referred to white people as the "more advanced race"—a perspective that at the time was not far out of the mainstream but nonetheless fueled the perception that conservatism was born of animus toward black people.

And when Buckley debated the famous black radical novelist James Baldwin in 1965 at the Cambridge Union in a televised affair over the prospect that "the American Dream has been achieved at the expense of the American Negro," Buckley was voted to have lost after making a spirited argument that black advancement should come as a result of black achievement rather than a turn to socialism. Much of Buckley's argument harkened back to the writings of Washington in *Up from Slavery*; that hardly registered with the Cambridge assembly.

The sum of these things accelerated a movement of black voters away from the Republican Party—something that had been happening for decades.

While Richard Nixon had won a third of the black vote in 1960, Goldwater's share of that demographic plummeted to a paltry 6 percent. This was a factor of Goldwater's opposition to the 1964 Civil Rights Act, of course. Martin Luther King Jr. threatened that a Goldwater election would trigger civil unrest in America's streets, something that happened anyway, and baseball great Jackie Robinson said Goldwater was "a hopeless captive of the lunatic, calculating right-wing extremists."

This was especially cruel given that Goldwater had been a staunch proponent of the 1950 and 1957 Civil Rights Acts, which both died in the Senate due to filibusters by Southern Democrats (including Johnson), and Goldwater, who was half-Jewish, had also been a supporter of both the NAACP and the Urban League back in Arizona. He simply thought the 1964 Civil Rights Act was unconstitutional in a pair of its components, including its compulsions about private sector employment, and therefore he couldn't vote for it.

Nobody in the conservative camp seemed to have a handle on how to provide an on-ramp for blacks into the movement. This was all policy, no politics. Meanwhile, of course, Johnson is said to have boasted in advance of the passage of his legislative agenda that "I'll have those n*****s voting Democrat for the next two hundred years."

When that conservative opposition to the big-government nature of the Great Society was then attached to the opposition by Southern whites to second-wave compulsive policies like forced busing in what was known as Nixon's Southern Strategy, the Democrat narrative of conservatism-as-racism was set in stone.

The truth of that narrative has never been particularly well established. Nixon won Southern states in the 1968 presidential election not so much because of his own support but because the Democrat Hubert Humphrey found his vote split there. Segregationist Alabama Governor George Wallace, running a third-party race, carried Louisiana, Arkansas, Mississippi, Alabama, and Georgia. What Southern states Nixon did win were the ones least "Southern"—Florida, with its many Northern transplants in the Miami metropolitan area, South and North Carolina, with the large military presences in both states, Virginia, and Tennessee. Humphrey managed to win Texas.

Yes, Nixon did very well in the South in 1972. He did very well everywhere else as well, considering that George McGovern was nothing short of an electoral disaster for the Democrats, and that election was one of the most thorough clobberings in American history.

But the supposed success of the "Southern Strategy" in which conservatives and Republicans stole away the votes of mouth-breathing racist rednecks and turned Dixie Republican is a canard, and a foolish one at that. It would take more than twenty years after Nixon before Southern states were regularly electing Republicans to statewide office or congressional seats, and really thirty years before the GOP had secured the electoral domination of the region.

By then the South was nothing like the segregationist backwater it had been, and its electorate was very different. A forty-year-old average voter in 1960 would be an eighty-year-old past his or her life expectancy in 2000, and it's fair to say a Southerner born in 1960 would have far different life experiences and attitudes than one born in 1920. The South clearly became less racist as the 1960s gave way to the 1970s, 1980s, 1990s, and 2000s—and as it became less racist it became more Republican.

But this lie has persisted. Conservatism failed to strangle it in its infancy, too concerned with academic discussions of free enterprise, federalism, and other high subjects to engage on a visceral level with a demographic to which it should have had ties.

Buckley's early bromides against desegregation surely didn't age well, but in comparison to prominent Democrat figures of the time who have largely gotten a pass he was a mere piker.

At the Cambridge Union debate, Buckley asked rhetorically exactly what a humble America should do to alleviate the sufferings of the American Negro. He was answered by a man in the audience, who hectored him with "Perhaps you should let them vote in Mississippi!" His response was that the problem was not so much that too few blacks in Mississippi had the franchise but that too many uneducated whites did—the implication being that those same mouth-breathing racist rednecks who would later be appended to the Republican Party as its supposed base vote were in truth responsible for electing the segregationist Democrat Ross Barnett as that state's powerful governor.

Conservatism was never and is not now a racist ideology. It is a calumny of the first order that the accusation was ever made and a terrible disgrace that the movement never found a suitably loud voice to defend itself against such charges.

Buckley was certainly a fighter and a brilliant orator for the cause. But his demeanor always reflected the idea that his side was perpetually doomed. And that was a fatal flaw in the formation of modern conservatism—its attitude, its priorities, and its actions all flowed from a fundamental lack of confidence.

And Buckley himself lacked the foresight for, and even the comfort with, the building of conservatism as a mass popular movement to counter liberalism. As such, he and many of his disciples saw themselves as forced into criticism of Kennedy/Johnson government expansionist policies rather than conjuring strategies for toppling them.

It would take a second wave of conservative operatives, activists, and politicians to build upon what Buckley and his colleagues at *National Review* had put in motion to expand beyond standing athwart history, yelling Stop.

Ronald Reagan won election as governor of California in 1966, after all.

CHAPTER 10

The Incomplete Victory of Ronald Reagan

If Bill Buckley was the father of modern conservatism, perhaps Ronald Reagan was the high school football coach who taught it how to win.

Reagan was a winner. He might have been one of the greatest winners in 20th century American history.

What people don't commonly perceive about Reagan was his versatility. Reagan was a man of many parts, beginning his career in Iowa, next door to his native Illinois, as a radio announcer and sportscaster and then heading out west.

Reagan became a Hollywood actor of some note, though he never achieved stardom at the level of a Humphrey Bogart or Cary Grant. But while Reagan might have been what was later called a "B-list" actor, he nevertheless earned enough respect among his peers that he was elected president of the Screen Actors Guild at a time when that job mattered.

Reagan's election as SAG's president coincided with the inception of the House Un-American Activities Committee, which conducted an inquiry into communist activity among America's cultural institutions and resulted in actors, writers, directors, and others in Hollywood being "blacklisted"—something that has been presented as a terrible abuse of free speech by the modern cultural Left but is in retrospect entirely defensible given Soviet fifth-column activity in the United States during the 1940s and beyond.

They'd have you believe such stories are conspiracy theories, the product of McCarthyite or John Birch Society fantasies, debunked as demagoguery by right-wing extremists. But there's a problem with that narrative; when the Soviet Union disintegrated, the Russian government for a time opened up its KGB files and allowed researchers a glimpse into its Cold War activities.

Those files, code-named Venona, surrendered a treasure trove of information that largely proved that the KGB was relentless in attempting to sabotage and erode American culture according to the Gramscian model.

And those revelations, which were covered sparsely at best by mainstream American media in the early 1990s, validated the concerns of anti-communists like Ronald Reagan during his time as SAG president.

Starting in the 1940s Reagan cooperated with the FBI in their probes of Communist activity in Hollywood, and reports dating from that time indicate that he had been a member, soon to his consternation, of a handful of organizations within the film industry that turned out to have communist ties. One of those was Hollywood Independent Citizens Committee of the Arts, Sciences and Professions, or HICCASP. When Reagan realized the red tinge of the organization, he proposed a resolution condemning Communism and voicing approval of capitalism in order to clarify its leanings. And when that resolution was defeated 60–10, he and his then-wife, the actress Jane Wyman, withdrew.

As SAG president he testified in front of HUAC, demonstrating a vigorous anti-Communist stance. But Reagan, at the time still a New Deal Democrat, was on record as opposing the committee's heavy-handed tactics and opposing attempts to blacklist Hollywood workers suspected of Communist ties without giving them a fair hearing.

Nevertheless, Reagan supported the passage of a SAG resolution that asked members to sign affidavits saying that they were not Communists before they could be eligible for guild office.

He became something of a controversial figure for his cooperation with efforts to block Communist infiltration of Hollywood, but Reagan was nevertheless afforded respect as one of SAG's most successful presidents. In fact, he was elected SAG president again in the late 1950s, despite the fact that he had evolved politically and was beginning to embrace conservatism—a migration that was greatly encouraged by his second wife, the former Nancy Davis, whom he married in 1952.

This evolution accelerated when Reagan was hired by General Electric, at the time an explicitly conservative company, to serve as a company spokesman and the director and host of its Sunday night *GE Theater* broadcast. That was one of several lucrative deals Reagan managed with the help of the Music Corporation of America (MCA), an uber-influential entertainment company headed up by the famous Hollywood agent Lew Wasserman. Through that association Reagan became a wealthy man even though his acting career was all but over; he began a transition from actor to politician.

Part of Reagan's job with GE was a role as a company talking head that put him on the road sixteen weeks a year from 1954–62, and that experience was a formative one for the former FDR devotee who later self-deprecatingly called himself a "hemophiliac" liberal in his younger days. During those tours, which Reagan made by train rather than by air, as he had a fear of flying he'd later conquer, he visited all of GE's 139 plants across the US, giving thousands of speeches to collections of the company's 250,000 employees and in front of civic forums all across the country.

The time spent traveling, Reagan used well—namely, by reading. At that time he gravitated toward conservative journals and books: *Human Events* and *Reader's Digest*, Whittaker Chambers's *Witness* and F. A. Hayek's *The Road to Serfdom*, and, of course, *National Review*. Reagan later called the GE tours a "postgraduate course in political science" and an "apprenticeship for public life." He read Sun Tzu and Henry Hazlitt, Jefferson, Madison, and Hamilton.

And the speeches Reagan gave to GE's employees reflected what he had learned. His 1964 oration in support of Barry Goldwater's presidential campaign that year, which shortly became famous as the "A Time for Choosing" speech, was hardly new to the GE employees he'd spoken to; Reagan spent several years giving variations of it during his tours. It was pro-capitalism, pro-liberty, anti-communist, and anti-Big Government.

But the general public, who knew Reagan mostly as a semi-successful actor appearing in a host of B-movies of yore, had little exposure to his political conversion. That changed with "A Time for Choosing."

It was one of the most compelling political orations in American history, and it brought the conservatism of Buckley, Kirk, Meyer, and others, which had percolated as an intellectual exercise, into the mainstream of America's conscience.

"I have spent most of my life as a Democrat," Reagan said near the beginning of the speech. "I recently have seen fit to follow another course. I believe that the issues confronting us cross party lines. Now, one side in this campaign has been telling us that the issues of this election are the maintenance of peace and prosperity. The line has been used, 'We've never had it so good.'"

But shortly thereafter, Reagan turned up the temperature:

> "No nation in history has ever survived a tax burden that reached a third of its national income. Today, thirty-seven cents out of every dollar earned in this country is the tax collector's share, and yet our government continues to spend seventeen million dollars a day more than the government takes in. We haven't balanced our budget twenty-eight out of the last thirty-four years. We've raised our debt limit three times in the last twelve months, and now our national debt is one and a half times bigger than all the combined debts of all the nations of the world. We have fifteen billion dollars in gold in our treasury; we don't own an ounce. Foreign dollar claims are 27.3 billion dollars. And we've just had announced that the dollar of 1939 will now purchase forty-five cents in its total value.
>
> "As for the peace that we would preserve, I wonder who among us would like to approach the wife or mother whose husband or son has died in

South Vietnam and ask them if they think this is a peace that should be maintained indefinitely. Do they mean peace, or do they mean we just want to be left in peace? There can be no real peace while one American is dying some place in the world for the rest of us. We're at war with the most dangerous enemy that has ever faced mankind in his long climb from the swamp to the stars, and it's been said if we lose that war, and in so doing lose this way of freedom of ours, history will record with the greatest astonishment that those who had the most to lose did the least to prevent its happening. Well I think it's time we ask ourselves if we still know the freedoms that were intended for us by the Founding Fathers.

"Not too long ago, two friends of mine were talking to a Cuban refugee, a businessman who had escaped from Castro, and in the midst of his story one of my friends turned to the other and said, 'We don't know how lucky we are.' And the Cuban stopped and said, 'How lucky you are? I had someplace to escape to.' And in that sentence he told us the entire story. If we lose freedom here, there's no place to escape to. This is the last stand on earth.

"And this idea that government is beholden to the people, that it has no other source of power except the sovereign people, is still the newest and the most unique idea in all the long history of man's relation to man."

Reagan took on a very similar, but far more relatable, message to Buckley's—that it was conservatism, rather than the liberalism of the time, that provided the safeguard for preserving American society:

> "You and I are told increasingly we have to choose between a left or right. Well I'd like to suggest there is no such thing as a left or right. There's only an up or down—[up] man's old-aged dream, the ultimate in individual freedom consistent with law and order, or down to the ant heap of totalitarianism. And regardless of their sincerity, their humanitarian motives, those who would trade our freedom for security have embarked on this downward course."

He related a few rather obnoxious quotes from leftist figures of the day disparaging the Constitution and extolling the virtues of an imperial presidency and centralized power as a force for good and then indicted those as nonsense or worse:

> "Well, I, for one, resent it when a representative of the people refers to you and me, the free men and women of this country, as 'the masses.' This is a term we haven't applied to ourselves in America. But beyond that, 'the full power of centralized government' this was the very thing the Founding Fathers sought to minimize. They knew that governments don't control things. A government can't control the economy without controlling people. And they know when a government sets out to do

> that, it must use force and coercion to achieve its purpose. They also knew, those Founding Fathers, that outside of its legitimate functions, government does nothing as well or as economically as the private sector of the economy."

Reagan embarked on a full refutation of the liberal argument for the regulatory and welfare state, a famous quote that would live on among conservatives to this day:

> "We have so many people who can't see a fat man standing beside a thin one without coming to the conclusion the fat man got that way by taking advantage of the thin one. So they're going to solve all the problems of human misery through government and government planning. Well, now, if government planning and welfare had the answer—and they've had almost thirty years of it—shouldn't we expect government to read the score to us once in a while? Shouldn't they be telling us about the decline each year in the number of people needing help? The reduction in the need for public housing?"

And another famous quote that became a Reagan staple:

> "Yet anytime you and I question the schemes of the do-gooders, we're denounced as being against their humanitarian goals. They say we're always 'against' things—we're never 'for' anything.

> "Well, the trouble with our liberal friends is not that they're ignorant; it's just that they know so much that isn't so."

Reagan delivered a fact-based condemnation of the underperformance and mendacity underlying the Social Security program. He trashed the Democrat program of deliberate inflation and its assault on purchasing power. He ridiculed the excesses of foreign aid, as it directly produced "dress suits for Greek undertakers" and "extra wives for Kenyan government officials" and a "thousand TV sets for a place where they have no electricity."

"A government bureau is the nearest thing to eternal life we'll ever see on this earth," Reagan said.

He extolled the personal virtues of Barry Goldwater, a friend for more than a decade whom he'd met through his father-in-law. And he defended the conservative anti-Communist stance.

"There's no argument over the choice between peace and war," he said, "but there's only one guaranteed way you can have peace—and you can have it in the next second—surrender."

And he closed with another timeless quote:

> "We'll preserve for our children this, the last best hope of man on earth, or we'll sentence them to take the last step into a thousand years of darkness."

Reaction to the speech was akin to a national gasp of shock. Many Americans had no idea the star of *Bedtime for Bonzo* was capable of such oratory. Others were dumbfounded that Reagan was so passionate in extolling a new ideological position not seen as mainstream in those times. Still others wondered why Reagan, whose oratorical skills significantly outstripped those of Goldwater, wasn't on the ballot. The syndicated columnist David S. Broder said it was "the most successful national political debut since William Jennings Bryan electrified the 1896 Democratic convention with the 'Cross of Gold' speech."

Reagan's speech couldn't save Goldwater, but it did put him on the political map. And two years later he was California's newly elected governor. Reagan was an upstart who was initially seen as an underdog to George Christopher, a former mayor of San Francisco, in the GOP primary. California's Democrat Governor Pat Brown intervened on Reagan's behalf in an attempt to sabotage Republican hopes; that was a miscalculation. Reagan throttled Christopher in the primary and destroyed Brown in the general election, reeling in more than 57 percent of the vote.

He ran on two promises; first, that he would "do something about the mess at Berkeley," where hippies and other anti-war protesters had turned the University of California into a sewer of lawlessness and sedition, and "to send the welfare bums back to work."

As to the former, he was somewhat successful, as Reagan engineered the firing of Cal's president and ended up calling in both the California Highway Patrol and National Guard to quell campus unrest in Berkeley—ultimately getting the chaos there under some semblance of control. His welfare reforms were hailed as major successes.

Reagan learned much as governor about how to negotiate with Democrats. He'd managed to cut property taxes but at the expense of income, business, and sales tax hikes, and he signed a bill legalizing abortion in cases where the life of the mother was at stake—a concession that opened the door to more than one hundred thousand abortions per year in California by the time he left office in January of 1975.

But despite his reputation as a conservative hard-liner, Reagan actually got along relatively well with the Democrats in the state legislature. His negotiating style, so notable in his later years as president, emerged during those years: Reagan would gladly accept part of his aims in one round of negotiations, then come back for more shortly thereafter.

By the end of his second term, Reagan was acclaimed as one of the greatest governors the Golden State had ever had. California had experienced runaway population and economic growth during his eight years; the state went from 15.7 million in the 1960 census to more than 20 million by 1970 and over 23 million in 1980, and burgeoning major industries flocked to the San Francisco and Los Angeles metro markets in droves. His leadership was credited with fueling the state's golden age.

It was only natural that Reagan would look to national politics as his next step. He had positioned himself as a third option in the 1968 GOP primary between Richard Nixon, an anti-communist political moderate who had made overtures to conservatives with a law-and-order platform, and liberal Republican Nelson Rockefeller. But Nixon quickly closed out any opportunity for alternatives and went on to win the general election in a blowout.

Nixon similarly won the 1972 election in a rout, though shortly thereafter came a break with the conservative movement. The president made an overture to Red China, which was anathema to conservatives, and embraced a series of compulsive economic policies, including wage and price controls.

"We are all Keynesians now," Nixon said. Buckley and others in the conservative camp seethed, and they refused to support him when the Watergate scandal broke a year later.

Amid the tumult of Nixon's second term, the conservative movement, of which Reagan had become the functional leader, was coming to maturity. In early 1974 the new American Conservative Union held its first annual Conservative Political Action Conference (CPAC), and Reagan was its headline speaker.

Reagan planned to make his ascension to the status of standard-bearer not just for the conservative movement but the GOP as a whole in the 1976 presidential election, but events derailed those plans. As Watergate deepened into an impeachment controversy, Nixon resigned in 1974, putting moderate Republican vice president Gerald Ford in the White House. The liberal Republican Rockefeller was installed as Ford's vice president, which further infuriated the party's conservatives.

At CPAC's second annual meeting in February 1975, there was much discussion of starting a third party to reflect the conservatism the Nixon/Ford GOP had for all practical purposes rejected. But Reagan, again the headliner of the conference, dismissed such talk. "Is it a third party that we need," came his rhetorical question, "or is it a new and revitalized second party, raising a banner of no pale pastels, but bold colors which could make it unmistakably clear where we stand on all the issues troubling the people?"

Ford then presided over the loss of Vietnam to the Communists, which was the result of the Democrat Congress's refusal to abide by the agreement to provide military aid to the South Vietnamese government. That disgrace infuriated the center-right in America, which began to look upon Ford as soft and a weak leader. That his

First Lady Betty Ford was busy championing abortion rights and the Equal Rights Amendment certainly didn't help.

Nor did Ford's agreement to cede the Panama Canal to its host country, something most of the country thought was ridiculous.

And when Ford, seeking to improve relations with the Soviets, refused to meet with prominent Russian dissident Aleksandr Solzhenitsyn when the latter was in Washington, conservative dissatisfaction began to boil over. Ford then traveled overseas and signed the infamous Helsinki Accords, which formally recognized the Eastern bloc and called its borders "inviolable by force," despite ample evidence most of the Warsaw Pact nations were held captive by Soviet troops against their will. It wasn't just conservatives who were displeased. Ford's approval rating sunk to 34 percent.

Reagan smelled blood and challenged Ford for the nomination in November of 1975, and one of the tightest primary campaigns in American history ensued.

Ford rattled off a string of early primary victories, and at one point it appeared Reagan would run out of money and be forced out of the race. But buoyed by Sen. Jesse Helms's powerful North Carolina organization, Reagan won a key victory there and followed that up with a massive rout of Ford in Texas. From there the race became a back-and-forth in the later primaries—Ford winning most of the north and east, while Reagan captured most in the west and south.

Reagan came awfully close to unseating a sitting president in a primary race. He won twenty-four state primary contests to Ford's twenty-six, and he earned 1,078 delegates to Ford's 1,121—nine short of the 1,130 needed to sew up the nomination.

There was a floor fight, and Reagan made a tactical mistake that cost him a shot at the nomination. He announced that his choice for vice president would be liberal Republican Senator Richard Schweiker of Pennsylvania, a move that alienated some in his base and attracted little interest from moderate delegates. Ford chose Kansas Senator Bob Dole as his running mate and captured the necessary delegates to finally end the contest.

And after Ford gave an entirely uninspiring acceptance speech, he turned the podium over to Reagan that the runner-up might say a few words. What followed was an eight-minute extemporaneous speech that extolled the virtues of individual liberty and peace through strength, during which the audience toggled between absolute silence and roaring applause. When it was over, it appeared well more than half the hall at the Kansas City convention was questioning whether they hadn't nominated the wrong man.

Reagan never explicitly endorsed Ford; his camp was sore over what they felt had been chicanery at the convention. And Ford went on to lose a close race to the Democrat Georgia Governor Jimmy Carter, who carried 50.1 percent of the popular vote and 294 delegates to Ford's 240.

The GOP had indeed nominated the wrong man.

What followed were four years that demonstrated more or less beyond a shadow of a doubt America's need for conservative governance. Carter was a disaster in nearly every respect, from his government's inflationary policies that badly debased the currency (13.3 percent inflation in 1979, 12.4 percent in 1980), his insistence on energy conservation rather than domestic oil production—which put America in thrall to the OPEC nations, most of which were hostile to our interests—and the resulting gas lines, his weak showing in front of the Soviet Union in terms of foreign policy, which ultimately led to the invasion of Afghanistan and the forty years and counting of untold misery afflicting that country, to the shuttering of factories and spiraling unemployment, and to the mismanagement of unrest in Iran that led to jihadist revolutionaries sacking the US embassy in Tehran and holding its personnel as prisoners for more than a year.

Additionally, in 1979 the communist Sandinista party seized power in Nicaragua, signaling the strong possibility Central American countries would fall one by one. It was quite plausible that the Panama Canal might fall under Soviet dominion, an eventuality that would amount to losing the Cold War.

Things were so bad in the Carter years that the president was moved to whining on television of the "crisis of confidence" that afflicted the country in what became known as the "Malaise speech," without much recognition that it was an acute deficit of intelligent and committed leadership emanating from the White House that was the primary cause. It began to look like Carter recognized the job was far too much for him, and by 1979, even much of his own party was fed up. Massachusetts Senator Ted Kennedy, the younger brother of John and Robert, threw his hat into the ring as a primary challenger to Carter.

And Reagan entered the race on the Republican side as the prohibitive favorite.

Kennedy had been seen at the outset of the Democratic primaries to be an odds-on favorite to wrest the nomination away from Carter, but he ran an abysmal campaign peppered with largely unintelligible media interviews, and by the time the Democrats convened in New York, Carter had twice as many pledged delegates as Kennedy. Though the latter refused to concede, and the convention was tumultuous, Carter nevertheless was the nominee. His acceptance speech was filled with fear-mongering about a

Reagan presidency; Carter offered little by way of reform or policy innovation.

The GOP primaries, on the other hand, were largely the Ronald Reagan Show. Reagan carried just under 60 percent of the popular vote in the various primary contests, winning forty-four states and piling up 1,222 delegates—nearly twice as many as George H. W. Bush, who finished second with 637. At the Republican convention in Detroit, Reagan chose Bush, largely a repeat of his strategy to unify with the moderate or liberal wing of the Republican Party.

And the liberals gave him the back of their hands nonetheless. Illinois Congressman John Anderson, who had won a mere 128 delegates and 12 percent of the primary vote, opted for a third-party run rather than endorse Reagan.

It didn't matter in the general election. Reagan won a monumental landslide victory over Carter, who spent the summer and fall spreading gloom over the dystopian reality Reagan's supply-side economics and supposed militarism would bring to America. The voters didn't buy it, as Reagan won forty-four states and throttled Carter by a 51–41 margin in the popular vote. He racked up an astounding 489 electoral votes to Carter's 49. Anderson carried just 6.6 percent of the vote and was largely never heard from again as a political figure.

"What happened in 1980," said the syndicated columnist George Will, "is that American conservatism came of age."

It was called the Reagan Revolution, but very little of what he offered was revolutionary. Much of Reagan's platform was quite recognizable from that of Goldwater, Nixon, and Ford.

On the other hand, with Reagan the nation finally got an opportunity to see the three-legged stool at work.

Upon taking office, in his first press conference as president in fact, Reagan displayed an aggressive realism toward the Soviet Union they'd not seen for some time:

> "I know of no leader of the Soviet Union since the revolution, and including the present leadership, that has not more than once repeated in the various Communist congresses they hold their determination that their goal must be the promotion of world revolution and a one-world Socialist or Communist state.... Now, as long as they do that and as long as they, at the same time, have openly and publicly declared that the only morality they recognize is what will further their cause, meaning they reserve unto themselves the right to commit any crime, to lie, to cheat, in order to attain that, that that is moral, not immoral, and we operate on a different set of standards, I think when you do business with them, even at a détente, you keep that in mind."

Official Washington blew a gasket at that kind of tough talk, but the consequences threatened by the dominant media and political establishment never materialized.

To Reagan the Cold War wasn't all that complicated. The Soviets were the bad guys, they were enemies of human freedom, and the world would be better off if the Soviet empire was consigned, in controversial words Reagan was unapologetic in uttering publicly, to the "ash-heap of history."

"We win, they lose," was Reagan's formulation. And for an American foreign policy establishment that had largely accepted the inevitable Communist victory and watched as country after country fell to totalitarian control prior to 1980, this was dangerous talk, likely to start a nuclear war.

The opposite happened. For example, on the day of Reagan's inauguration, Iran set loose the hostages from the Tehran embassy they'd held for more than four hundred days. In Poland, the Solidarity movement consisting of trade unionists under Lech Walesa began, with Reagan's help along with that of Margaret Thatcher and Pope John Paul II, to undermine the Soviet puppet Jaruzelski government. Afghan mujahideen fighters, equipped with American weapons smuggled in from Pakistan, began bleeding the Soviet Red Army.

And when Cuban-backed Communist revolutionaries attempted to seize power on the tiny Caribbean island of Grenada, Reagan sent in the US Marines to put the coup down and protect hundreds of Americans, particularly a number of them attending medical school there.

No country fell to Communist aggression in the entire eight years Reagan was in office, and within a year of his retirement back to his Santa Barbara, California, ranch, the Berlin Wall came down, and the Soviet empire collapsed entirely.

But it wasn't without strife that the Communist advance was halted. In Central America, the fall of Nicaragua in 1979 led to Marxist agitation in next-door El Salvador—and a nasty blowback from the American-backed government, which employed death squads to put down the insurrection. Reagan wanted to challenge the Sandinista communist regime in Nicaragua in order to keep them busy at home and prevent them from fomenting revolution elsewhere, and to do that ruthlessness was necessary. Mines were laid in the Managua harbor, and US-backed guerillas, known as the *contras*, began an insurgency against the Nicaraguan regime.

Congressional Democrats balked at funding the *contras* in Reagan's second term, the second time in a decade that party had come up short in appropriating funds to fight communism amid a direct challenge. This ultimately led to the scandal known as the Iran-Contra Affair, in which a scheme was concocted to sell equipment, including spare parts, to the jihadist regime in Iran for its warplanes, in return for the release of a number of Americans being held by the Iranians' proxies in Lebanon, and then to use the proceeds from those sales to replace congressional funding of the *contras*.

That evidence began to emerge that the *contras* were funding themselves through narcotics trafficking didn't help the public relations of the administration's Central American project.

But when the Democrat-led Iran-Contra hearings began, a star emerged in Marine Col. Oliver North, whose testimony covering his role in the affair dominated the proceedings and captured the nation's imagination. Public outrage over Iran-Contra was largely limited to the East Coast press and Democrat partisans; everyone else largely wondered why congressional funding hadn't been forthcoming in the first place.

And Reagan didn't suffer much in popularity from the affair, given the somewhat plausible deniability afforded him. His leadership style was relatively hands-off, went the explanation, and sometimes that could get a little bumpy.

Whether people believed that line or not, most were willing to shrug off Iran-Contra given Reagan's record of success overall.

Partisan Democrats in the media seethed and began calling Reagan the "Teflon President" for their failure to ensnare him. Later there were accusations Reagan's CIA had engaged in the drug trade wholesale to fund the *contras* and other initiatives; those weren't given particular credibility by most Americans, who by then had gotten at least somewhat used to the lengths the Dems would go to in order to smear their political opponents.

But clearly, fearless anti-communism and "Peace through Strength" worked. It created the most successful foreign policy in American history and produced a world-changing result thought impossible by the conventional wisdom in place upon Reagan's first inauguration.

Reagan's commitment to a small-government economic policy was similarly successful. He sought and secured a massive tax cut in his first term, while endorsing then-Fed chairman Paul Volcker's program of raising interest rates in order to strangle inflation. Reagan's first two years in office were rough; unemployment mounted to double figures, and the economy plunged into a recession.

But by 1983 the troubles were past. While US GDP grew at a modest 2.54 percent in 1981 and sank to negative 1.8 percent during the 1982 downturn, it rebounded to grow at 4.58 percent in 1983 and a shocking 7.24 percent in 1984. The Reagan recovery was on, American business was booming, and the country had shaken off the "crisis of confidence" Carter had whined over. The US economy's positive reaction to Reagan's tax cuts and deregulation produced growth hovering around 4 percent for the whole of his second term, but that wasn't all. With exceptions, including the betrayal of George H. W. Bush's key campaign promise of "no new taxes" in 1991, the basic thrust of Reagan's economic policy was held in place for two decades, and the US economy grew by an astounding third between 1980 and 2005.

Bush had derided Reagan's supply-side philosophy, cutting taxes on producers to free up capital for investment and job creation, and riding the resulting economic activity to general prosperity, as "voodoo economics" owing to disbelief that tax cuts might produce increased government revenues. But the federal government's intake did grow—for fiscal year 1981 federal revenues were $599 billion. By fiscal year 1989 they had risen to $991 billion. Reagan was precisely correct in his forecast.

Unfortunately, the Democrats controlled the House of Representatives, where the federal budget originated. And Reagan's attempts to rein in domestic spending were an abject defeat. What was a $79 billion budget deficit when he took office had grown to $153 billion by 1989, and in three of the years in that time frame the deficit had topped $200 billion.

Much of that was attributable to the defense buildup that ultimately helped to end the Cold War. But much more was entitlement spending, which proved to be impossible to stop. He inveighed against the fiscal incontinence of Congress, and he demanded again and again to be afforded the power of a line-item veto as a means of imposing some semblance of budget discipline, but it was not to be.

And Reagan embraced the social conservatism of the traditional conservatives and the newer "religious Right" of organizations like the Moral Majority and other church-based groups motivated by a number of issues, abortion prominent among them, which reflected opposition to the increasing secularization of American culture.

But from a policy standpoint Reagan couldn't offer much more than a good word from the bully pulpit. Abortion was legal on the day he took office, and it was legal when he left. Reagan stated his support for bringing prayer back in schools; that proved impossible. Reagan, noting the alarming rise in drug use on America's streets and the tertiary effect on crime rates, embarked on a national program to fight drug abuse. That was an utter failure, though one could argue things might have been even worse had he not made the effort.

The mainstream media and the political Left looked upon the Reagan years as something akin to a theocracy, but this was pure propaganda. The 1980s were a decade in which pop culture exploded—it was a Golden Age for the music business, theaters were jammed with audiences for blockbuster films debuting two at a time, the art world saw a flowering of sorts, though traditionalists were less than impressed with the predominance of "modern" art at auction and on display. And very little of this cultural flowering was especially religious or traditional.

A perfect example of the difficulties Reagan encountered in attempting to score points for social conservatives came in 1987, when he nominated the brilliant jurist Robert Bork, a judge on the DC Circuit Court of Appeals, to fill a Supreme Court vacancy. Bork was recognized as one of the most qualified judges in the country, on or off the Supreme Court. He had made partner at a major Chicago firm before joining the faculty at Yale Law School in 1962. Bork had served as the solicitor general from 1973 to 1977 under Presidents Nixon and Ford, and he argued over thirty cases at the Supreme Court during that time. His 1978 book, *The Antitrust Paradox*, revolutionized antitrust law. Retired Chief Justice Burger said there was no one with better qualifications than Judge Bork.

But he was a proponent of the conservative legal doctrine of originalism, which holds that constitutional legal issues must be decided with adherence to the intent of the Framers and not some fuzzy, politically tinged desire to reach contemporary policy ends.

"The judge's responsibility is to discern how the framers' values, defined in the context of the world they knew, apply in the world we know," he told the Senate in his opening speech at the confirmation hearings. "If a judge abandons intention as his guide, there is no law available to him, and he begins to legislate a social agenda for the American people. That goes well beyond his legitimate power."

This scared the pants off the Democrats, for they knew a Robert H. Bork on the Supreme Court would ultimately make for a reversal of the famous abortion case decision in *Roe v. Wade*, which conservatives have always believed was decided horribly as a matter of constitutional interpretation. Abortion would then return to state legislatures to be decided according to local values, something the Left refuses to accept.

At the time, the custom for judicial vacancies was that unless very severe infirmities were found in their qualifications, the president's choices were to be given great deference, and blocking them was considered a very serious affront to the good order of government. Reagan's first Supreme Court appointment had been Sandra Day O'Connor, the first female to serve on the Court, and she had been confirmed 99–0. His choice of sitting Justice William Rehnquist to succeed the retiring Warren Burger as Chief Justice had been approved 65–33. And his nomination of Antonin Scalia to replace Burger on the Court had gone off with a 98–0 vote in favor. There was little precedent to kill the nomination of a qualified candidate at the time.

Which didn't slow the Democrats down in the slightest.

Bork's confirmation hearing was turned into a circus, with the Democrat members of the Senate Judiciary Committee taking turns savaging the man's character and smearing him as a fascist and theocrat. Kennedy, who had apparently recovered from the unintelligible babbling of his 1980 presidential campaign, was quite eloquent in slurring Bork in terms unrecognizable to his friends and colleagues:

> "Robert Bork's America is a land in which women would be forced into back-alley abortions, blacks would sit at segregated lunch counters, rogue police could break down citizens' doors in midnight raids, schoolchildren could not be taught about evolution, writers and artists would be censored at the whim of government, and the doors of the federal courts would be shut on the fingers of millions of citizens for whom the judiciary is often the only protector of the individual rights that are the heart of our democracy."

It certainly didn't get any better during the hearings. Bork's wife, Mary Ellen, would later write:

> "Most people don't remember the hearings on Robert Bork for nomination to the Supreme Court, but I do. I was there during the four months of vicious political campaigning against this judicial nominee, my husband, and in the Senate hearing room as then-Sen. Biden presided over a rigged hearing full of an unprecedented level of lying and distortion of a man known for his integrity and judicial wisdom. Democrats flagrantly lied about Bob's record of opinions. On day four

> of the hearings Sen. Biden was accused of plagiarism and had to drop out of the presidential race. In the course of one week Sen. Biden orchestrated a vicious lying assault and was caught passing off someone else's words as his own."

Ultimately the acrimony of the hearings wore Bork down, and he wasn't able to win over the public. Six Republican senators voted against him, and his nomination failed, 42–58. And the loss of Bork denied Reagan the ability to appoint a fifth conservative to the Court. After the nomination of another conservative, Judge Douglas Ginsburg of the DC Court of Appeals, was aborted when it was discovered Ginsburg had smoked a joint with a student while a professor at Harvard in the 1970s, Reagan settled on Anthony Kennedy.

And Kennedy spent three decades writing insipid "swing vote" opinions on the Court that perpetuated bad law and allowed the Left's cultural march to continue with the sanction of the highest court in the land.

The social conservatives might have had Reagan on their side. Nevertheless, no objective observer could say that they won the 1980s.

But Reagan, and the conservatism he espoused, did win the 1980s. After one term in office that was clear.

Carter's vice president Walter Mondale was the Democrat presidential nominee for 1984, and Mondale nominated a woman, New York congresswoman Geraldine Ferraro, in hopes that it might generate some novelty and momentum for his campaign.

It didn't. Reagan crushed Mondale in one of the most savage routs in the history of American presidential politics, carrying 59 percent of the popular vote and 525 of the 538 electoral votes. Mondale won only his home state of Minnesota and the District of Columbia.

Reagan's 1984 election might have been the pinnacle political moment for the conservative movement, so much so that in December of that year, following the rout of the Democrats, there were ample discussions about whether liberalism wasn't on the ropes.

There are an awful lot of great things that can be said about Ronald Reagan, who by any intelligent standard was the most accomplished and successful American president of this Third Era that is now ending. It was Reagan who took the Buckley-Meyer-Kirk philosophical vision of conservatism and made it a popular—and populist—movement.

Reagan thought big. Reagan rejected both the lazy fatalism and delusional utopianism of the smart set of the time and set America on a path to prosperity and victory.

And by 1989, when Reagan was wrapping up his two terms, America was at the pinnacle of its prestige and geopolitical influence. The Cold War was ending, and we had won, and we were amid a boom of economic prosperity his policies had touched off that would last for a generation.

All that was needed was a standard-bearer to continue and consolidate Reagan's advances, and conservatism would have what it needed to create the next era of American political consensus and reform.

But alas, that isn't what happened.

CHAPTER 11

Bush Republicanism

In his 1984 book, *The Liberal Crack-Up, The American Spectator* founder R. Emmett Tyrrell Jr. summed up a major limitation of center-right politics.

"The Democrat has the political libido of a nymphomaniac," said Tyrrell. "The Democrat politicizes practically everything and lusts for it madly. The Republican has the political libido of a eunuch."

What happened to conservatism after Ronald Reagan exited the political stage in January of 1989 can be quite well explained by Tyrrell's quote.

Reagan had chosen George H. W. Bush as his vice president in 1980 in an effort to placate the moderates in the Republican Party behind his nomination. Bush had been a congressman from Texas, where he had moved from New England as a young man, director of the CIA, and chairman of the Republican National Committee. He was a well-connected moderate and an asset to Reagan's ticket in broadening its appeal.

But Reagan and Bush were never particular political pals.

In his autobiography *Bare Knuckles and Back Rooms: My Life in American Politics,* veteran political consultant and Reagan inner-circle member Ed Rollins recounts his impressions of the marriage of convenience on the 1980 presidential ticket following the selection:

> "En route to Los Angeles, I was exhausted, but couldn't sleep. Even three weeks of twenty-hour work days couldn't begin to overcome my adrenaline. My mind was racing. Even though the Reagans and Bushes were getting along and the press had reacted well to the choice, I was uncomfortable with the shotgun marriage. On this flight, a phrase popped into my mind for the first time to describe my feelings about George Bush: Trojan Horse. The enemy was in our camp."

Bush was happy to play second fiddle to Reagan. He didn't rock the boat, and he happily sailed along in Reagan's wake for those eight years, particularly when things went so well. But as Reagan prepared to step away, Bush was already preparing to depart radically from the conservatism of the Reagan Revolution.

In his 1988 convention speech, Bush spoke ebulliently about creating a "kinder, gentler nation," and conjured up the image of a "thousand points of light"—a reference, it was to be understood, to all the wonderful charitable acts and impulses that a Bush-led America would bring on.

That was a quiet insult to Reagan, whose policies were aimed at freeing up the kind of money among regular Americans and creating the kind of prosperity that would enable precisely the thing

Bush was talking about. Nancy Reagan, upon hearing the "kinder, gentler nation" line, asked her seatmate at the convention, "kinder and gentler than whom?"

And Lee Atwater's interpretation was that this was "a thousand points of bullshit."

America in 1988 was quite possibly the kindest, gentlest nation it had ever been.

Just a few weeks before Bush's convention address in New Orleans, the American Association of Fund-Raising Counsel Trust for Philanthropy, a mouthful of an organizational name if ever there was one, put out a report on charitable donations in America. The report said that in the previous year, some $93 billion in charitable gifts were recorded, up from $88 billion in 1986. And that came despite the October 1987 stock market plunge and uncertainties about the economy maintaining its pace of growth.

"From the estimates of giving in 1987, the message is clear: the philanthropic impulse in the United States has never been stronger," the report said. "And that should not be surprising. We Americans are not indifferent inheritors of a long tradition of giving and sharing."

This, according to George H. W. Bush, whom we'll refer to from here on in as Bush 41 for clarity's sake, was what his administration would improve on.

Bush 41 won a convincing victory over the utterly hapless Democrat Michael Dukakis, a diminutive Massachusetts governor who came off as Jimmy Carter with a Greek accent. At one point, voters had Dukakis ahead of the vice president, but the Bush campaign was very effective in destroying Dukakis based on his almost comic record of clown-show liberalism—including a furlough program whereby violent criminals incarcerated in state prisons would be let out for unsupervised adventures in the wilds of Massachusetts's cities and towns, which resulted in a number of highly predictable disastrous outcomes.

The most famous of those, which was featured in Bush 41's campaign ads, involved a convicted murderer serving a life sentence named Willie Horton, who was let loose for a weekend and had a grand old time, committing assault, armed robbery, and rape before being captured and sentenced in Maryland where he remains incarcerated to this day.

Once that incandescent example of what a Dukakis's America would look like played out on TV screens, the flirtation with that party possessing the vigorous political libido was greatly curtailed, and Bush 41 took 426 electoral votes to the Democrat's 111.

The Bush 41 team took over from the Reagan team, and it wasn't seamless. When Jim Baker moved into the state department in 1989 to replace George Shultz, he said, "This is not a friendly takeover." When the conservative Heritage Foundation criticized Bush, Baker said, "Screw the Heritage Foundation." When various conservatives peeled off from Bush in that period, Bush and Baker said, "We don't need them."

That was how the Bush era began. Here's how it ended: with something Tim Young said in September of 2021.

Young, the excellent conservative comedian and political commentator, took to Twitter after viewing the Shanksville speech former president George W. Bush gave at the 20th anniversary of the 9/11 terrorist attacks.

"The more I hear from George W Bush," he tweeted, "the more I realize there was never really a choice in presidential elections in my lifetime until 2016."

What was it that Bush said which prompted Young's outburst? Most notably, this obnoxious statement:

> "There is little cultural overlap between violent extremists abroad and violent extremists at home. But in their disdain for pluralism, in their disregard for human life, in their determination to defile national symbols, they are children of the same foul spirit. And it is our continuing duty to confront them."

That has to be the dumbest, most contemptuous statement ever made by an American president about people who mostly voted for him.

Bush was clearly talking about the protesters who demonstrated at the US Capitol on January 6 of 2021. At least, that's how his statement was taken, and he did nothing to disabuse people of that notion. Had he clarified that the rioters of Black Lives Matter and Antifa were his real target, seeing as though the "mostly peaceful" riots and carnage they put on display all summer long in 2020 created scenes much more reminiscent of 9/11 than anything on January 6, Bush's statement would have been only partially awful.

But nope—Bush said what he said, and then he went back to his primitive portrait studio in Dallas. We've seen the last of him until he has another opportunity to insult his own voters.

So you'll know, and you surely already do, insulting and betraying supporters is the defining characteristic of Bush Republicanism.

George Herbert Walker Bush was insulting conservatives and conservatism all the way back in 1980 with his "voodoo economics" blatherings, only to tell a bald-faced lie to us in 1988 when he promised he'd never raise taxes. Then he sold out his own voters in the name of surrender to the Democrat wolves on Capitol Hill; apparently, that was how he expected to produce the "kinder, gentler nation" he was so keen to promise us.

This was after Ronald Reagan had created untold economic prosperity, won the Cold War, and placed America in a position of cultural dominance no nation in world history had ever achieved. Somehow that wasn't good enough for Bush *père,* who so insulted his own voters that a third of them bolted to Ross Perot in 1992 and made Bill Clinton president.

And then, in 2000, along came W., who held out that he was a "compassionate" conservative—as though conservatives, who give the lion's share of the money flowing into American charities and dominate the most loving and peaceful communities in the country, lack compassion. It's a terrible shame that he was the best the GOP could do that year. He got the nomination for the simple reason that everybody understood John McCain was worse.

As Young said, there was no real choice in that election. You were going to get a terrible excuse for a leader either way in the 2000 primaries, and then you were going to be stuck with either W. or the unhinged loon Al Gore, who might actually have been a less disastrous president over the long haul.

George W. Bush was the Jimmy Carter of the Republican Party. He sold out his voters on immigration, refusing to do anything about the border and allowing for the demographic changes the Democrats are so sure will create their mythical future dominance, on behalf of corporate America and the cheap labor demanded by the US Chamber of Commerce. He did nothing about Bill Clinton's housing time bomb, which led to the 2008 economic crash.

And he responded to 9/11 by launching America into two wars we lost.

Why is Khalid Sheikh Mohammed still alive? Why wasn't he tried and executed within twenty months of his capture? It's been twenty years, and he still languishes in Guantanamo Bay at US taxpayer expense. Bush meanwhile failed to get Osama bin Laden, Ayman al-Zawahiri, or Mullah Omar for seven years between 9/11 and the end of his presidency despite hundreds of billions of dollars and thousands of American lives spent. He found a way to make America synonymous with torture, did nothing about the clear Saudi funding of Islamic terrorism leading up to 9/11, launched us on a stupid campaign of globalist fancy by pretending that inside every Pashtun, Bedouin, or Tuareg tribesman is a Jeffersonian democrat pining to get out, and delivered nothing of the slightest value to his own voters on domestic policy.

Bush forced the Republican Party to defend corporate bailouts and hopeless nation-building in the most backward country on earth. He single-handedly created Iran as the most dominant force in Middle East politics, and he greatly accelerated, with just less than the earnest aplomb of Clinton or Barack Obama, the rise of China as a global superpower through awful trade policy.

And he created the Orwellian security state that predictably metastasized into a weapon used by the ruling class against the American people.

We haven't had a declaration of war in more than a half-century, and we've been at war more years than not in my adult life. Bush couldn't even get a declaration of war against Afghanistan when they didn't agree to cough up bin Laden and his goons. Instead it was an amorphous "authorization for the use of military force," which has been used as a blank check for troop deployments seemingly everywhere in the world but our southern border.

Worse than that, Bush funded the Pakistani government from whose meddling and manipulation the Taliban had come—and still comes—in the first place. He sent American troops off to fight a war in which he was funding both sides. And no, the fact that Bush's successors never bothered to fix that idiocy doesn't excuse him.

Bush fixed nothing. Of value, he created nothing. He was given the trust of the American people in a moment where we were more unified than since World War II, and he abused and wasted it. Even Bush admits the justification for the Iraq War was false.

His management of American foreign policy was so incompetent that America got no significant oil contracts out of Iraq and no significant rare earth mining contracts out of Afghanistan. News flash: if you're going to waste our tax dollars on nation-building, we'd like to at least get some economic justification out of it.

But we got nothing out of it. We got nothing out of Bush's eight years in office other than the satisfaction of knowing that the French-looking nincompoop gigolo John Kerry was never president. And we got almost nothing out of the four years his father was in office before the American people categorically rejected his reelection in 1992.

And then we were given the stupid and insulting equivalence of Ashli Babbitt with Mohammed Atta. You really can't get more clarity than that statement as a summation of what Bush Republicanism thinks of Republican voters.

The Reagan Revolution wasn't good enough, and we needed a "kinder, gentler nation," and conservatism wasn't good enough, so we needed "compassionate conservatism" instead. And then, when multiple states broke their election laws to run a highly suspect and deeply flawed presidential contest where thousands of votes were added to one side in the middle of the night, and the results were flipped, which obviously was going to engender objections, it was terrorism when some Americans protested and things got sloppy.

George W. Bush had nothing whatsoever to say about Hillary Clinton's campaign attempting to harass Trump electors into going faithless after the 2016 election, and he had nothing at all to say about the fact that Clinton's team created a hoax scandal out of Trump's nonexistent collusion with Putin, a hoax now fully exposed by Special Prosecutor John Durham's stream of filings that outline the most egregious political crime in American history.

Why doesn't George W. Bush have anything to say? Because the Bushes are friendly with the Clintons. They like Hillary better than Donald Trump. And that's nothing new—Bushes, and Bush-style Republicans, have been simping for the other side since the day Reagan left office.

But how was this allowed? How did we end up with essentially twenty-eight years of Republican retreat, broken only by the few years during which Newt Gingrich and his conservative reformers ruled Congress and brought Bill Clinton to heel following the 1994 midterm elections?

It isn't a complete answer, but consider Jonah Goldberg and Steve Hayes.

I'm so old that I remember when Jonah Goldberg was primarily known for writing an excellent political book. *Liberal Fascism,* which came out in 2009, skillfully skewered the modern Left for its illiberal, statist tendencies.

One wonders if Goldberg shouldn't reread his famous tome. Perhaps he's repudiated it. He seems so determined of late to make himself useful to the people he once castigated.

There's a certain brand of weak-sauce conservative pundit, many of whom have populated the airwaves of cable news channels and other corporate media venues, that depends for its sustenance on remaining "acceptable" to those who are not conservatives. This brand has for two decades or more been recognizable by its willingness to make The Conservative Case for virtually every kind of leftist policy aggression. There were times, in the early days of conservatism, that this critique was made of Buckley. But today's "acceptable" conservatives would never have taken on some of the fights Buckley did.

More notable conduct by today's "acceptable" conservative commentariat is its constant scolding of others within the Republican Party or conservative movement.

For a time, that *Mean Girls* repertoire was defensible, in that the Right could supposedly boast of better quality control than the Left. Political figures and culture-makers on the Right were held to a higher standard, and the Right's self-policing, we were told, kept the conservative movement closer to the center. The much-ballyhooed excommunication of the Birchers was exemplary of this self-regulation.

But after 1988, the scolds and "acceptable" conservatives who populated our media and cultural institutions were so busy picking up checks and seeking to please decision-makers who didn't agree with them that they failed to fight for those institutions.

All of which have become so hostile not just to conservatives but to ordinary Americans that we're no longer even welcome there.

It was inevitable that such figures would eventually lose currency with their core audiences when the situation turned sour enough. And in 2016, the American people turned on first the Republican status quo political class, which includes its pundit class, and then the political class at large by making Donald Trump the president. Don't worry; we'll give that subject an ample airing in our next chapter.

There's a direct line between that event, which was wholly predictable though it took so many by surprise, and the announcement in January 2021 that Goldberg and Stephen Hayes, the former editor of the now-defunct *Weekly Standard,* had ejected from paid contributor gigs at Fox News over Tucker Carlson's documentary about the January 6 protesters and their treatment by the Biden regime.

Goldberg and Hayes are founders and proprietors of *The Dispatch,* a middling site offering Never Trump-style conservative political analysis that has existed basically since the demise of the *Weekly Standard* in late 2018. Goldberg's main outlets to the public have been Fox News and his syndicated column based out of the *Los Angeles Times*. Nobody really reads *The Dispatch*.

And why? Because the public has moved on from Jonah Goldberg and Steve Hayes. And David French, another Dispatchik formerly occupying a high place in the conservative pundit class.

We've moved on from corporate-funded "acceptable" conservatism, and we've moved on from allowing the Left's paid liars—who showed us exactly who they are in the Kyle Rittenhouse case, and before that, the Trump-Russia debacle—to define what we're entitled to believe.

Tucker Carlson, who of all the analysts and opinion-makers on the Right probably has the best handle on the current mood of the movement, is a great example of that. To boil Carlson's brand down to its essence, he looks upon the American political status quo with deep dissatisfaction and is willing to skewer every element of its foundation from the perspective of someone who understands what the country is supposed to be—an open, Judeo-Christian society where markets are free, corruption is shameful, and power is given very little trust.

It shouldn't have been much of a surprise, then, when Carlson produced a three-part documentary titled *Patriot Purge*, covering the events during and following the January 6 protest at the US Capitol, available via the Fox Nation streaming service and not actually airing on Fox News itself. Two main themes emerge from the documentary series: first, that there was a governmental role in fomenting the January 6 protests into something that could be weaponized against those viewing the conduct of the 2020 presidential election suspiciously, and second, that the treatment of the people who entered the Capitol on that date, most of whom have never been charged with insurrection or treason but rather with various kinds of trespassing or minor property crimes, has been wholly out of proportion with their offenses.

You can see January 6 as a black mark on our national escutcheon and nonetheless concede Carlson's basic points are valid.

The documentary should have generated discussion. But on the part of Goldberg and Hayes, the opposite occurred. They took their balls and went home. In a letter justifying their "Take This Job and Shove It" exit, they said:

> "The special…is presented in the style of an exposé, a hard-hitting piece of investigative journalism. In reality, it is a collection of incoherent conspiracy-mongering, riddled with factual inaccuracies, half-truths, deceptive imagery, and damning omissions. And its message is clear: The U.S. government is targeting patriotic Americans in the same manner—and with the same tools—that it used to target al Qaeda.
>
> "'The domestic war on terror is here. It's coming after half of the country,' says one protagonist. 'The left is hunting the right, sticking them in Guantanamo Bay for American citizens—leaving them there to rot,' says another, over video of an individual in an orange jumpsuit being waterboarded.
>
> "This is not happening. And we think it's dangerous to pretend it is. If a person with such a platform shares such misinformation loud enough and long enough, there are Americans who will believe—and act upon—it.'"

One gets a clear image of a young Kevin Bacon in an ROTC uniform, nervously screeching, "All is well!" as chaos unfurls around him, from this statement of resignation. The attorney general of the United States of America had begun training the FBI's eyes on angry parents at school boards while lying about it to Congress, and an idiot in a Viking helmet who trespassed at the Capitol had just been sentenced to forty-one months in prison by a supposedly responsible federal judge, and these two has-beens thought there was nothing to question?

Let's remember that *The Dispatch,* and Goldberg specifically, echoed the false claim that Capitol Police Officer Brian Sicknick was bludgeoned to death on January 6. Who is he to castigate Tucker Carlson for questioning the "acceptable" January 6 narrative?

And one also gets an image of the suits at Fox News passively shrugging their shoulders. Goldberg and Hayes were coming up for contract renewals at Fox at the time, and they weren't being asked back. When Goldberg instead appeared as a "pet" conservative on CNN, the cycle was complete.

The fact is, Tucker Carlson is the only member of the corporate media willing to challenge the "acceptable" narrative of January 6, something anyone willing to objectively analyze recognizes is full of lies. And the fact that rather than defend that narrative against Carlson's challenge in the public square, Goldberg and Hayes instead commenced a virtue-signaling retreat, is yet another example.

But it's fine if they're not willing to debate January 6. Most of the people who used to pay attention to Goldberg and Hayes don't care what they've got to say anymore. And if they're gone from Fox News, that means somebody more relevant might replace them.

Let's hope that somebody is less "acceptable" and more willing to accurately assess the state of America brought on by two decades of weak-sauce conservatism's constant retreat.

And it has been a constant retreat. Bush Republicanism—we could call it Bush conservatism, as that's what the Bushies have called it, and that's a reason I prefer to use revivalism as an alternative to conservatism going forward—has had all of the cooperative elements of Buckley's early-days conservatism, which was reflective of the movement's nascency and lack of political power, and none of Buckley's passion for the fight.

Which was why it was so easy for George Mitchell to take Bush 41's no-new-taxes pledge away as though it were his lunch money. Or for Ted Kennedy to drink W.'s milkshake on the Medicare drug benefit. Or for Chuck Schumer to popularize "Bush lied; people died" as an anti-Iraq War slogan when Democrats signed off on that war based on the same bad intelligence the president got, with the president just sitting there silent and watching his job approval sink into the twenties. The Bush Republicans were so wedded to the idea of getting an increasingly bitter and radical Democrat Party to like them that they'd allow the worst kinds of abuses in pursuit of a belly rub.

And it all came at the expense of the suckers, the Republican voters who kept nominating them and, decreasingly, electing them because there were no charismatic or worthy successors to Reagan for us to choose from.

Here's another example of just how bereft of political libido, in Tyrrell's phrasing, the Bush Republican era was.

Let's come back to race, and race relations, for just a minute.

Can we agree that the period between, say, 1964 and 2008 represents the single fastest advance in race relations within one society in human history? America went from having the segregationist South on fire amid the prospect of Congress passing legislation to enforce the promise of the Fourteenth Amendment to electing as president a man whose chief selling point was that he was black.

There is no real precedent in world history for a nation to peacefully go from actively oppressing a minority in much of its territory to electing, in a landslide, a member of that minority to lead it in the space of two generations.

It should be noted that of the eleven presidential terms represented during that period, seven of them saw Republicans in executive leadership. That's a fact somewhat inconvenient to the Left as it continues to press the fraudulent case that the GOP is the home of racists and bigots.

What accounted for this sea change? An idea, one the vast majority of Americans of all races bought into.

Credit the idea to King's popularizing the notion that what America wanted was a color-blind society. "I have a dream," he said, "that my four little children will one day live in a nation where they will not be judged by the color of their skin but by the content of their character."

America bought into that vision, first gradually and then all at once. It was a unifying concept that led to black entertainers and athletes earning untold fortunes courtesy of the patronage of often mostly white audiences, black entrepreneurs thriving, and the growth of a black middle class where almost none existed—all despite the sharp decline of the black family and the attendant waste of human talent resulting from it.

We want the color-blind society. But it isn't what we're getting. The people taking credit for selling it to us—though King would, one imagines, be horrified at the state of the modern Left in this country—are determined to go much further than that.

Take what happened at Coca-Cola in 2021, for example. It was revealed that the company, one of America's great worldwide brands, was conducting diversity and sensitivity training seminars, which fit under no possible concept of a color-blind society and should offend, to the point of fighting words, every single American.

Among the messages on slides that emerged from the seminars:

> "Confronting Racism: Understanding What It Means To Be White, Challenging What It Means To Be Racist....
>
> To be less white is to:
> be less oppressive
> be less arrogant
> be less certain
> be less defensive
> be less ignorant
> be more humble
> listen
> believe
> break with apathy
> break with white solidarity....
>
> "In the U.S. and other Western nations, white people are socialized to feel that they are inherently superior because they are white. Research shows that by the age of 3 or 4, children understand that it is better to be white."

And the eye-opener:

> "Try to be less white."

This is at Coca-Cola. Not Ben & Jerry's or Nike.

The level of cultural aggression involved in presenting something like this in a corporate seminar is astounding. It validates the Instagram post Gina Carano was canceled for sharing, except for the fact Carano was decrying the possibility of a psychotic government actively promoting hatred of an ethnic group, and this is supposed to be one of the most mainstream corporate entities imaginable.

It makes you wonder what else is being taught at those corporate seminars.

Which brings us back to Bush Republicanism, because since 1988, when most of the sea change in race relations since 1964 had taken place, and a sizable chunk of the economic and social advancement of Black America, if not most of it, had also occurred, the "compassionate conservative" crowd hoping for a "kinder, gentler America" while refusing to engage on icky cultural issues held sway within the GOP.

There can be little argument that despite all the think tank white papers, top-dollar political messaging, money spent on "outreach," and *National Review* columns over that time frame the performance of the Republican Establishment can only be described as a failure.

The America Ronald Reagan left to his party had a right-leaning culture to match a right-leaning populace. We've gone from that to Coca-Cola preaching outright anti-white racism in its employee seminars.

How can you call yourself a conservative if you aren't willing to fight to conserve your societal values and traditions?

We aren't talking about preserving segregation. We're talking about preserving King's color-blind society against a cadre of lunatics marinating in Critical Race Theory and its dog's breakfast of envy and victimization concocted mostly by white Europeans like Herbert Marcuse. Nobody seems to recognize that pretty much everything the anti-white crowd is using was invented by white guys.

When something like this has taken hold so completely that it happens at Coca-Cola, you'd better believe that you need some warriors to roll it back.

Does anybody think Mitch McConnell, Bill Cassidy, Mitt Romney, and Liz Cheney have what it takes to do that? Will Jonah Goldberg and David French do it? Or Adam Kinzinger?

Please.

We're in a war for the survival of our very culture. And we've been in a fairly disorganized retreat for a long time. To those who think Donald Trump, who at least recognized the necessity of the fight, isn't good enough for them—if you wish to fantasize about retaking the GOP for the failed brand of conservatism that Trump shook out, then let's hear a plan to stop the Coca-Cola-style corporate aggressions.

We already know the answer, which is that they have no such plan. They've sat around for decades watching things progress to this point and even defended those cultural aggressions at times. They've lectured us that private companies can do as they please because that's capitalism, they've squandered mountains of lucre on secondary schools and universities pumping out the worst sort of academic bilge, and they've refused to match the political libido of the Left over the very future of America.

In April 2022 some of these same people proceeded to scold Florida governor Ron DeSantis for signing a bill to do away with special tax protections that state had afforded to Disney. The bill was a fairly unambiguous response to the corporation's over-the-top advocacy against that state's anti-grooming law; Disney's corporate management team was caught on a leaked video call sharing stories of how they planned to insert promotion of the queer lifestyle in upcoming children's programming while commiserating over the passage of a bill barring school officials from discussing sexuality with kids younger than eight.

Disney's stock proceeded to tank as a disgusted America scowled. And yet the "responsible" and "acceptable" Republicans whined about DeSantis' overreach in eliminating a long-standing corporate welfare plan for a company which abused its position of influence to engage in partisan politics. The stupidity of this was exceeded only by its predictability.

The Bush Republicans, the establishment gang who pretended to be fanatical soldiers in Reagan's revolutionary army until the coast was clear and then proceeded to sell out their voters time and again, gave away most of what Reagan proved true conservatism could achieve. By the time that era was finally over, things had gotten so bad that Mitt Romney, who might have been more of a Bush Republican than any of the Bushes even were, was being shushed off a presidential debate stage—and out of a perfectly winnable 2012 presidential election—by CNN's Candy Crowley. That came just two years after the breakout of the Tea Party movement, which all of establishment Washington banded together to suffocate.

To list all of the betrayals of Republican voters, from *père* Bush's tax treason to *fils* Bush's disgraceful Shanksville speech, would fill volumes, and I only have one chapter here. Anyone older than forty-five could probably recount them from memory, and I'd be cursed by the conservatives for suggesting the exercise.

But the denouement of Goldberg and Hayes as pundits of mass exposure is a nice metaphor for the fading away of Bush Republicanism. When Jeb Bush saw what was once thought to be an odds-on nomination in 2016 devolve into laughter once Donald Trump derided him as "low-energy," it was a sure sign the brand had lost its luster.

Americans were fed up with "kinder, gentler, compassionate" Republicans who couldn't stop sending troops off to fight wars against third world bogeymen around 2005. The Tea Party movement wasn't just a reaction to the radicalism of the Obama administration; it thumbed its nose at the Bushy establishment as well, but the party and its "acceptable" pundits wouldn't listen.

Then Trump rode that escalator down to that lobby, and everything changed.

CHAPTER 12

Trump (and MAGA) Cometh

The rise and, perhaps, temporary fall of Donald Trump teaches us, or at least those among us who adhere to the political center-right, that one can have two almost directly opposite impressions in his head at the same time.

Specifically, amazement that something should happen coinciding with a recognition of its utter inevitability.

Trump, or something like him, was inevitable. As the famous neoconservative pundit Charles Krauthammer, who was given to discovery of pure truths equally as often as puzzling follies, noted, "That which cannot continue will not continue."

And the governmental performance of what people had come to call the Uniparty in Washington, DC, could not continue.

After Mitt Romney's flaccid presidential campaign failed to dislodge Barack Obama from the White House in 2012, the paid political consultants of Bush Republicanism vomited forth what was known as "The Autopsy," and its conclusions for why the race was lost and how to avoid future humiliations were…more cowbell.

"The Autopsy" concluded, essentially, that the GOP had to surrender to the Obama agenda and increase its efforts to pander to minority groups and younger voters. It placed a high priority on "outreach" to those groups and, on policy, its suggestion was to adopt an even more pro-corporate agenda.

The media loved "The Autopsy." It was given wonderful reviews. But two years later when the Republican presidential primary field began to form, the candidates with the biggest followings had mostly decided to ignore its blueprint.

In particular, Ted Cruz and Donald Trump ran as far away from "The Autopsy" as they could, casting themselves as a stark departure from business as usual. Cruz offered a detailed policy platform and a record as a conservative iconoclast in the Senate unafraid of forcing government shutdowns and fiery disputes even with his own party's leadership.

But Cruz didn't have the social cache of Trump, who'd spent three decades as a TV personality, bestselling author, iconic business tycoon, and celebrity brand. When Trump came down the escalator of his namesake skyscraper in New York to the cheers of a crowd it was said consisted at least partly of paid actors and let loose a long-winded broadside on the political establishment of the time, it was something nobody had seen in national politics since…

Never. Ross Perot's disorganized 1992 and 1996 independent presidential campaigns, which were a mix of vanity and protest, had some of the fire of the Trump Tower spectacle but none of its showmanship.

The media and commentariat laughed it off as a curiosity. But they weren't laughing long.

Trashed as a racist by Sen. John McCain, one of the more obnoxious exemplars of the Bush Republican brand, for his passionate criticism of illegal immigration, Trump went for the jugular. He attacked McCain's military service, noting that his five years spent in the infamous Hanoi Hilton during the Vietnam War after having his fighter plane shot down didn't entitle him to the deference he sought.

"He was a war hero because he was captured," Trump said. "I like people who weren't captured."

That elicited gasps of outrage among all the best people, but it was literally the quote that made Trump the next president.

Was it a boorish comment? Of course it was. Even Trump's most fervent supporters agreed it was rude. But that wasn't the point.

Everybody in the Republican Party who had followed politics since the mid-1980s knew all about John McCain, and they all knew that McCain had used his time in a North Vietnamese hellhole as a political get-out-of-jail-free card. He'd skated out of any consequences for being part of the Keating Five, a corrupt group of Capitol Hill politicians greased by the oozy Charles Keating of savings-and-loan collapse fame. McCain had a record of screwing over his fellow Republicans in the Senate going back two decades or more; it was commonly known that anything said at GOP caucus meetings when McCain was around could be leaked to the media for maximum possible political damage if he was so inclined, and because of Hanoi, no retaliation was possible.

McCain even blocked drilling in a small patch of the Alaska National Wildlife Refuge, a featureless tundra field largely barren of flora or fauna, because he and that state's senior Senator Ted Stevens didn't get along, and he therefore refused to give Stevens a deliverable for his constituents. That's what an unmitigated jerk he was.

There were the pitifully cynical "Just build the damn wall!" TV ads McCain ran back home in his Senate campaigns when his voting record was the opposite.

And then there was the shameful way McCain's 2008 presidential campaign treated his vice presidential pick, Sarah Palin, who might have been in over her head but lent that moribund effort the only living flesh and blood it had.

None of this stuff was a secret. It was perfectly well-known. Trump could have hit McCain on all of it and perhaps scored a cleaner kill. Instead, he just dropped a nuke.

Anybody can get shot down, was the message. *This guy's a loser. Sure, I'll say it. I'm not afraid of the consequences.*

The American political system, particularly on the Republican side, couldn't process that kind of bravado.

And when Trump made it clear that he'd drop a neutron bomb on anybody else in the race who crossed him—from Lyin' Ted to Little Marco to Low-Energy Jeb—it quickly became clear that while he might have had fewer policy chops than any of the others in what was truly an impressive 2016 primary field, Trump was the alpha male in the race.

And after sixteen years of George W. Bush and Barack Obama attempting to fleece America into thinking they were compassionate and in touch with their feminine side in order to chase the women's vote, Trump was a breath of fresh air even when he trash-talked like a street kid from Queens.

Working-class Americans lined up around the block to vote for him in the primaries. Trump was a juggernaut the collection of governors, senators, congressmen, and other political veterans who made up that field found themselves powerless to stop.

Evangelicals, a key GOP constituency, backed Trump even though his personal history made him anything but righteous. The establishment and media were appalled; to this day their poison pens drip with bile for the Religious Right over its embrace of a man they claim is the antithesis of their values.

You don't understand us at all, came the response in various forms. *We chose Trump because you hate him as much as you hate us, and because he's committed to fight back against you on our behalf.*

The Religious Right had been the only constituency in the conservative coalition consistently willing to fight the Left's cultural aggressions, and only Reagan among Republican nominees had shown any interest in taking up their cause. But Trump did so, unapologetically and with some rhetorical skill. That was enough.

Cruz, who had made his career as a committed Christian and a fighter for that cause, was aghast that he couldn't count on the evangelical vote against Trump. As the only candidate left with a chance to knock Trump off late in the primaries, he kept pointing out Trump's lack of a conservative pedigree and the distinct lack of righteousness on display in his very public personal life.

Trump's response was to insinuate Cruz's father, a Cuban émigré, had something to do with the John F. Kennedy assassination.

He didn't care. It was just politics, and politics is a circus. Say whatever wins the news cycle, and the voters will be amused and reward you.

Cruz was livid, as he had every right to be. But he learned a valuable lesson, which is that if you're a politician, absolutely nobody cares about your problems. Trump took the nomination, and Cruz refused to endorse him at the convention. That was a problem for Cruz, not Trump; he nearly paid a terrible price for it two years later when he barely survived a challenge from the ridiculous cross-dressing, gun-grabbing, drunk-driving Democrat "Beto" O'Rourke for his reelection to the Senate.

After that, Cruz and Trump had no more problems.

The GOP establishment was apoplectic over Trump's rise, and to some extent there was reason for trepidation. Since Reagan politicians calling themselves conservatives had come and gone without actually doing anything to help the movement or keep faith with their promises, went the reasoning, how could anyone trust a political gadfly like Trump who had donated often to Democrats and hadn't even been a consistent registered Republican?

National Review dedicated an entire issue to the "Never Trump" cause. The usual-suspect pundits, among them Bill Kristol, Jonah Goldberg, Steve Hayes, Quin Hillyer, and David French, declared themselves enemies. Kristol found a sanctimonious political neophyte named Evan McMullin, who was quickly derided as "Egg McMuffin" by many on social media, to run as a third-party candidate; in interviews, McMullin showed the presence of a new school board member, or perhaps a first-term state representative. Kristol declared that McMullin was the wild card in the race.

And then there was Hillary Clinton, who would clearly win.

Except Clinton was a supernova of malfeasance and corruption as Obama's secretary of state, arrogant to the core. So much so that she refused to use the State Department's secure email server and instead had her own private email account that was hosted on a server in a bathroom closet. The server, which violated federal law as employed, was found to hold over one hundred emails containing classified information, including sixty-five emails deemed "Secret" and twenty-two deemed "Top Secret." An additional 2,093 emails not marked classified were retroactively designated confidential by the State Department.

Congress investigated. Clinton laughed at their questions, asking, "What difference does it make?" when it was pointed out she'd flagrantly broken the law.

Then a computer hacker named "Guccifer" produced dozens of emails from Clinton to her crony, longtime political hatchet man Sidney Blumenthal, which clearly showed she was trafficking in classified information on an unsecure email server. The congressional panel demanded she produce emails from her server, and she held back more than thirty thousand, claiming they were "personal."

But this coincided largely with another scandal, that of the Clinton family non-profit foundation that was a sleazy influence-peddling operation. Millions of dollars poured into the Clinton Foundation, and her husband, the former president Bill Clinton, was pocketing hundreds of thousands of dollars in speaking fees paid by shadowy interests. In one case, a Bill Clinton speech in Moscow was paid for by Renaissance Bank to the tune of a half-million dollars; that bank was involved in a Russian enterprise that ultimately bought control of a sizable share of America's domestic uranium resources. Hillary Clinton, as Secretary of State, had signed off on the purchase.

And then the contents of the Democratic National Committee's email server were turned over to WikiLeaks by an unknown party, and all hell broke loose.

The cover story about the DNC email release was that Russian hackers had broken in and stolen them. But despite the fact that twelve Russians were later indicted for supposedly hacking into the DNC server, the technical details of what happened to the server didn't support it. On the contrary, it was much more likely that the theft of the emails was an inside job. A DNC employee named Seth Rich was then murdered on a Washington, DC, street; none of his personal property was taken. That led to speculation that Rich had been the one who turned the emails over to WikiLeaks.

A major story erupted from what was on the DNC server. The release produced proof that the Democrat Party had been conspiring to give Clinton the nomination over Bernie Sanders, an independent socialist senator from Vermont whom they had every right to screw over. Sanders hadn't been a registered Democrat, ever; he only caucused with them in the Senate. Having done nothing for the party, he now demanded its nomination; of course the party establishment would deny it to him.

But Sanders's supporters were absolutely furious that the fix was in during the Democrats' primaries, and that would be costly to Clinton when a small but significant number of them ended up voting for Trump.

Then another email breach happened; this one had to do with the Clintons' campaign guru, John Podesta.

Podesta, one of the creepiest individuals in the history of American politics, had his Gmail server hacked into thanks to a weak password, and nearly twenty thousand pages of his emails were released by WikiLeaks. In them were all kinds of nuggets of information that wasn't helpful to Hillary Clinton's cause.

There were copies of speeches she'd given to Wall Street firms that cast her as a puppet of Big Finance.

There was proof that Donna Brazile, a longtime friend of the Clintons and a CNN talking head, had shared questions to be asked to Hillary at a CNN town hall debate. Brazile was later given the chair of the DNC after Wasserman Schultz's forced resignation following the DNC email release.

There were discussions of the formation of groups intended to politicize the Catholic church and force it to accept a progressive agenda, which caused a stir among Catholic voters.

And creepiest of all were the nonsensical and unexplained references to things like hot dogs and pizza, which created an immense amount of speculation that Podesta and some of his friends might have been involved in child sex trafficking, as those references were—perhaps coincidentally—similar to code words used by pedophiles. The Pizzagate scandal was born, and though some of the most outlandish allegations made in it were clearly disproven, other elements were not; the whole thing just seemed to be dismissed as debunked, and no explanation was ever given.

But the political toll of the Clinton and Democrat scandals was high, enough to overcome the conventional wisdom that the obnoxious Donald Trump, tape of whom discussing in locker-room-talk terms the effect on celebrity on one's sexual desirability surfaced a month before the election and was supposedly disqualifying, had no chance to win.

He won. By a very tight margin, Trump ran the table of a whole host of swing states and posted a highly improbable 306–232 electoral college victory. Clinton refused to concede on Election Night, sending Podesta out to thank her campaign workers and then giving a rather defiant speech the next day acknowledging her loss.

Her campaign then began harassing Trump electors demanding they refuse to vote for him, which failed miserably.

And then Team Clinton pressed on something it had already concocted, which was a "dossier" dummied up by a former British spy named Christopher Steele using a host of bogus sources and making lots of unfounded and untrue allegations against Trump. The dossier had been released to the media before the election and generally dismissed as a fraud.

But Fusion GPS, the political hit-job firm that commissioned the dossier on behalf of the Clinton campaign, kept pushing it, and Trump's transition and inauguration were marred by the media narrative that surfaced as a result. It was alleged that Russian meddling in the election on Trump's behalf had produced a scary situation, that Trump had essentially colluded with Russian premier Vladimir Putin to steal an election.

The Trump-Russia collusion allegations had literally been spun up out of thin air. But the dead-ender Obama administration, it was later discovered, had used the dossier to fraudulently seek warrants under the Foreign Intelligence Surveillance Act (FISA) to spy on members of Trump's campaign team.

It was a scandal worse than Watergate by an order of magnitude, but it was largely buried under false allegations of Russian collusion.

And those allegations crippled Trump's administration in its first two years, particularly when one of his weaknesses surfaced almost immediately.

Trump had a lot of trouble hiring well.

His first choice for attorney general was Jeff Sessions, an old senator from Alabama who had come up as a US Attorney and was one of the first major political figures to endorse him. Sessions looked on paper to be an outstanding choice, but based on an irrelevant contact with a Russian official here and there, Sessions recused himself from the Trump-Russia matter.

And that meant Trump had no ability to manage the special counsel investigation that followed. It was staffed by a cadre of corrupt Clinton-supporting lawyers out for a witch hunt, and it went on for two and a half years before grudgingly concluding that Trump had done nothing wrong.

A clear lesson was learned from the experience, which is that whatever modern Democrats accuse others of, they're almost certainly doing themselves. But in the case of the Trump-Russia hoax, it worked for them; national unease over the prospect of a tainted 2016 election played big into the 2018 congressional midterm disaster that befell the GOP and put Nancy Pelosi back in as Speaker of the House.

Amid that awful 2018 election cycle, though, came a result that was more than a silver lining—it was, as my *American Spectator* colleague Jack Cashill called it, an election that saved America (and maybe the world).

We're speaking about Ron DeSantis's close win against the Democrats' flavor-of-the-month charismatic Marxist hopeful, then-Tallahassee mayor Andrew Gillum.

As Cashill tells it:

"People forget that out of more than eight million votes cast in the 2018 governor's race, Gillum came within 33,000 votes of beating DeSantis. It was that close. Had Gillum won, he would have had no compunction about turning Florida into California—or worse. That Florida would have become just another lockdown state is a given. No Democratic governor has bucked that expectation, but it was not Gillum's COVID response that Floridians had cause to fear.

...

"The Florida gubernatorial election of 2018 may well prove to have more impact on the history of the nation than the 2020 presidential election. Unlike Gillum, who used 'freedom' as a code word for its very opposite, DeSantis has modeled freedom to the world. With no income tax and the lowest per capita tax burden in America, Florida is leading the nation in almost every relevant economic category. 'Freedom works,' said DeSantis. 'Our economy is the envy of the nation.'

"DeSantis gets it. More than any governor in recent memory, he understands the power of 'freedom' to liberate and inspire. 'Florida,' he said, 'has become the escape hatch for those chafing under authoritarian, arbitrary and seemingly never-ending mandates and restrictions.' And yes,

> those doing the chafing and escaping include even Alexandria Ocasio-Cortez."

DeSantis wasn't the only silver lining for the GOP in 2018. The winners that year included a good cast of Trump-inspired conservative politicians who were clearly not of the Bush Republican mold, like DeSantis's fellow governors Kristi Noem of South Dakota and Bill Lee of Tennessee and new senators Marsha Blackburn, Josh Hawley, and Rick Scott. On the whole it was a terrible cycle, but the new Republicans have greatly outshone the new blood (Ilhan Omar, Alexandria Ocasio-Cortez, Gretchen Whitmer, Tony Evers, Steve Sisolak) on the Democrat side.

And a major silver lining of the 2018 election was that then-Speaker of the House Paul Ryan, an establishment conservative openly hostile to Trump, was no longer in charge of the House Republicans. Other than working to pass Trump's signature tax reform package, which gave the economy a sizable boost almost immediately, Ryan was an impediment, not an asset, to the president's legislative agenda.

The inability to break the Democrats' filibuster on anything but fiscal matters and federal appointments meant the Senate was a dead letter for those first two years. Particularly when McCain, just before dying of cancer, cast the deciding vote against a repeal of Obamacare solely to spite Trump.

All of this makes it sound like Trump was a failure. By no means is that true. I recount the above to demonstrate just how desperate the fight to drain the DC Swamp was for a political outsider with ideas of fundamental change.

The Trump administration certainly had its moments, many of which served as anecdotal lessons for Republicans willing to move beyond the Failure Theater of the Bush era. For example, shortly after taking office in 2017 Trump acted to make good on a campaign promise Republican politicians had given lip service to for decades without result.

He moved the US embassy in Israel to Jerusalem.

Gasps audible on the Lower West Side emanated from UN headquarters in Turtle Bay, and all hell broke loose as conventional wisdom suggested would happen. But something unexpected then happened.

Nikki Haley, Trump's UN ambassador at the time, had the duty to represent America during the diplomatic "crisis" that ensued.

A resolution went in front of the United Nations' full body shortly after the decision was made public. It condemned the USA for placing the embassy in Jerusalem, and some 128 countries—including the usual suspects like Iran and Egypt, but also others like Denmark, France, Austria, and Germany—voted for the resolution.

Eight countries—Israel, Honduras, Guatemala, Nauru, the Marshall Islands, Micronesia, Palau, and Togo, not to mention the USA—did the honorable thing and voted against the resolution. Some thirty-five others, including Argentina, Australia, Canada, the Bahamas, Poland, Romania, Croatia, Mexico, Jamaica, Haiti, South Sudan, and a few others, did the defensible thing and abstained.

Israel is, after all, an American ally, and a pretty good one. It was unseemly that our embassy wouldn't be in their capital. The US embassy is in the capital of every other country where we have one, so it's only proper that we would have the one in Israel in Jerusalem—which is, after all, the city Israel has chosen to serve in that capacity.

And our choice to place the embassy in Jerusalem is nobody else's business but ours and Israel's. It's not Britain's business, or China's, or Afghanistan's, or Cuba's.

The conventional-wisdom crowd, the ruling elite, lambasted the new administration for committing an unforced diplomatic error. That Trump had won an election after making a promise to site the embassy in Jerusalem made no difference whatsoever to them. But it mattered to Trump, and it was a great example of why his voters were so unshakable in supporting him.

Trump and Haley warned the anti-American crowd that we would not be lectured to on morality by the likes of Bolivia and Belarus, and that some of those countries are the recipients of American foreign aid—a spigot he would happily cut off if they followed through on their threats of condemnation.

"They take hundreds of millions of dollars and even billions of dollars, and then they vote against us," Trump said. "Well, we're watching those votes. Let them vote against us, we'll save a lot. We don't care."

And Haley, just before the vote, was even more spot on.

"The United States will remember this day in which it was singled out in this assembly for the very act of exercising our right as a sovereign nation," she said. "We will remember it when, once again, we are called up to make the world's largest contribution to the U.N., and we will remember it when many countries come calling on us to pay even more and to use our influence for their benefit."

Previous American administrations lacked the sand to do the simple, obvious thing and place the embassy in Jerusalem. Previous American administrations would have let themselves be mau-maued into backing off such a position out of a fear of "world opinion."

But Trump's was the first administration in a long time to recognize that "world opinion" consists of the bloviations of Third World kleptocrats, Islamic supremacists from the Organisation of Islamic Cooperation, Russian satrapies, and Eurotrash *sitzpinklers* from countries torpidly micturating on their own cultural patrimony as a *hijra* of millions descend upon them from places where female genital mutilation is the rule rather than the exception, and homosexuals are commonly thrown from the roofs of tall buildings. In short, Trump recognized the UN is a collection of crooks and frauds, not statesmen, and deserves no better treatment than it gives its host and patron.

The American people have long recognized this. It hardly requires much attention to understand that when Iran and Cuba are put in charge of the Human Rights Commission, the whole organization isn't to be taken seriously, and when the UN is given a mission like peacekeeping or arms control, and the result turns out to be a series of prostitution rings and massive bribery schemes, any intelligent person would recognize that to support those missions with American tax dollars is to compound the theft.

The embassy in Jerusalem officially opened in May of 2018 without notable incident. And when Joe Biden took office three years later, his Secretary of State Antony Blinken quietly announced that it would stay there.

The Jerusalem embassy kerfuffle was a perfect example of how much of what's said to be impossible in American politics is anything but—it merely requires a willingness to suffer a rough news cycle or two before the shallow legacy media moves on to something else, and then the positive effects of doing the right and obvious begin to kick in. When you point out that the emperor doesn't, in fact, have any clothes on, such courage is inevitably rewarded.

Trump's immigration policy was another similar example.

He wasn't able, particularly after the 2018 elections, to get much help in building the border wall it seemed so obvious the country needed. But border enforcement under Trump became an actual strength as he negotiated a remain-in-Mexico policy for asylum-seekers coming up from Central America or other countries, rather than simply allow them to come to US soil and press their case for political asylum while operating as uninvited immigrants. That and other policies slowed the flood of immigrants to a trickle, and for the first time in a generation, real wages for American workers increased.

Trump promised to renegotiate our trade arrangements with China, which had so badly taken advantage of the bipartisan willingness to sell out America to an implacable geopolitical rival if not an outright enemy, and he did, launching a trade war that dislodged a reasonable share of our supply chain from that country.

And the US economy benefitted from his management, posting incredible stock market gains, household earnings growth, a labor shortage that was a healthy thing, and solid GDP numbers.

Until COVID came along.

As said in a previous chapter, this is not a book about COVID. But the fact is that had that Chinese virus, almost certainly the product of a lab leak at the Wuhan Institute of Virology in the fall of 2019, not spread across the planet in early 2020, Donald Trump would be in his second presidential term.

Managing the pandemic that followed given the media-driven hysteria and utter, sinister incompetence of our public health bureaucracy, which Trump had neither selected nor knew much about, proved impossible.

In late January 2022, an anonymous former Trump official writing under the pen name Thelonious posted a fascinating piece at *American Greatness* discussing the difficulties of the Trump administration. After noting the sea change in Republican politics Trump brought on and the great service he did the country in exposing just how rotten the DC establishment had become, among a few other items, the piece ultimately got around to the COVID-19 experience:

> "Enter the Wuhan lab leak of the novel coronavirus in late 2019. Intentional or not, the criminal enterprise in charge in Beijing immediately recognized the potential of a global scare over the virus to reverse the dynamic of the Trump years and make China ascendent again. Through a combination of carefully choreographed media propaganda about their own lockdown measures, an almost total lack of information sharing about the virus and its origins, and a seeding of the virus abroad by means of an intentional diaspora of infected residents around the world before Western nations had gotten a handle on the situation, Beijing set the stage for the global catastrophe that was about to ensue.
>
> "The Chinese could not have accomplished their ambitious end of shutting down the economies of their competitors, however, without the collaboration of their pawns at the World Health Organization, and at the U.S. National Institutes of Health and Centers for Disease Control and

Prevention who had secretly sponsored the calamitous 'gain of function' research responsible for creating COVID-19.

"Trump's handling of the pandemic and its consequences throughout the watershed year of 2020 illustrated, in dramatic fashion, every single one of his weaknesses as the leader of the MAGA movement. His initial instincts to shut down travel from China were sound, and he followed through with it on the advice of China hawk Peter Navarro and over the objections of Dr. Anthony Fauci and the pro-China contingent over at the NIH and the CDC. But the travel ban did not extend to infected Europe, and it proved too little too late since the virus already had been intentionally seeded worldwide.

"Trump appointed the treacherous Pence as head of the Coronavirus Task Force, preferring to spend his energies at directionless and combative daily press conferences sparring with a press corps that saw its opportunity to finally bring down the hated Orange Man with a disastrous pandemic on his watch.

"As his task force moved towards the hard economic lockdowns promoted by China and their useful dupes ensconced at the WHO and throughout the U.S. health establishment, Trump objected that the 'cure' of economic lockdowns shouldn't be worse than the 'disease' of the pandemic. The president put Dr. Scott Atlas (who had argued persuasively that the economic, social, and public health costs of economic shutdowns, including school closures, were completely unjustified by the risks of the virus) on the task force. Atlas was quickly marginalized by the Fauci-led cabal, and was subsequently destroyed by Fauci and his minions with orchestrated attacks in the media and back at Stanford University where he had, before accepting the fateful appointment, been a tenured professor in good standing with his peers.

"As 'two weeks to flatten the curve' of infections (supposedly risking a hospital system overwhelmed with COVID patients) morphed into indefinite general shutdowns of business and social activity in state after state, grinding the national economy virtually to a halt, Trump watched helplessly as Fauci became the de facto policy maker not only on public health, but on social interaction, economics, and even whether Americans could safely celebrate holidays together or visit family members on their deathbeds. As schools shut down that spring amidst the generalized panic (stoked by the task force's prognostications of millions of COVID casualties), the warnings of Atlas and others about the social and psychological costs to shutting down all of society over a virus went unheeded. The results were, again, utterly predictable."

Just so. There were three major problems in Trump's handling of COVID that could have lasting effects from a political standpoint should he run again in 2024.

The first was that Trump didn't fire Anthony Fauci. That would have engendered a great deal of uproar among the media, and he would have been crucified for it, but Trump's COVID response was greatly hamstrung by the consistent undermining of the president Fauci gleefully applied. He needed to have been gone by Tax Day 2020, along with his boss at NIH, Francis Collins, White House Coronavirus Response Coordinator Deborah Birx, who was a Pence appointment, and US Centers for Disease Control and Prevention Director Robert Redfield.

Trump needed to replace the whole lot of them with people willing to brave the media headwinds and focus on what was his initial instinct about the virus—that it wasn't deadly to the majority of people and that early treatment would produce recovery and therefore natural immunity.

What he got from the public health bureaucrats was destined, if not intended, for failure—and maximum political fallout at that. When we later found out despite vituperative denials that Fauci had funded the very Wuhan Institute of Virology research that seems to have led to the pandemic, something which was in evidence in the spring of 2020, Trump could have used it as a cause for cleaning out the stables.

The second problem was Operation Warp Speed, in which billions of federal dollars were paid to pharmaceutical companies for COVID vaccines that went into mass production before anybody really knew whether they would work.

As it turned out, the vaccines, which did come on the market at lightning speed, are really more like a pre-treatment for COVID. You can still get sick from the virus after being vaccinated, and you can still spread it. Your symptoms might be less. As to their side effects, those are still being debated—but it's clear there is some risk, if small, of heart problems and blood clots particularly among the young.

And vaccine immunity is clearly not as effective as natural immunity. The pursuit of fast vaccines was unsound compared to Trump's first instinct, and the subsequent attempts at federal and state vaccine mandates by Democrats, a gross civil rights violation invalidated by the courts, was made possible by the Trump vaccine push.

Which is unfortunate, because it isn't like Trump was trying to do harm. But at Trump rallies in late 2021 and early 2022, he found himself heckled and even jeered by the crowds when boasting of the success of Operation Warp Speed. It seems as though he won't be able to use it as an asset in future campaigns.

The third problem, which has perhaps become the fulcrum upon which American politics rests today, was the Left's use of COVID to corrupt the electoral process by shifting to widespread use of mail-in ballots and ballot harvesting as an "emergency" measure. These practices, which it was said were necessary because it wasn't safe for voters to show up at voting precincts due to the virus, were put in place in several states without passage by state legislatures—a direct violation of the US Constitution, which puts responsibility for the time, manner, and place of elections in state legislators' hands—and the effect of their implementation was chaos on Election Night 2020.

Suspiciously, vote-counting was halted late into the night with Trump leading in a number of key swing states, and when it was restarted, Joe Biden, a muddled old man lacking the energy and cognitive capability even to mount a presidential campaign, had shockingly caught and passed Trump in vote counts. Perhaps that happened legitimately, but very many of Trump's voters smelled a rat. Later, in a self-congratulatory *TIME* magazine article, the "cabal"—that was the word used in the article—of political activists, billionaire donors, and others who had funded and managed the effort to use COVID to institute these irregular practices boasted that they had "fortified" democracy.

Conservatives have been livid ever since.

On January 6, 2021, when Congress was set to meet to certify the results of the Electoral College, a massive "Stop the Steal" protest took place in Washington. The crowd appeared to be well into six figures' worth of people. A small number of them took to the US Capitol and made their way inside, some let in by the strangely undermanned Capitol Police presence at the building, and the "mostly peaceful" protest did turn into what appeared to be a minor riot. One of the protesters, an Air Force veteran named Ashli Babbitt, was shot to death by a Capitol policeman named Lt. Michael Byrd for simply attempting to step through a broken window into a corridor.

Trump was impeached following Biden's inauguration, and for the second time, the first being over an entirely meritless charge that he had sought help from the government of Ukraine to "get dirt" on Biden's dealings there, for simply telling the Stop the Steal crowd to peaceably assemble at the Capitol and make their voices heard.

And hundreds of the protesters from that day have been arrested and jailed in federal prisons, often in solitary confinement and without bail or trial, on charges not of violent crimes but essentially of trespassing. As of this writing the vast majority of them have no prospect of release or the disposition of their cases. They're political prisoners in every meaningful sense of the term, and it's an American disgrace.

The Trump years were good ones for the American people, at least until COVID hit. He returned America to a sound foreign policy, his economic policies were producing results and held the promise of more, he was doing some damage to the entrenched corruption of the federal government despite terrible adversity, and he gave Americans permission to see their national interest again.

But the job he took on was too big to be accomplished in one term, his team didn't give him enough help, and given the odds he faced, he couldn't afford to make mistakes, and he did make some.

But the Make America Great Again movement Trump led had been waiting for someone like him to carry its standard. And despite all the lengths our ruling elite has gone in trying to kill it, it survived Trump's 2020 defeat. It continues to grow, and with or without Trump at its helm, it appears the single most potent ingredient in American politics.

Bush Republicanism is gone. Trump killed it. The corruption of the establishment has been laid bare to the horror of the public. And despite their best efforts, Trump is, as of this writing, the early favorite to return to the White House in 2024, perhaps to finish what he started.

The movement that put him in the White House needs to be better focused, better organized, and better able to partner with him—or someone else, if Trump isn't the nominee—in changing American politics. If that happens, the Revivalist Era can begin.

PART FOUR

AN AMERICAN REVIVAL

CHAPTER 13

The Fourth Revolution and the End of Conservatism

In what might have been a seminal moment in American political history, NASCAR driver Brandon Brown won his first race on the circuit in September of 2021. Brown took his national series victory with a win in the Xfinity Series race shortened by darkness at Talladega Superspeedway.

But the race was not the seminal moment. That came in the interview after the race, in which a female NBC Sports anchor noted the rather loud, spirited chant from the fans in the stands and deliberately mistook the ubiquitous "F*ck Joe Biden!" which has become de rigueur in virtually every public gathering in America, as "Let's Go, Brandon!"

It was a difficult mistake to make, and, as Sen. Ted Cruz said, it was perfectly emblematic of the lengths to which the corporate legacy media will go to push fake news on the American people.

But because lots of Americans who agreed wholeheartedly with the sentiment behind "F*ck Joe Biden!" are still uncomfortable with the loud dropping of F-bombs, "Let's Go, Brandon!" is the Delta Variant of derisive civil disobedience. Now the whole family can chime in.

And so when Biden traveled to Michigan to shill for his increasingly unlikely nation-killing $3.5 trillion federal spending orgy, he was met by hundreds of protesters yelling, "Let's Go, Brandon!"

As well as the other Bronx cheer.

Biden—and the media propping him up—are now officially the figures of ridicule they always should have been. The "Let's Go, Brandon!" meme comes within a context that is unmistakable. It's a stand-in for perhaps the most vulgar and dismissive rejectionist—and justifiably so—outpouring of invective against an American president in close to two decades, and everybody knows it.

And it's also a direct shot at corporate legacy media for their obvious and shameful lies.

"Let's Go, Brandon!" ought to scare the living hell out of Democrats everywhere. Because once they're ridiculing you, and having fun doing it, the game is over. That Team Biden couldn't get nine months into an administration before the wheels fell off and the country was laughing in their faces is damning.

And those wheels are off. Make no mistake about it.

Quinnipiac University runs polling that has always been just shy of a push-poll for Democrats. The Q-poll sample is generally slanted by several percent to the left, and Q-poll questions are often framed to generate a specific result. Republican consultants will tell you often of their irritation with Quinnipiac's polling.

But when Quinnipiac came out with their latest numbers on Biden's approval rating just after the emergence of the "Let's Go Brandon!" meme, well:

"A new Quinnipiac University poll released Wednesday shows just 38 percent of Americans approve of the job Biden is doing, down from 42 percent in the same poll three weeks ago and 50 percent approval in mid-February.

"'Battered on trust, doubted on leadership, and challenged on overall competency, President Biden is being hammered on all sides as his approval rating continues its downward slide to a number not seen since the tough scrutiny of the Trump administration,' Quinnipiac polling analyst Tim Malloy said in a statement summarizing the devastating findings.

"The poll puts Biden underwater on his handling of every major issue. Approval of the president's response to the COVID-19 pandemic, which Quinnipiac put at 65 percent in late May, was down to 48 percent in Wednesday's poll. Disapproval of Biden's handling of the pandemic, by contrast, has shot up to 50 percent from 30 percent in late May.

"Biden also gets failing marks on the economy (39 percent approval, 55 percent disapproval), foreign policy (34 percent approval, 58 percent disapproval), and taxation (37 percent approval, 54 percent disapproval).

"In addition, just 37 percent approve of the job he is doing as commander-in-chief of the armed forces, while 58 percent disapprove.

"But the president's worst issue score comes on his handling of immigration (25 percent approval, 67 percent disapproval) and specifically the ongoing migrant crisis at the US-Mexico border (23 percent approval, 67 percent disapproval).

"A plurality of respondents (46 percent) say the administration is not being aggressive enough in deporting immigrants, while just 15 percent say the White House is being too aggressive with immigration enforcement.

"Biden still has 80 percent approval among Democrats. He's down 60-32 with independents and 94-4 with Republicans. The poll release doesn't give a D-R-I breakdown of those surveyed, so it's hard to pin down whether things aren't actually worse than 38-53."

Quinnipiac wasn't the only one. There was Gallup:

"Americans by significant margins now view the Republican Party as better than the Democratic Party at protecting the nation from international threats (54% to 39%, respectively) and at ensuring the nation remains prosperous (50% to 41%). The 15-percentage-point GOP advantage on security matters is its largest since 2015, while its nine-point edge on prosperity is its largest since 2014. Last year, the GOP had a narrow advantage on international matters while the parties were essentially tied on economic matters. More of this change has come from declines in Americans perceiving the Democratic Party as better on these issues than from increases for the Republican Party.

...

> "Americans typically see the Republican Party as more capable on national security matters, but the 15-point gap in favor of the GOP this year is the largest since a 16-point advantage in 2015. The party had an even larger 23-point gap in 2014, a time when the Obama administration was struggling to deal with the rise of the Islamic State in Iraq and renewed Middle East violence, among other issues."

And there was Morning Consult:

> "40% of voters say Biden has accomplished less than they expected since taking office in January, up 12 points since June, and matching the share who say the same of congressional Democrats.
>
> "The shares of independent and Democratic voters who say Biden has underperformed expectations have doubled over the past three months.
>
> "52% of all voters disapprove of Biden's job performance, his worst rating in a Morning Consult/Politico poll so far."

Things never got better for Team Biden. The approval numbers fell under water, and they've stayed there despite a Herculean effort at distraction by the administration, its congressional allies, and the legacy corporate media. By February 2022 the Quinnipiac poll had Biden's approval at 35 percent, with 55 percent disapproving. At the end of April 2022 the president's RealClear Politics polling average on approval was a mere 41.7 percent, with 53 percent disapproving.

Bad approval numbers for a man like Biden and the people handling him are dangerous, at least in the short term. But they're a necessary condition to the prolonged political earthquake that would shake us into the next political era we so desperately need. Biden looks for all the world to be the next in the line of transformational presidential failures—Adams, Buchanan, and Hoover being the precedents—who have ushered in a whole new national consensus for the other side.

Nonetheless, the drowning man is always a threat to pull his rescuer under the water, and Biden is a man of such low character (as are his handlers) that pulling America down to save themselves is likely a feature rather than a bug in the eyes of the regime.

It was always likely that as Team Biden failed, the thuggery and totalitarianism and contempt would only grow.

So while you're delighting in "Let's Go, Brandon!" at a ball game or a car race, the Justice Department has been siccing the FBI on moms expressing distaste about Critical Race Theory at school board meetings, which might be the tipping point for things to get even worse. Team Biden wants to sic the IRS on your bank account. Biden and most of the Democrats on Capitol Hill tacitly approved that George Soros mob chasing Kyrsten Sinema into the Arizona State University women's restroom to berate her over her refusal to spend $3.5 trillion on socialist fantasy. After what was quite obviously a leftist publicity stunt in which Facebook "whistleblower," Hunter Biden laptop story suppressor, and social justice warrior Frances Haugen showed up at Congress with documents proving the social media platform was an outrage engine, Team Biden began promising to impose online censorship. And that promise was shortly fulfilled as in December 2021 and January 2022 a fresh spate of Twitter and YouTube cancellations tumbled forth.

And in April of 2022, the Department of Homeland Security, not content to sit on its hands as more than two million illegal aliens invaded the United States over the course of the previous twelve months, announced the creation of an Orwellian "Board of Disinformation Governance," directed by a left-wing propagandist named Nina Jankowicz. Victor Davis Hanson, noting that Jankowicz had called the New York Post's reporting of the Hunter Biden laptop scandal "Russian disinformation," mused that to hire her to purportedly expose disinformation was to validate the old saying, "takes one to know one." Republicans in Congress weighed impeachment of DHS secretary Alejandro Mayorkas for his new Ministry of Truth as well as the vacation of the border.

The forces of authoritarianism are gathering, undeterred by the ridicule and rejection of the American public. But there's a problem, which is that the authoritarian woke Left can't seem to improve any of the institutions over which it has won control.

In January 2022, Joel Kotkin offered a quite optimistic view of the future. Writing at UnHerd.com, Kotkin questioned whether wokeism has reached its peak and is now on the wane:

"Over the past several decades, the progressive Left has successfully fulfilled Antonio Gramsci's famed admonition of a 'long march through the institutions.' In almost every Western country, its adherents now dominate the education system, media, cultural institutions, and financial behemoths.

"But what do they have to show for it? Not as much as they might have expected. Rather than a Bolshevik-style assumption of power, there's every chance this institutional triumph will not produce an enduring political victory, let alone substantially change public opinion.

"Even before Biden's botched Build Back Better initiative, American progressives faced opposition to their wildly impractical claims about achieving 'zero Covid' and 'zero emissions,' confronting 'systemic racism' by defunding the police, regulating speech, and redefining two biological sexes into a multiplicity.

"Increasingly, the 'march' has started to falter. Like the French generals in 1940 who thought they could defeat the Germans by perfecting World War One tactics, the progressive establishment has built its own impressive Maginot Line which may be difficult to breach, but can still be flanked.

"That is not to deny the progressives' limited successes. It has certainly developed a remarkable ability to besmirch even the most respected institutions, including the US military. But that is where its achievements stop.

"While the Pentagon's top brass focused on 'domestic terrorists' and a progressive social agenda, it calamitously bungled its withdrawal from Afghanistan and appears utterly unprepared for Chinese or Russian competitors. And the effect of this progressive march is plain to see: the percentage of Americans who feel 'a great deal of trust and confidence in the military' has dropped in just three years to 45% from 70%.

"This decline in trust in major institutions, so evident in America, is also rife across Europe and Australia. In Europe, for example, young people express less pride in their cultural and religious heritage, and are almost three times as likely as their elders to believe that democracy is failing.

"The great paradox of progressivism is that nowhere are its shortcomings more evident than in its geographic heartland: the dense urban centre. Conventional wisdom has dictated that America's high-tech economic future will be shaped in dense urban areas, where superstar companies stand the best chance of recruiting superstar employees.

"But while the upper crust of the labour force continue to head to the dense urban cores, on the ground people are moving in the other direction. Across the high-income world, not only in America but Europe as well, the vast preponderance of

> growth has taken place in suburbs and exurbs. In the last decade over 90% of all US metropolitan population growth and 80% of job growth took place on the periphery. On the ground, then, the progressive dream is withering."

Kotkin is correct on the out-migration from the deep blue cities. Democrat stronghold New York lost 319,000 people in 2021. Washington, DC, shed 2.9 percent of its population in just one year at a time when the federal government grew larger than ever. Hawaii, Massachusetts, Louisiana, California, and Illinois, all states with Democrat governors, shed population in 2021. Meanwhile, Texas grew by 311,000 people and Florida by 211,000. Idaho gained a 3 percent population increase in just one year. It's been a staggering amount of population migration out of the Left's core jurisdictions. People vote on Hard Left policies with their feet in America just as they have elsewhere in the world.

And college attendance is down. As Kotkin reports, it fell by 5 percent in the past decade, and then another 6.5 percent in 2020 and 2021. Parents are recognizing the ripoff woke higher education has become, and particularly in the case of straight white males college attendance has fallen off markedly.

A *Wall Street Journal* article in early September 2021 noted the exodus:

> "Men are abandoning higher education in such numbers that they now trail female college students by record levels.
>
> "At the close of the 2020-21 academic year, women made up 59.5% of college students,

> an all-time high, and men 40.5%, according to enrollment data from the National Student Clearinghouse, a nonprofit research group. U.S. colleges and universities had 1.5 million fewer students compared with five years ago, and men accounted for 71% of the decline. This education gap, which holds at both two- and four-year colleges, has been slowly widening for 40 years. The divergence increases at graduation: After six years of college, 65% of women in the U.S. who started a four-year university in 2012 received diplomas by 2018 compared with 59% of men during the same period, according to the U.S. Department of Education. In the next few years, two women will earn a college degree for every man, if the trend continues, said Douglas Shapiro, executive director of the research center at the National Student Clearinghouse.
>
> "No reversal is in sight. Women increased their lead over men in college applications for the 2021-22 school year—3,805,978 to 2,815,810—by nearly a percentage point compared with the previous academic year, according to Common Application, a nonprofit that transmits applications to more than 900 schools."

As the article notes, the largest falloff among the male population comes among poor and working-class whites, for whom there are lower enrollment rates than among blacks and other minorities.

What's surprising about this is that anybody should find it surprising. If you've spent any time at all on a college campus recently, what you know is that American higher education, just like American elementary and secondary education, is specifically calibrated to demonize, inconvenience, and oppress straight white men.

That the enrollment rates should fall off is not just unsurprising, it's the desired result.

The *WSJ* piece makes clear that nobody at any institution of higher education is willing to devote resources to recruiting more straight white males to attend college. They don't want them.

If they did, they wouldn't have destroyed so many things that attracted straight white guys to college in the first place.

Let's bear in mind that elementary and secondary education in this country is dominated, almost in an exclusory manner, by females—and the women who run the K-12 schools treat boys not as boys but as bad girls who need to be managed. Any male who survives past high school in such an environment (and males graduate high school at lower rates now than females do) is likely exhausted at the idea of sitting in an estrogen-soaked classroom for the next four years rather than going out and living.

The education establishment has already poisoned the well for straight white males by attempting to indoctrinate them into its woke fantasies, and given the natural tendency of teenagers to rebel, it's a pretty good bet that a lot of them have objections to overcome when it comes to spending the next four years being lectured to—and, frankly, being ripped off.

What is it that colleges offer straight white men these days, anyway?

Is it money? You're supposed to go to college so you can make more money. But colleges are pushing degree programs that are more likely to make you a debt slave than prosperous. Practical males who aren't bought in to the status argument and simply look at the objective aspect of it—particularly after having been dragged through the utter tedium and insult that is modern secondary education—look at those crazy tuition bills and question whether it's worth the investment. If you're bent on becoming a lawyer, doctor, engineer, scientist, or accountant, then yeah—you need a college degree, though you might be able to get one online while you're working a job. Even then, everybody knows that by the time you're in your late twenties, nobody cares where your degree is from.

By the way, you literally can make more money going to trade school and filling the massive hole in the workforce that exists for plumbers, welders, machinists, carpenters, and other skilled tradesmen, wherein you can very likely become a business owner by your early thirties and make a nice living while being completely in control of your time, than you can getting a BA in a run-of-the-mill college major that prepares you for white-collar corporate drudgery and workplace irrelevance by your late forties.

College used to be known not just for the higher learning one could find there (something which is questionable; go check out the syllabus for any 1000-level English or history class nowadays, and you might see these institutions as adult day care more than higher education) but for the development of social skills students could attain. But is college really preparatory for real life now? Or does it just coddle kids and keep them as children?

They've destroyed the Greek system at all the colleges, you know. For college men, fraternities used to represent the single most important learning experience anybody could get in his formative years. In a fraternity you got a great education as to how organizations work, how interpersonal relationships are built and maintained, how to sell (rush is nothing but an intensive course in sales), and how adverse circumstances can create bonds between people who would never have them otherwise (which is what pledgeship is for, and the worse pledges had it, the closer the pledge class became).

Take that experience away and all college really amounts to, in far too many cases, is paying too much to sit in a classroom and listen to some institutionalized loser pontificate and demand you parrot his or her rants for a grade. Girls will put up with that far more readily than boys will, especially when girls are pandered to on college campuses.

Then, of course, there is the fact that American colleges are nonstop leftist indoctrination camps. White American males, particularly those from non-privileged backgrounds, generally are repulsed by all of it.

They're particularly repulsed by the gay and trans advocacy that festers on campus, the intersectional feminism, and especially the guilty-until-proven-innocent kangaroo courts policing "sexual assault." Nobody thinks date rape is OK, but there are so many incidents of hoaxes, or situations where the guy and the girl are both so hammered neither one remembers sleeping with each other, that lots of these guys look at the college social life as a trap not worth their time.

Not that long ago, you went to college and you'd major in something that would give you a window into real-world productive work, you'd take core classes and electives that would make you well-rounded and culturally literate, you'd engage in Greek life or other extracurricular activities that taught you how to make friends the way adults do, and you'd find somebody you might like to marry.

When colleges enthusiastically embraced that role in society, there was a near universal consensus that everybody who had a smidgeon of academic talent should go.

But the people who run academia now have no interest in that role. Drunk on the power and money their predecessors left them, and unfettered by any accountability that politicians (at state schools) and donors should have imposed on them, they decided a couple of decades ago that they were to be the molders of a brand new kind of American. Our colleges teach kids that gender is a social construct, that America was founded to facilitate slavery, and that in a decade or so the world will end because of climate change.

It isn't surprising that straight white males whose parents don't have a quarter of a million dollars handy to burn on four years of adult day care, or who aren't committed to a career path colleges are the gatekeepers for, are losing interest in the project.

What's surprising is that anybody still wants to put themselves through this wringer at all.

So they've poisoned the public against the cities they run, they're busily destroying higher education, and they're hard at work destroying K-12 public education as noted earlier in this book.

The news media? Kotkin notes that's virtually a dead letter:

> "Meanwhile, the mass media, particularly its legacy outlets, constitute another progressive bastion losing credibility. One recent survey found that barely one in three Americans trusts the media, including a majority of Democrats, while only

> 15% of Americans have confidence in newspapers. Part of this surely stems from their bias: although there remain some powerful conservative voices, notably on talk radio and News Corp properties, the vast majority of journalistic power lies with the Left. It's the same story with social media, which increasingly dominates news access and is also widely distrusted.
>
> "But the media's Maginot Line may prove more vulnerable than expected, and this breach is certainly a far better prospect than those that came with the German flanking. There is a definite challenge not just from the traditional Right but a plethora of new publications which offer intelligent analysis outside the establishmentarian party line, as well as from Substack. Unless the media oligarchs find ways to repress these elements, a resurgence of free thinking may rescue journalism from progressive editors and journalism schools."

And then there's Hollywood, which is run by a small cadre of incompetents who destroy virtually everything they touch by demanding most, if not all, of its products are tainted with woke propaganda.

How well does that work? Well, in the first box office weekend of 2022 a $60 million Jessica Chastain-Penelope Cruz-Diane Kruger blockbuster, *The 355*, opened on more than three thousand screens nationwide. The movie had everything going for it—and it flopped badly, generating only $4.3 million in revenues.

Why? *The 355* is a shoot-'em-up spy movie starring a multicultural cast of five female leads and no male ones. It offers the usual fare of females beating up men twice their size.

Audiences took one look at the trailer and said, "Nope."

Nobody cares about woke propaganda disguised as entertainment. When Hollywood relents and allows its products to tell stories that reach us as human beings, it's rewarded. But it doesn't go there much anymore. That's a key reason why Netflix and Disney have both seen their stocks collapse.

And in the meantime, independent Christian filmmakers crank out low-budget films like *I Can Only Imagine*, *The Shack*, *War Room*, and *Fireproof* that routinely turn $1–3 million productions into $80 million revenue engines. None of these are great films—they're watchable, but "conservative" filmmaking still has a long way to go—but the "bomb" ratio is far, far less than the Hollywood in-crowd is generating. A Christian film company created *The Chosen*, an excellent streaming series telling the stories of the Gospels in a realistic portrayal, and has crowd-funded its operations to the tune of an astonishing $350 million or more in donations.

What does all this failure add up to? A revolution, that's what. A major upheaval in all of these key political, economic, and cultural institutions that have "gone woke" and no longer serve the American public's interests.

America is begging for major changes. Everybody knows it. The Left, in fact, is counting on turning that dissatisfaction, the end of this current era, into its own utopian moment.

But the public doesn't want to be governed by the woke commies. The public is running away from them as best it can.

Which means whoever can offer the clearest, most cogent, and most competent alternative to authoritarian woke leftism will win the fourth revolution of American history and control the coming era.

Right now, whether you're a Democrat, Independent, or Republican, you're likely scoffing at the idea today's Republican Party is capable of making a majority that can govern—politically, culturally, and economically—for the next three generations. And you aren't wrong.

But the revolution has to start *within* the GOP. It has to fundamentally change the nature of conservatism and Republicanism. It has to inject a strong dose of testosterone and human growth hormone into the American Right. I'd suggest giving the movement a new name better reflective of the challenge it seeks to meet, and demanding that it go on offense and stop losing ground to the Hard Left.

Conservatism hasn't conserved enough. We know this. The Marxist crowd figured out how best to weaponize its oppressor-vs.-oppressed binary critique of Western civilization in America, namely by using race and sex to create its new revolutionary proletarian vanguard, and in so doing they turned a dead economic philosophy into a live cultural virus that has swallowed up all of our institutions and has gain-of-functioned its way into the halls of political power.

Conservatism wasn't built for that fight. Conservatism was built for polite conversations with liberal Democrats. It was built for *Firing Line* and for *The McLaughlin Group*. Conservatism, as it was constructed by people like William F. Buckley, aimed to "stand athwart history, yelling 'Stop!'"

It was never built for offensive maneuvers. And for a time, that was all right. For a time, the opponents of conservatism largely shared the same set of cultural and political values as the center-right.

But that time is over. And again and again the people who have called themselves conservatives have proven they lack the firepower to beat the Marxists in the real fight in which we're currently engaged for the soul of not just America but the Western world.

Take Sen. Bill Cassidy, for example, whose self-immolation in the eyes of the Louisiana Republicans who elected him in 2014 and 2020 was immediate when he voted to impeach Trump in February 2021. Cassidy likes to boast about his reasonably high marks on the American Conservative Union scorecard (he scored a 67 percent in 2021, which wasn't very high at all), but he's a perfect example of the ineffectiveness of "conservatism" to conserve America.

Cassidy spent 2021 lecturing the Right about its future as ordinary Americans scowled at him. He kept whining about how "relitigating" the 2020 election wouldn't get Republicans anywhere. But what caused his political problem in the first place was his vote on an illegal impeachment of a private citizen over a political protest that got out of hand. And Cassidy said it was "bringing solutions to the American people" that would be the party's salvation.

Tell that to Jack Kemp, who spent two decades in a failed crusade to convince urban black voters to choose the GOP. Kemp offered lots of "solutions" that, if implemented, would have made things better in the inner city, and almost none of them ever became law. Why? Because the people who run the inner city have zero interest in "solutions." "Solutions" upset the political formula that insures they're going to have power for the foreseeable future.

When you're in an era of consensus politics, you can win arguments about policies and craft the kind of bipartisan legislation with which Bill Cassidy thinks Republicans will prevail.

But the naivete and blindness involved in his assumptions are breathtaking. To illustrate just how stupid this all is, in 2017 when Trump was just getting started in his first year and needed to lean on Republican majorities in both the House and Senate, the budget produced under threat of a Democrat filibuster was an unmitigated disaster.

How bad was it?

Democrats blocked funding for Trump's border wall. They managed to secure billions of dollars in Obamacare subsidies that Trump's administration had previously vowed to cut. Democrats also forced the House, led by the "conservative" Trump critic Paul Ryan, to balk on a vote to partially repeal Obamacare. They were able to block cuts to Planned Parenthood (which was soon after providing puberty blockers to "trans" kids even without their parents' approval) and fully funded the Environmental Protection Agency. There was a $295 million Medicaid bailout for Puerto Rico, ongoing high-speed rail funding for California, and the creation of a $100 million fund to check "Russian influence" in Europe.

What else? Democrats preserved a $3.1 billion refugee resettlement program and increased funding for the National Institute of Health, where Anthony Fauci works, of course, by $2 billion. Both of those line items were supposed to have been cut. The "Food for Peace" program in Africa, which was supposed to have been cut, got a $1 billion funding increase.

Daniel Horowitz of *Conservative Review* was livid. "People voted for a revolution—to drain the swamp—and out popped a

Democrat budget," he noted. "In fact, one would be hard pressed to find anything different about this budget from the one we would have gotten if Hillary (Clinton) had been elected."

Did Bill Cassidy vote against any of that GOP-led bacchanal? What do *you* think?

When Hillary Clinton lost the 2016 election, the Democrats didn't "move on" from it, by the way. They attempted to bully Trump electors into going faithless, they fed every moronic conspiracy theory they could, and in particular the Trump-Russia fraud that the Clinton campaign, through its Perkins Coie attorney Michael Sussman and its spin-doctor political skunkworks Fusion GPS, had concocted and fed to the corrupt FBI.

And for two years they conducted an active sedition campaign against the Trump administration, which paid off in the 2018 midterm shellacking.

Doesn't seem like there was any negative consequence to their failure to "move on," and that was from an election that was more or less honestly conducted. The great allegation of Russian "meddling" in the 2016 presidential election was that a couple hundred thousand dollars was spent on Facebook ads.

As opposed to $400 million in Zuckerbucks being spent to turn local elections offices in heavily Democrat areas into ballot-harvesting machines and to promote highly suspicious, unconstitutional departures from state elections laws. A retired Wisconsin Supreme Court justice, tasked to lead a special investigation into the conduct of the 2020 election, found copious examples of crimes committed and suggested the state legislature consider decertifying the results based on the abuses funded by Zuckerbucks in that state.

Those dark-money abuses gave a potato-brained addlepate incapable of running an actual presidential campaign, we're told, the highest vote total in American history.

Bill Cassidy wants you not to question what happened in 2020, when America is burning down to cinders based on the abject lack of leadership that election produced.

We're entitled to respond that what Bill Cassidy really wants is for people to forget that he voted for what he'd already said was an unconstitutional post-presidential impeachment, something the people of Louisiana had absolute contempt for his doing. And he wants people to forget that he's been nuzzling up to the treasonous, tyrannical, and quite possibly illegitimate regime the questionable 2020 election has produced in order to trail in a few shekels of infrastructure spending. Cassidy was one of the Washington Generals in the US Senate who voted for the $2 trillion infrastructure bill that contributed to a 7 percent inflation rate by the end of the year, a massive effective tax increase on the American people that can't be offset by a bunch of government swag dropped from helicopters onto local governments.

What are these "good policies" Bill Cassidy wants the GOP to run on? Deals he cuts on rearrange-the-Titanic-deck-chairs bills with the Chris Coonses and Mazie Hironos of the world?

Nobody should take Bill Cassidy's political advice. He's the most Washington General of the Washington Generals of the US Senate. Bill Cassidy is committed to losing nonstop in DC, and then defending his Failure Theater politics in front of the home folks he hopes either aren't paying attention or are getting their news from the Chuck Todds and Jake Tappers of the world.

Bill Cassidy is how you lose. He's how you dispirit your base so they fail to turn out and throw the bums to the curb.

He's the utter personification of why the Right has to move beyond "conservatism" and into Revivalism. There is no room for Bill Cassidy in a movement to right the American ship before she sinks beneath the waves; he's no conservative in his own right, but he's nonetheless an anchor tied to the feet of the conservative movement. Cut him loose, let him sink to the bottom, and let's retake our country in the next two cycles animated by righteous indignation over the usurpation of power that was the 2020 election.

Another great illustration of the insufficiencies of the "conservative" establishment in the face of America's current condition came when Bob Woodward and Robert Costa's book, *Peril*, was released in the summer of 2021. In it, Chairman of the Joint Chiefs of Staff Mark Milley is said to have told the Chinese he would warn them if war between our nations was imminent. Whether you take those breathtaking revelations at face value and see Milley's reported words and deeds as treason or whether you think those may have been embellished, perhaps by Milley himself, what's unmistakably true and perhaps most disturbing about the controversy is the American Left's reaction showed they were perfectly fine with the utter dysfunction the story represented.

Do you think Daniel Patrick Moynihan would have been all right with the chairman of the Joint Chiefs of Staff demanding loyalty oaths from top military personnel to the exclusion of the elected President of the United States? Would Joe Lieberman have said it was fine to tell the Chinese they'd get a heads-up in the event war with them was in the offing?

And yet hourly on CNN and MSNBC there were wild-eyed leftists and ruling-class sycophants calling Milley a hero. Rep. Adam Kinzinger, who spent 2021 determined to catch and pass his colleague Liz Cheney as the most hated Republican in Congress by Republican voters, went on CNN to declare that, while Milley needed to "answer questions," he was fit to continue in his job.

This was before the Afghanistan pullout.

Consider the left's COVIDgasms as well. You can't successfully make common cause with people whose response to a recall effort against Gavin Newsom based on public outrage over hypocritical, unscientific, and authoritarian abuses of power to create COVID lockdowns was to (1) invoke the specter of Donald Trump's unpopularity in that state and then (2) claim a mandate for more COVID lockdowns when the Trump demonization worked as an electoral strategy.

The Left, who've routed the liberals out of the Democrat Party's leadership and even reprogrammed a not-insignificant number of them into running-dog communist lackeys, wasn't interested in an honest debate about Newsom's Branch Covidian power grabs. What they wanted was to hold on to, and grow, their power. So they called Larry Elder, the conservative talk host who ran against Newsom in the California recall election, the black face of white supremacy, and they covered California with "Orange Man Bad," and then they claimed a national consensus for things the Constitution clearly doesn't allow.

It isn't David French's world anymore, if it ever was. You can't beat the Insane Clown Cult that rules the Democrat Party with Bill Cassidys, Adam Kinzingers, and David Frenches. The enemy is now well past their Maginot Line.

But the good news is a revivalist movement, if it even takes on that name, is right there waiting to launch. The foundations, intellectual, spiritual, and political, are already in place.

Go and read the text of the speech Mollie Hemingway gave upon receipt of the Bradley Prize last year, with an audience full of Old Regular conservative attendees, where, in talking about the cultural aggressions and bullying of the Left, she said this:

> "For conservatism to mean anything now, it has to be about rejecting this rigged system. Don't just say 'stop.' Our duty is to not to say 'stop' but then bend the knee in cowardice when the mob comes. That brings even more harm to our more vulnerable neighbors and does nothing to prevent the destruction of the country.
>
> "It's not comfortable for conservatives who value order and civility to even think or speak this way. But the fact is that many Americans are alienated from and no longer feel at home in their own country. The moral climate has been degraded as the left has taken over every single one of the powerful institutions in the country and is actively pushing people to lead a life of godlessness, barrenness, selfishness, gluttony, and addiction to outrage and dopamine.
>
> "All of a sudden, the conservative project is not a conservative one, so much as a counter-revolutionary one."

That's about as revivalist a message as you can get.

Or have a look at the scalding indictment of the military-industrial complex former Marine Josiah Lippincott delivered at *American Mind* distilling much of the new critique of our woke generals and their paymasters into concrete ideas for reform:

> "Our generals are losers abroad, and grifters at home. They parrot MSNBC talking points on Twitter and grovel before Fauci. This is bad enough. But Milley's actions show that America's top military officers have reached another level of delusion. They fancy themselves a new praetorian guard to protect the nation—as construed by elite editorial boards—from the people's elected representatives.
>
> "This deep state is in control. It is clear that no populist elected leader can trust America's security establishment. As Senator Chuck Schumer warned President Trump on Rachel Maddow's show in 2017, the intelligence community has 'six ways from Sunday of getting back at you.'
>
> "The military establishment is gloating now and flexing its muscle. After the election, outgoing Syria envoy Jim Jeffrey admitted that the Pentagon and State Department had consistently lied to Trump about troop levels in Syria. Before he left office, Trump's order to have troops out of Afghanistan by January 15 was overruled by the establishment. Trump, far from trying to start a war on his way out of office, sought to end one.

"White House spokesperson Jen Psaki claims that Milley was following 'constitutional orders to prevent unlawful military actions.' According to her, Trump 'was implementing an insurrection.' The claim that Trump wished to start a war to distract from the election, upon which Milley based his collusion with the Chinese government, was an utter lie. Nor was Trump implementing an insurrection; the FBI has dispensed with this myth, finding that there was no coordinated plot associated with the Capitol riot.

"There will be no hearings, serious journalistic investigations, or outcry from the establishment. Milley will go unpunished. He will retire with full honors and full pension. The Pentagon will never reform itself from the inside. The entire military-industrial complex (MIC) must be dismantled if we are ever to have again an armed forces consistent with the Founders' republican virtues.

"The American Right must be willing to starve the Pentagon of its lifeblood. The most important asset the people have is their bodies. American mothers and fathers need to stop feeding their children into the machine. Heartland American boys and girls have better things to do and better leaders to serve under. The American people must go on strike until the generals once again learn to subordinate themselves to the people.

> "GOP politicians must assist their constituents in this noble task. They must find real courage and demand radical institutional change. This starts with deep and abiding budget cuts for the Pentagon and the rest of the MIC. The Founders' distrust of permanent standing armies must be restored.
>
> "America should once again rely on true citizen soldiers for national defense."

Lippincott suggests that near-universal gun ownership and the conversion of the citizenry into a nationwide militia recruitment pool is a far greater guarantee of American liberty than our hyper-wasteful, newly woke, and externally aggressive military complex. He isn't wrong, and public sentiment is moving in his direction. American support for and confidence in the military, as reflected in a Beacon Research survey on behalf of the Ronald Reagan Foundation, cratered from 70 percent in October 2018 to 45 percent in November 2021.

There is little reason to believe that direction will change. Our current military leadership hasn't won a war since, arguably, Desert Storm in 1991, just unquestionably lost one to a collection of Pashtun tribesmen in Toyota trucks last year after trillions of dollars and thousands of lives spent over two decades, and will almost certainly lose, or at least fail to win, in the next kinetic military conflict the hawks push us into.

Or that our swampy political leadership bungles us into. Which by the time this book is published could happen in Taiwan or Ukraine.

The public doesn't want to lack confidence in the military. The public was so outraged at Biden's ugly denouement in Afghanistan that the bottom fell out of his public approval and changed the course of his presidency. He'll never recover from being the president who lost that war, regardless of whether it's fair to term him such. General George S. Patton, in a famous speech to the Third Army on June 3, 1944, practically on the eve of D-Day, summed up the essence of our national nature with respect to matters military:

> "Men, all this stuff you hear about America not wanting to fight, wanting to stay out of the war, is a lot of bullshit. Americans love to fight. All real Americans love the sting and clash of battle. When you were kids, you all admired the champion marble shooter, the fastest runner, the big-league ball players and the toughest boxers. Americans love a winner and will not tolerate a loser. Americans play to win all the time. That's why Americans have never lost and will never lose a war. The very thought of losing is hateful to Americans. Battle is the most significant competition in which a man can indulge. It brings out all that is best and it removes all that is base."

Subsequent events cast some doubt on Patton's prognostications, but he was correct about the public's reaction to them. Americans will not tolerate a loser, and that's precisely what "Let's Go Brandon" Joe Biden is. It's also what our top military brass is.

Rapidly declining public support for this woke military leadership, which is persecuting those in its ranks who resist taking a vaccine of dubious effectiveness for COVID and which is demanding senseless sensitivity training and other inanities for people who are supposed to be our trained killer patriots, reflects our intolerance for losers.

As Krauthammer said, "What cannot continue, will not continue." The failure of our woke military leadership cannot continue. The public will demand change. It's up to a revivalist political movement to produce it.

Bruce Abramson, writing at *RealClearPolitics* last summer, declared the Buckley conservative formulation obsolete in the modern fight against the woke Left. Abramson was clearly calling for revivalism:

> "William F. Buckley's desire to 'stand athwart history and yell "Stop!"' described a personality type more than a political agenda. Conservatives, by well-earned reputation, tend to revere traditions and institutions, trust authority, and favor measured, incremental change. Dana Carvey's impersonation of George H. W. Bush caricatured the type brilliantly: 'Wouldn't be prudent, wouldn't be prudent at this juncture.'
>
> "Without knocking prudence, however, shouting 'Stop!' is only a smart strategy when you're ahead. It doesn't help when you're losing.
>
> "In the 21st century, the right has lost control of every important American institution. Academia, K-12, the media, Silicon Valley, Hollywood, Wall Street, the civil service, the unions, most

professional organizations, and corporate boardrooms. Even the top military brass trip over themselves flaunting their woke credentials.

"Stopping time now would enshrine the stupidity, cruelty, and moral bankruptcy of radical leftist wokeism.

"Conservatism—Bill Buckley's version of it, anyway—is dead. It's just as well. It failed to conserve much of anything. A movement standing athwart history and yelling stop in 2021 will remember four score and seven only as the number of genders.

"There's precious little in contemporary American life worth conserving. There's a tremendous amount to cherish, however, in this country's grand traditions. What America needs today is a counterrevolutionary restoration.

"And that's a problem. The GOP has spent decades promoting respectable, cautious, incrementalists like Mitch McConnell, John Roberts, and Kevin McCarthy—fine men blessed with none of the skills necessary to lead a counterrevolution.

"Worse, conservatism has always held a particular attraction for people who view prudence, risk-aversion, reverence, and obedience as virtues. These traits are as overrepresented among rank-and-file Republicans as they are within party leadership. America's 'Great Awokening' has thrown them into a state of deep inner turmoil.

> After all, a corrupted American institution is still an American institution. Even when all available evidence screams that institutional leadership has betrayed America, noncompliance feels wrong.
>
> "Such feelings, though laudable in other settings, are self-defeating when a society's elite institutions and authorities have turned against its own people—as they have in the United States today. Current circumstances call for a very different personality type: bold, irreverent, eagerly noncompliant, and hypervigilant of the corruption that can render even legitimate authority unworthy of respect."

Brandon Morse at the conservative site RedState.com echoes that exhortation to the Right to give up its retreatist mentality when tough fights are afoot, particularly in the culture:

> "We're going to lose and we're going to lose a lot. They're so entrenched that driving them out will take years of hard-fought battles ranging from the legal to the physical. People will suffer character assassinations, cancelation, heartbreak, and threats to their well-being...but it's a battle worth fighting because America is worth fighting for.
>
> "The final goal of the culture war isn't to make someone pull a lever for a certain side, it's for the very heart of the citizen. Currently, conservatives are appealing to an emotion that the left is starving out of Americans, and soon there

> won't be anything left to appeal to. Gone will be the desire to keep freedom, capitalism, and true equality alive.
>
> "These losing battles need to be fought, but losing battles doesn't mean losing the war. You can ask George Washington about that."

Revivalism is on its way to becoming the zeitgeist of the Right.

Its critics will dismiss this as mere Trumpism. But Donald Trump was not Ronald Reagan, and even Reagan didn't invent conservative populism. Trump merely appropriated what was already there, and then he showed two things in his four years in office: first, that the application of some of what we're calling revivalist politics and policy actually works, and second, that the entrenched elites and Establishment types are so threatened by it as to actively tear the country apart in defense of their power structure when confronted by a potential revivalist future.

You didn't just see that with Trump; you saw it even more intensely with Marjorie Taylor Greene before she'd even done anything. They threw MTG off all of her committee assignments immediately after her inauguration, and for what? That she expressed some agreement with a few items being discussed online by the Q crowd?

Greene, freed from committee assignments, spent 2021 becoming a fundraising and political-culture behemoth. She's turned into one of the biggest stars in all of conservatism, because she has no reason to hold back. There may not be a Republican elected official the Left and the political in-crowd hates more than Marjorie Taylor Greene, and it makes no difference.

What happens when there are fifty Marjorie Taylor Greenes? What happens when they're the majority of the House GOP caucus or the Republican delegation in your state legislature? What happens when Republicans who are no longer interested in standing athwart history yelling "Stop!" are running the place? And what happens when they develop the kind of institutional competence and confidence in leadership of a McConnell, Schumer, or Pelosi?

What happens when Buckley's defensive admonition gives way to a revivalist impetus for grabbing history by the throat and dragging it where it needs to go?

You get a new political era. That's what happens.

Trump's future as a political force is unknown as of this writing. He's likely to run for president in 2024, and if he does, he'll be the odds-on favorite to win the GOP nomination. Trump is also quite likely to resume office as president in the event he catches Biden as an opponent. *RealClearPolitics'* polling average at the end of 2021 showed Trump beating Biden in a hypothetical 2024 head-to-head by a 46–41 margin.

That said, Trump will be seventy-eight years old on Election Day 2024. The movement this book describes certainly includes Trump, but it isn't defined by him, it didn't start with him, and it certainly won't end with him.

It can't.

Revivalism summoned Trump into being, not the other way around. Don't forget that if Trump hadn't been the GOP nominee in 2016, it would have been Ted Cruz, who despite an annoying penchant for occasional swings and misses is nonetheless a revivalist in his own right, at least in his better moments. And if Trump isn't the nominee in 2024, it's quite likely going to be Florida's Governor Ron DeSantis, who is arguably more revivalist than Trump is.

The public has taken the measure of the Paul Ryans and Bill Cassidys and Liz Cheneys of the world and wants no more to do with them. Those are the people who lead you to scoff at the idea the GOP could be the party at the center of American political life in this next era. This book suggests it's the shedding of them, the sidelining of those "prudent" men and women Abramson discusses that is central to building the next consensus.

A movement larger and longer-lasting than Trump, though perhaps led by him for a time, is waiting to take shape. It's present in green shoots all across America that are growing despite the toxic spray of the Biden administration and the neo-communist regime that props him up.

In Florida, the governor and the legislature might share a political party with the Bill Cassidys and Liz Cheneys, but that's about all. And in Florida, one gets the strong impression that the state's present is the nation's future. Conservatism is on offense in Florida, and in a few other states as well.

Revivalism is coming. It'll be unmistakable by November 2022.

CHAPTER 14

The Limbaugh/Breitbart/ Codevilla Legacy

I was really hoping in early February 2021 that I could put off an *American Spectator* column I knew I'd soon have to write. Millions of Americans shared my sense of dread about its subject.

But there was no denying the end was coming for Rush Limbaugh, the greatest radio personality in the history of the medium. The lung cancer that afflicted Limbaugh had been chipping away at him for well over a year, and his program had only sometimes been his own during that time. Various guest hosts, many of them excellent in their own right, had filled the space behind the EIB microphone, but none had covered the void Limbaugh's cancer-related absence left.

And none will. Losing Limbaugh has created a gaping hole in the conservative movement that will never be filled. All that's left is to work around that chasm while remembering his legacy.

Thanks to Rush, talk radio became the mass-media answer to the Left's dominance of television news and newspapers. It still largely is.

Rush Limbaugh burst onto the national scene in 1988, syndicating a daytime talk radio program and giving life to an industry that was all but dead. Talk radio had been the province of a number of local hosts, most of whom little more than disc jockeys with more to say but not much to hold an audience. The medium for talk radio was the AM dial, which was in deep decline after rock and roll had turned FM radio into the dominant choice of listeners and advertisers alike.

But Rush didn't just electrify an industry. He showed America what it could do. And he spawned an entire movement in media, which is still growing and evolving.

When Rush came along, conservatism was predominantly a political philosophy of the haves, something to be sniffed at by the "practical" political set. It was a think tank–driven enterprise, the stuff of long-dead philosophers and egghead academics on their way to being pushed out of the universities by the ascendant post–Cold War socialist Left. Building on the work of the founders of the modern conservative movement, Ronald Reagan had made conservatism a winning electoral force and injected it with a patriotic, populist energy, and Reagan was seen as the Great Communicator—a backhanded compliment in that it lauded his message-making skills while diminishing the magnetism of the message.

But Rush married Reagan's understanding of human existence, and conservatism's relationship thereto, with a middle-class sense of humor that was joyously optimistic and more than a little cynical at the same time. He offered blistering satire and flew directly in the face of the Left's early attempts to impose political correctness. Limbaugh had no compunction whatsoever about slaughtering each and every one of the Left's sacred cows—but he did so in a way that was undeniably honest and lighthearted.

I'm eviscerating you, was the underlying message, *but I'm doing it effortlessly. There is much more I'm holding back.*

He joked throughout his thirty-two years as a national talk host that he had "half my brain tied behind my back just to make it fair." That wasn't just a boast; it was a warning to his detractors. It signified that conservatives didn't need to go to the lengths the Left commonly goes in order to win the argument. Limbaugh won the argument for three hours every day just by offering up what was on his mind.

And it was validation for those of us who already agreed with him, who had figured it out on our own with almost no help from the media or the culture (and that was before the culture completely disintegrated into the left-wing abyss it currently is). Rush brought us together, and he made us realize not only weren't we alone, but there were millions and millions of us.

Enough to make a majority. Enough to win.

Once in a while he would interview guests on his show. He would take phone calls from listeners but more infrequently than most hosts would. Limbaugh's show was mostly a three-hour tour de force, an exposition of his understanding of the human condition.

He believed as Margaret Thatcher said: the facts of life are conservative. Limbaugh drove that point home again and again for over three decades. It's one main reason why he persuaded so many Americans and brought so many of them into the conservative movement. He led the way as his success spawned a wealth of talented radio hosts. Talk radio became, for a huge portion of the American public, the principal medium for political discussion. Even with the advent of the internet, talk radio is still a huge factor in the public's perception of events. And right up to his death—he was still broadcasting multiple times a week even as his body was giving way—Rush was the best player in the game.

And along the way, Rush maintained a spirit of humility, humor, and professionalism.

For someone who generated an audience of more than twenty million through the sheer force of his personality, Limbaugh was also shockingly lacking in ambition. That giant radio audience would easily have translated into success on television, and Limbaugh made a brief foray into that medium with a late-night syndicated show. But local TV stations kept parking it into after-midnight time slots, and Limbaugh hated television. He disliked the scripted nature of it and the chopped-up time slots between commercial breaks. Rather than push forward, he refocused on his core competency.

He wrote books that sold millions of copies. But then he trailed off. He kept his focus on the radio show. Limbaugh could have hired ghostwriters to keep the books coming, but that wasn't who he was.

The kind of success Rush Limbaugh had would corrupt almost anyone. It never corrupted Limbaugh.

He suffered through medical issues, especially in the second half of his national career. Limbaugh struggled with hearing loss and had cochlear implant surgery in 2001. That led to a bout with dependence on OxyContin, the opioid painkiller with which so many Americans have struggled. Limbaugh didn't let either diminish his effectiveness. He underwent rehabilitation, overcame the Oxy issue, and came back stronger than ever.

And he wouldn't let himself be canceled by the Left, no matter how thoroughly he infuriated them.

In 2012, after Andrew Breitbart's death, Limbaugh eulogized his friend by noting the absolute nastiness of those rejoicing over it on Twitter. Limbaugh opined that Breitbart would delight in publicly exposing those detractors for the vitriol and mean-spiritedness of their words.

Those same vitriolic carpers rejoiced over Limbaugh's death. It was a disgusting display of hatred.

But we rejoice over his life, cut short though it may have been. For Limbaugh was a titan whose shadow plunged his detractors in darkness. He created an industry and fueled a movement that has won the modern American argument. Thanks in large measure to Rush Limbaugh, the Left doesn't even bother trying to persuade anyone of their ideas; instead they invented cancel culture to stop the argument altogether.

They couldn't cancel Rush, so they're trying to cancel the rest of us.

We should honor him by continuing the fight. It will take all of us to paper over the void his passing leaves behind.

Rush might have been the greatest media figure of the conservative movement, and what we learned from him is invaluable. He taught us that it's all right to speak our minds, to be unafraid, to keep a smile on our faces as we fight to save and revive our country. He taught us that elan and confidence and good cheer are infectious, that happy warriors are winning warriors.

There will never be another Rush Limbaugh. But the more Limbaugh disciples in radio, in podcasting, and in other venues who are willing to copy his style and his cheerful confidence in seeking and telling the truth, the greater his legacy will be.

Revivalism takes much from Limbaugh. He's one of three of its spiritual founders.

I never met Angelo Codevilla, just as I never met Limbaugh. I did meet Andrew Breitbart and spent more than hour with him in 2010, just a few months after launching a career as a blogger.

That makes me one for three in earning face time with the three great prophets of a 21st century conservative America.

Breitbart's contribution, over a much shorter time frame—a true tragedy if ever there was one—was no less significant than Limbaugh's. As Rush showed that the Left couldn't dominate the airwaves, Breitbart proved it also couldn't dominate the internet. Breitbart filled the conservative movement with the courage to call out the pampered and perfumed princes of the legacy media for the frauds and nincompoops so many of them are, and over the relatively few years he was a national new media figure, he put them utterly to shame by exposing their refusal to act as the Fourth Estate American custom and constitutional law expects them to be.

Limbaugh and Breitbart were masters of conveying the message and relaying the truth. What Codevilla, who died in California in the fall of 2021 after being hit by a car, did as an even longer-standing luminary on the Right was to divine that truth and educate others.

You might notice that all three of the great figures noted above were self-made men. None were elevated by corporate or government elites. And none were beholden to anyone for their success. That matters.

It's a great pleasure to write for a publication that hosted so much of Codevilla's insight over the years, and to have been influenced by his writings at *The American Spectator* and elsewhere for particularly the past decade is an honor a great many of us in conservative media are now challenged to capitalize on.

Perhaps the most influential of those writings, which appeared at *TAS* on July 16, 2010, was the aforementioned essay entitled "America's Ruling Class and the Perils of Revolution." That work, delivered at the very height of the Tea Party movement in advance of the 2010 midterm elections that swept away Barack Obama's governing majority in the House of Representatives, made such an impact on Limbaugh that he read the entire thing over the three hours of a show and unfailingly referred to it for months if not years later.

Indeed, any understanding of the modern Right, to include the 2016 election of Donald Trump and the way forward for the Republican Party—in fact, to understand the utter collapse of the GOP's traditional leadership with the party's own voters that has persisted and metastasized even today—must begin with that essay. Codevilla shortly published it as a booklet, for which Limbaugh wrote an introduction.

His formulation was an incandescently true one, much of which is discussed in this book: America, particularly in the half-century since the social upheaval of the 1960s, has developed into an oligarchy, and there is a ruling class in the country that shares a number of characteristics in common. Those include an unfailing belief in a credentialed elite, a contempt for the lifestyle and values of the country at large, a globalist, anti-patriotic mindset, and the arrogance of power not just political but financial and cultural.

Codevilla contrasted that ruling class, which he indicted for its almost comic misperformance, with what he called "The Country

Class," the two-thirds of the American people who either didn't go to college or, if they did, were not fully indoctrinated into the values and pieties of the faculty lounge, whose livelihoods don't depend on government, and whose attitudes give primacy to meritocracy and productivity (competence, if you're looking for a succinct term) rather than the "fairness" required by the redistributive state.

Codevilla held that the ruling class and the country class are headed for an inevitable showdown. This was five years before Trump descended that escalator and became the embodiment of his thesis.

This is not to say that Codevilla was the ultimate Trumper. He was perfectly willing to criticize Trump harshly when the president deserved it. It is to say that Codevilla put into words what vast swaths of America felt, accurately contextualized it, and framed the battle.

From the perspective of someone who has committed to exhortations that the Right move beyond conservatism toward an embrace of Revivalism, the significance of "America's Ruling Class" is that what created Trump as a political phenomenon was not Trump. MAGA, or Trumpism in the vernacular of the Left and its modern-day mugwump allies, has always been misconstrued as a personality cult. Trump's genius was to make himself fit into the country class's yearning for a champion. As Codevilla wrote in July 2021:

> "In 2015 and 2016, candidate Trump's disrespectful, disdainful attitude toward the ruling class put him at the head of presidential preference polls ab initio, and kept him there. Throughout the

campaign, he said little of substance—just enough to give the impression that he was on the side of conservatives on just about everything. His leitmotif was, 'I despise those whom you despise because they despise you. I'm on your side, America's side.'

"Trump promised to 'make America great again,' but did not explain what had made it great in the first place nor how to restore it. Never a religious person, and one who had once expressed support for abortion, Trump delivered more stirring thoughts on religious freedom and the right to life than any candidate ever, including Ronald Reagan.

"Trump believed in the unity between himself and his followers, and that they would stay with him, even if he were to shoot somebody on Fifth Avenue. Millions of them reciprocated. The political, and even the moral content of that unity mattered less. He did not try to support his many accusations with facts. Millions who disagreed with him or who disliked him personally voted to make Trump president, and even more voted to reelect him.

"But whatever Trump might have thought, his voters knew that hatred for the ruling class—not Trump himself—was why they supported him. It was about themselves, not Trump. The ruling class knew it, too. That is why, for most of the past six years, it brayed so much disdain from

> every available venue on him personally, trying to convince at least some of his followers that he is unworthy of decent people's allegiance."

Codevilla went on to say that Trump's practical accomplishments on behalf of the country class, vis-à-vis the ruling class, were grossly insufficient. Which is, sadly, mostly correct; particularly, for example, given the effect COVID-19 had in enriching the Facebooks, Amazons, and Pfizers at the expense of Main Street USA.

I bring this up not to diminish Trump but to point out that what is indispensable about MAGA, or revivalism, as they're certainly related ideological emphases if the latter isn't a distillation of the former, isn't the candidate but what he stands for and commits to deliver. It is Codevilla's work over the many years he was prolific in hammering out the truth of the American condition and the perils of our decline that is essential; a country class public that demands its embodiment in political candidates, and crucially is vigilant in maintaining that demand, will find them.

As Codevilla's *American Greatness* editor Ben Boychuk said in a heartfelt and insightful tribute to his friend upon his death:

> "The shopworn cliché of any remembrance is that we will never see his like again—that the man was one of a kind. Of course, all of us are 'one of a kind.' But Angelo Codevilla was surely unique as a teacher. He left us a great many lessons. We are blessed to be able to return to those lessons, learn and re-learn from them, and carry on—even build upon—the work he did not live to finish.

> "The man is gone, but after we grieve our loss,
> we can see to it that the teaching endures."

Very much so. As is the case with Limbaugh and Breitbart, whose work is no less relevant today than when they were creating it, Codevilla's insights and lessons form the patrimony from which those of us who follow may draw.

It's our responsibility not to fail their memory. We mustn't merely keep up the fight. Armed with what they've given us, we have to win it.

CHAPTER 15

Renewing America's Values and Our Role in the World

The great foundation upon which a revivalist movement ought to be built owes much to Ronald Reagan, paradoxically the most successful president, as a Republican, of this current Democratic era.

It was Reagan's formulation of conservatism as a populist political ideology that prevented the Democrats' welfare-regulatory-intelligence-globalist state from careening into disaster at the height of the Cold War. Your author yields to no one in the admiration of Reagan, who accomplished, through courage and foresight, what upon his election was considered impossible—total victory over the Soviet Union without firing a single shot in a direct war.

Reagan was a masterful politician, but furthermore he was a visionary statesman and leader. His political adversaries sought to damn him with the faint praise of terming him "The Great Communicator" and "The Teflon President," appellations meant to minimize the substance of a man against whom they had no real defense.

Ronald Reagan saw very clearly the reality of geopolitical life in the second half of the 20th century. He recognized that Soviet and communist tyranny was a whitened sepulcher, a horrific human disaster covered up only by political power in the nations where it was practiced and cowardice among fellow travelers and other weaklings in the West. Reagan knew that to stand up to that tyranny was to beat it into remission, and that's exactly what he did—from being the first to rhetorically deposit it into the ash-heap of history to standing in Berlin and demanding that Mr. Gorbachev tear down his wall.

Reagan won, and so did America. Within a year or two of his leaving office in triumph, the United States reached the zenith of its political, cultural, moral, and economic power. It is not inaccurate to say that the United States of America at the end of the 1980s had reached a point in world history that will never be matched in terms of peaceful hegemony across the globe. We were at war with no one, we held economic power never before seen, and American culture so dominated the world that Reagan's detractors were busily touting Hollywood and Bruce Springsteen as the real reason the Soviets collapsed.

And Reagan galvanized the American electorate with a very simple political formula later called the "three-legged stool," which formed the basis for American conservatism for four decades.

It was a good formula. It encapsulated the times extremely well. It included staunch anti-communism, social conservatism, and supply-side economics. Reagan was right in all three particulars, though there were holes in the execution of them, as would be expected.

We won the Cold War without question, but that victory didn't include sweeping communism out of Cuba and North Korea, and the Chinese Communist Party simply lay in wait for its opportunity to renew the fight for tyranny against freedom on a global stage.

Reagan's cultural renaissance gave America its pride again, and the American family made a comeback after the utter disaster of the 1960s and 1970s. But that victory wasn't complete—the dissolution of the nuclear family halted only slightly throughout the 1980s before accelerating later.

And while Reagan won the war over taxes, the federal government became unmoored from its budgetary constraints, particularly under the administration of his successors. What was called "voodoo economics" at the time now looks like abject austerity, with an unpayable price looming before us.

None of this is intended to blame Reagan for our current troubles. No political victories are permanent, and neither are political doctrines. We do our best to uphold the philosophical virtues behind our Constitution, but we know how difficult it is to keep them relevant as they certainly must be in a free society.

As such, it's past time to recognize Reagan's three-legged stool is no longer the formula that can command a majority of the American electorate in service to conservative ideals. That's an unfortunate reality, since the stool has been a comfortable formulation for so long and deserves, if nothing else, a gold watch and a proper retirement party.

It's time for a new conservative formulation, one built upon the successes of Donald Trump's four years in office.

Many of the Never Trump variety within the conservative movement have insisted on keeping the three-legged stool as the foundation of the Right, though the credibility for such arguments has waned. If David French is unwilling to condemn the purveyors of Drag Queen Story Hour as they groom young children for the LGBTQ agenda, for example, exactly how does social conservatism survive?

Our new formulation should build upon the successes, and there were certainly some, of Donald Trump's four years in office. Those successes are due for dramatically increasing appreciation, given the unmitigated catastrophe the Biden administration is becoming. Biden is a transformationally awful president, destined for status alongside Buchanan and Hoover as the worst we've seen. A February 2022 poll by Rasmussen for the website National Pulse confirms this: the survey asked respondents to rank Biden as likely to be seen as one of the best presidents, about average, or one of the worst, and 54 percent of likely voters saw Biden as feeding from the bottom.

Only 15 percent said he will rank as one of America's best presidents. The other 25 percent expect his presidency to be seen in the future as "about average."

And he's only been in office for a year, without much prospect of things improving. The damage Biden will do to America will be visited, history teaches us clearly, upon his party in catastrophic measure.

America is going to be looking for something better.

That something is going to need to be tangible, and it can't depend on the personality of one man, most notably because the next federal election is a midterm, and one man isn't on the ballot—instead it's 435 House seats and 35 Senate seats. You can't count on winning that many personality contests; you need an agenda.

Thankfully, there is one. It simply needs to be articulated. The good news is we can distill the essence of what got Trump elected and worked for MAGA conservatives up and down the 2020 ballot even if Trump didn't win reelection on November 3 (we'll table that discussion, while conceding little, for now) into five things.

And here they are. Consider this a platform to replace and update Reagan's three-legged stool:

1. Resisting China and its rise as the single largest threat to human liberty on the planet.

That one is pretty easy, considering that the Chinese Communist Party has become everything we should have been most worried about where the USSR was concerned. In retrospect, the Soviets and the KGB were clownish and laughable compared to the perfidy and sophistication of a CCP that buys up American media and cultural properties, co-opts political leaders, engages in aggressions in the tech space to make opposition to them impossible, and acts with a ruthlessness Joe Stalin would be offended by in dealing with dissidents like the Uighurs, Tibetans, and Falun Gong.

Everybody knows this. The only people who doubt it are being paid by the Chinese to doubt it. Politically it's a no-brainer. And it must be done if America is to have a future.

2. Protecting American working-class wages and working conditions by controlling and managing immigration.

If ever there was a doubt that this needed to be a major part of a conservative agenda going forward, it's gone now, considering what Biden and his handlers have done to our southern border. Of course, in the aftermath of the destruction the Chinese COVID-19 virus has wrought upon our economy, we're even less capable of accommodating the kind of mass immigration for political purposes the Democrats are bent upon inflicting on us. So resisting that is a bedrock agenda item for which Americans of virtually every ethnic and demographic stripe would reward the GOP.

3. Keeping our economy open for entrepreneurship and small business growth by restricting, if not breaking up, oligopolistic companies like Walmart, Amazon, and Google.

This one is also quite easy, as it brings together both the MAGA conservative crowd and what members of the Bernie Sanders fan club are willing to adjust their approach to dealing with a problem they're accurate in recognizing.

America is too much an oligarchy, and particularly in the tech space. Big Tech is homogenous, radical, largely anti-American, and viciously anti-competitive. The Bernie Bros, who are wrong in virtually every particular as to solutions, nevertheless aren't wrong in recognizing the problem; many of them have had it in their crosshairs since Occupy Wall Street. They just don't know how to fix it. But the Right, who can draw upon the historical experience of Teddy Roosevelt and his contemporaries, does.

Make an issue of it, and don't back down when Big Tech acts as the entrenched special interest it has become.

4. Rolling back the political and legal corruption of the Left, which has created a dual-track legal system for elites and common Americans.

Everyone knows this is a problem. Everyone hates that this is a problem. This is a problem that deeply offends everyone who doesn't benefit from it, which is virtually everyone.

Trump didn't press on this button remotely as hard as he should have. He knew lots of people who benefited from their elite status when it came to privilege and favorable treatment from the political, judicial, and media/opinion establishments, but while he touched upon the subject, he largely left it alone outside of his fights to preserve himself against the abuses of the systemically corrupt in Washington. Trump wasted two and a half years defeating the lie that he was essentially a Russian agent running a Manchurian candidacy because members of the corrupt cabal at the center of our abusive political elite chose to slander him thus.

And now Joe Biden is president despite clear evidence he and his family members have run a long-standing pay-for-play operation the Clintons would be proud of, including selling out American interests to China.

There is no better time for the GOP to stand for one legal and political system, one standard applying to all, and no more cultural and political elites not accountable to the American people.

5. Breaking the power of American elites to corrupt and degrade our cultural institutions with things like wokeism, cancel culture, and Critical Race Theory, and bringing America back as a country based on Judeo-Christian values.

When Reagan established the three-legged stool, there were detractors on the Right who didn't like the social-conservatism piece much. They thought the pro-life argument was preachy and tedious, and they didn't want to talk about God. They believed, and spread, the lie that if the GOP married itself to the Religious Right it would never win elections.

That was a colossal mistake.

Not so much because the Religious Right commanded the allegiance of a majority of the American people, but because when those social moderates abstained from the culture wars, and the Christian crowd was routed out of bedrooms, classrooms, and television rooms, the Left never recognized the limits the moderates expected. The culture war devolved from birth control to no-fault divorce to gay marriage to this insane trans movement, and now we're on the cusp of normalizing pedophilia. And the definition of racism is now literally whatever the Left thinks will benefit it in the next election cycle.

That's what you get when you refuse to fight in the culture. Trump gets credit for recognizing this and being willing to fight not on the Christian conservative side so much as that of the traditional American value set. It's an entirely majority stance, one that a decade ago would have been seen as soft to the point of being left-of-center, but it's entirely defensible.

The line is Martin Luther King Jr.'s color-blind society. It's the simple formulation that a man who thinks he's a woman has the same problem as a man who thinks he's Napoleon. It's the understanding that you can be and do whatever you want so long as it doesn't impinge on the same freedom enjoyed by others. It's the insistence that your desire to exchange ideas even on controversial topics does not make you untouchable and should not destroy your livelihood or social acceptability. And it's the recognition that for whatever flaws America is a beautiful, righteous, moral place founded on the best principles, and our imperfections do not invalidate our experience.

Revivalism carries with it a bit of a religious context. Periodically in America there have been religious revivals; in fact historically we're as overdue for one as we are for a new political era. In fact, we're the least religious country we've ever been. It might even seem risky to use a word that carries a hint of religion as descriptive of a movement seeking to build a lasting American majority.

But that's OK. Because we're not asking for a return to Puritanism, and we're not trying to impose the old-time religion here. You certainly don't have to memorize Leviticus to be a revivalist in the context of this book's discussion.

All we're saying is that America was founded on the moral principles of Judaism and Christianity, which are the founding principles of Western civilization, and even as a fairly secular country as we now are, it's a good idea to keep those values as the basis of our society.

Especially since the Left has shown us the alternative. Would you rather have the Golden Rule or Cancel Culture? Would you like to live according to the Ten Commandments or Ibram X. Kendi's crackpot demands for "antiracist" recriminations? The Gospels or the transgender agenda?

All this time we've been told that Christianity is a millstone around the Right's political neck. Compared to what the Left is slinging, Billy Graham is a breath of fresh air.

Proof of the utter bald-faced stupidity of the American Left is that they've transformed their list of cultural enemies from a reasonably well-marginalized Religious Right to something so expansive that it includes Joe Rogan and maybe even Whoopi Goldberg.

To take or ally with a traditional American cultural position now can simply mean you're slightly to the right of Mao Zedong. It takes a pretty stout level of incompetence for the Left to unify this many people against them.

The American people understand each of the five principles above. They will make a majority. Each of them was present in Trumpian politics, though they were never presented holistically as the essence of his political doctrine.

And thankfully, they are not dependent on Trump's presence on the ballot. Any Republican with credibility to espouse them can win with them. Ron DeSantis is a pretty good example.

Take education, which is destined to be one of the most significantly changed sectors of the American economy as the current New Deal/Post-War/Information Age era gives way to the next. We saw a preview of the changes to come in technicolor in the 2021 Virginia gubernatorial election, when overreach by the unions and educational establishment ran badly afoul of the will of the marketplace. Even after Virginia, the teachers' unions and the Left's educational establishment continued attempting to shut schools down, force kids to take the jab, and impose mask mandates. It's utter insanity, and parents are furious.

The Democrats have always controlled the narrative on education. This is partly due to the fact almost everybody working in education is a Democrat, and Democrats control all the key institutions that drive that system, at least in the public sector. It's also partly due to the fact that Republicans have been completely passive on the educational issue for most of the last half-century.

Those colleges pumping out anti-American leftist indoctrination? Don't forget that the funding which fuels that parade of horribles came in many or most cases thanks to Republican governors and state legislatures, or Republican alumni and donors. Nobody bothered to check on what our overfed higher ed institutions were doing with all that cash. If they had, they'd have recoiled in horror, because the cancer billowing out of the universities has poisoned K-12 education all across the country.

This happened, and people didn't notice it much. Not until the cocktail of climate change lunacy, Critical Race Theory, intersectional feminism, and transgenderism hit a critical mass and began coagulating into the religion of woke, and kids barely out of diapers began reciting it. Even then, lots of parents didn't realize the source.

Not until COVID.

Then the teacher unions bullied the wimps and collaborators on school boards into shuttering the schools and holding classes via Zoom, thus drafting parents across the country into duty as proctors for their kids' education. That was one of the greatest tactical mistakes in American political history, for it had three intensely negative effects on the public education establishment.

First, parents were extremely put out over the sudden inconvenience of not having somebody taking care of their kids while they went off to work.

Second, those parents, once they got accustomed to essentially homeschooling their kids, in many cases realized it was doable. Homeschooling as a segment of the education market grew from 5 percent to 11 percent in only one year, and a giant chunk of the population now reports in surveys that homeschooling or other educational alternatives is an acceptable option.

And third, those parents drafted into duty as proctors got a firsthand look at what was being taught to their kids—and they didn't like it at all.

School board meetings around the country have turned into circuses because the parents are now showing up and demanding better. They have no use for the idiotic mask mandates school systems want to impose on kids not at serious risk for symptomatic COVID, and they have zero interest in Critical Race Theory or transgenderism.

This has been true all over the country, but it so happens that its epicenter is Virginia, and Loudoun County, Virginia, in particular. There, a ninth-grader was raped by a boy in a dress in a girls' bathroom. But the school district refused to acknowledge the incident, despite an ongoing criminal prosecution that ultimately resulted in a conviction and sentence. And the girl's father, a middle-aged plumber named Scott Smith, raised hell with the school board over their refusal to properly respond to the incident.

It was a critical point in American politics that needed to be managed well by the party in charge—both in Virginia and nationally.

The Democrats have absolutely failed. They literally couldn't have flubbed this any worse.

The Biden administration, in response to the Loudoun County incident, had the National School Boards Association send them a letter demanding that the Justice Department sic the FBI on unruly parents voicing their opposition to the misrule of public education by the current Powers That Be, and with lightning speed Attorney General Merrick Garland said he'd do just that.

The resulting uproar was so loud that in several states the state school board associations repudiated the letter. In Ohio, the state association canceled its NSBA membership. Parents around the country are seeing blood over the suggestion that exercising their First Amendment rights brands them as "domestic terrorists."

And in Virginia, McAuliffe traipsed around the state shilling for the school boards and teacher unions, which the public didn't notice until he committed a monstrous gaffe at a debate with Youngkin.

"I'm not going to let parents come into schools and actually take books out and make their own decisions," he said. "I don't think parents should be telling schools what they should teach."

That statement turbocharged Youngkin's campaign, and it ultimately led to his victory. Not only did Youngkin catch McAuliffe and knock him out in the gubernatorial race by focusing on the insanity of the educational establishment and emphasizing parents' rights in the schooling of their kids, but the GOP won the other two statewide races plus a majority in the state House of Delegates.

But the Democrat Party didn't walk anything back, even in the face of the Virginia results. In fact, they've been leaning in.

Garland was utterly defiant in a disastrous appearance before a House committee in fall 2021, refusing to admit a mistake in insulting activist public school parents despite withering criticism from Republican congressmen on the issue. And former President Barack

Obama locked in the Democrats' position on parental influence in public schools by denying it's even an issue.

"We don't have time to be wasting on these phony trumped-up culture wars, this fake outrage that right-wing media peddles to juice their ratings," said Obama. "Instead of stoking anger aimed at school boards and administrators, who are just trying to keep our kids safe…[W]e should be making it easier for teachers and schools to give our kids the world-class education they deserve, and to do so safely while they are in the classrooms."

He said that one day before the skirt-wearing rapist was sentenced and two days before the students of Loudoun County staged a mass walkout to protest the system's woke tyranny. It seems the outrage is a lot less fake than Obama's pre-White House *curriculum vitae*.

And then Youngkin led the GOP tsunami in the statewide Virginia elections, with education as the forefront issue in the campaign.

The 2022 midterms, not to mention the statewide elections, will almost assuredly be more of the same. The real question is how far the public is willing to go and how fast. If the educational Left were smart and humble, they would be scrambling to get in front of the issue and embrace reforms.

But they aren't, and the possibility of a sea change is now very much on the table.

You'll have lots of Republicans running on money-follows-the-student school choice policies, promoting homeschools, private schools, microschools, learning pods, and all kinds of alternatives and promising to fight to fuel them with educational savings accounts, refundable tax breaks, and the like.

And winning on those issues. Because the Democrats are in abject thrall to those teacher unions, and Randi Weingarten and Lily Eskelsen García, who respectively run the American Federation of Teachers and the National Education Association, are hardly going to agree to allow Democrat candidates to moderate their positions in opposition to aggressive school choice measures. And they're certainly not going to allow their candidates to turn against transgenderism or Critical Race Theory.

It's worse. You may have heard about an obnoxious *Washington Post* op-ed by Jack Schneider, a professor in the University of Massachusetts Lowell education department, and left-wing journalist Jennifer Berkshire, which ran right after the Virginia elections and vigorously denied that parents have the right to determine the course of their children's education. That only heated up this controversy. It was a terrific exposition of the public education complex's hostile, elitist mindset.

They're not going to give up control without a fight. The problem is the battlefield is becoming very unfriendly to them.

They're going to lose the fight. If they don't back down, they're going to lose it in the midterms and all the state and local races down the ballot. And when the Democrats take a hard spanking from the public, with the insanity and incompetence of the education establishment as a front-and-center issue that brings suburban moms home to the GOP from their anti-Trump vacation in 2018 and 2020, it's entirely likely that Weingarten and Garcia and some of the other education establishment figures out there will begin taking fire as scapegoats for the Democrats' losses.

Consider what happens if Democrat politicians start seeing the teacher unions as net liabilities in election campaigns.

They can't abandon those unions, obviously. The teacher unions funnel far too much money into the Democrat Party for them to go cold turkey. But if a few vulnerable "centrists" here and there who survive what's coming in 2022 (or, like Joe Manchin and Kyrsten Sinema, come up for reelection in 2024) begin peeling off in order to save themselves and agree to work with Republicans on expanded school choice, well...

It could be Randi, bar the door.

Public policy is the only thing preventing the creation of a true educational marketplace. Nothing about public education really serves the needs of parents and kids anymore, and polls show it. The market is already moving toward diversity in educational methods and institutions. The minute funding is freed up for those alternatives, they're going to explode, and they'll do so at traditional government schools' expense.

There's an old saw about how someone goes broke: a little at a time and then all at once. We're beginning to see how that might happen to the public-school mafia. The cascade of policy implications that is just on the horizon is long overdue.

Higher education is due for a massive upheaval as well, and it's really just a matter of time before three things begin to metastasize as our next era begins, all three of which are necessary and healthy—if more than a bit disconcerting for many of those immediately affected.

First, you're going to see bankruptcies and closings of institutions of higher education. This is inevitable when college enrollment begins to shrink as is currently the case over the course of the past decade. The arrogance and intersectional tribalism of the modern rulers of the academy have directly produced this decline, but with fewer customers comes a smaller pot of revenue to dip from.

HigherEdDive.com has been tracking the closings of colleges and universities since 2016 with a running list, and as of December 2021 the tally is up to seventy-two in more than two dozen states. These are mostly small, private liberal arts colleges—Burlington College in Vermont, Trinity Lutheran College in Washington state, MacMurray College in Illinois, and Shepherd College in California among them—but they're the leading elements of a reorganization to come. Institutions of higher education have let their costs run wild by investing far too heavily in administration and too little in faculty, and they've let tuition inflation price them beyond the willingness to pay of many marginal, and marginally interested, students.

And so the bull market in higher ed is giving way to a bear market that is going to claim not just the small, tuition-dependent players with little endowment but a few "name" institutions as well.

Second, there will be disruption in the higher education market, and the obvious sector of that market poised for growth will be institutions that serve a conservative counterculture.

Liberty University and Hillsdale College, which have obdurately resisted the intrusion of critical theory and woke activism on their campuses, are thriving. While there are few new entries into the market, one which was announced in the fall of 2021, the University of Austin, promises an unapologetic commitment to free expression and open scholarship.

And with online education expanding rapidly—partially out of necessity as traditional colleges and universities pander to Branch Covidian faculty who refuse to do their jobs—it's inevitable that the University of Phoenix/Southern New Hampshire University model will evolve to replace most institutions.

It's also only a matter of time before Republicans in state legislatures begin paring back the outrageous budgets and wasteful administrative infrastructure extant on state college and university campuses, not to mention grilling those administrators about the lack of free speech and the open viewpoint discrimination within their institutions. There is already more than a seed of public approval for "de-wokifying" the ivory tower, and when GOP politicians, perhaps of a revivalist bent, begin messaging their intention to use the purse strings to force public higher education institutions in red states to give up their status as indoctrination centers, it's going to play well with the voters.

In February 2022 the Wyoming state senate voted to advance a budget amendment that defunded the University of Wyoming's Gender and Women's Studies department. That was the first of what are likely to be many intrusions by the people's representatives into the enemy's camp, and those are overdue.

And the public in Wyoming loved it. Because people are beginning to notice who's on those campuses in those suspect departments.

There are so many examples. On every campus is the professor who spends too much of his time on Twitter posting utterly offensive, fascistic, anti-American, and deliciously boorish hot takes, and by now these people are relatively well known. If these loons are made the poster children for State U, and if State U's administrators are made to sing for their suppers in front of the state Senate Finance or House Appropriations Committee, it'll get uncomfortable.

Why? Because it'll inevitably go like this. Asked about Professor McRanty's long train of wacko leftist statements, President Dodger will claim he has to defend the professor because of "academic freedom." Then comes the response that State U ranks terribly in the Foundation for Individual Rights in Education's free speech survey, along with three examples of students and/or faculty being persecuted, censored, expelled, or otherwise mistreated based on speech much less out of the mainstream than that of Professor McRanty.

It's a guarantee that President Dodger at State U has never been thus called on the carpet and will not possess the rhetorical skill to defuse that bomb. All it'll take is enough Republicans truly willing to see woke public universities who are trapping students in debt to chase degrees that aren't worth their cost while indoctrinating their victims into radical ideologies as what they are, and the whole conversation turns into a question of, "Why should my constituents pay for this?"

Do we have such Republicans now? Not enough. But they're coming. There are more of them in every election cycle.

The disruption of the current higher ed model will come from above, as the politics turns on it, and below, as alternative institutions and low-cost online entries to the market redefine what a "good" college is.

James Piereson, who created the formulations of American political eras so much of this book's analysis rests on, suggests a number of things necessary to reforming higher education back into an institution worth applying resources to. It would be a good idea, particularly for Republican policymakers and donors interested in applying some pressure along those lines, to turn these into firm demands:

> "A few preferred reforms in higher education... would include these high on the list: (1) Shelve the utopian idea that every young person attend college, and along with it the dubious claim that the nation's prosperity depends on universal college attendance. (2) Terminate nearly all Ph.D. programs in the humanities and most of them in the social sciences. (3) Replace them with postgraduate programs in the liberal arts that allow students to earn graduate degrees based upon teaching rather than research and permit them to master broad fields that cross existing disciplinary boundaries. (4) Reverse the expansion of administrative layers, especially offices and programs created to satisfy campus pressure groups. (5) Bring back general education requirements and core curricula to ensure that every undergraduate student is exposed to the important ideas in the humanities and sciences that have shaped our civilization."

The higher education bubble, so often discussed within academia and without, is going to break. When it does it's a wonderful opportunity for revivalists to insure that what remains is forced to serve the entire public, not just the parochial needs of a coddled and eccentric leftist elite. After all, when student debt in America is well more than $1 trillion, and much of it simply can't be paid off given the often-worthless degrees that debt financed, and when the Democrat Party continues raising the issue as one of their new planned public policy giveaways, there is a perfect environment to call that bluff.

It's said that political parties are really just coalitions of various interest groups, which in one sense is less true than it used to be. Most die-hard Democrats and Republicans will tell you they're party members not because of a particular spot at the trough they wish to dip their snouts but because the Democrat or Republican ideological platforms most accurately reflect their tastes.

That's probably truer of Republicans, or better put some Republicans, than Democrats—only for the reason that the GOP is generally more resistant to identity politics than is the party of Jackson and Jefferson...and Jackson and Sharpton. That might be changing, though, since straight white people who work in the private sector and pay taxes have more and more begun to regard themselves as an identity group of their own.

On the Democrat side, it's really all identity politics these days—pandering to identity groups is basically all they do. That pandering is what gave us the demand for student loan relief, made most prominently by noted Communist Bernie Sanders and academic affirmative action fraud Liz Warren, to spend some $1 trillion or more on forgiveness of college loans so many former college students just can't pay.

As such, the victims of American academia operate as both an identity group, indoctrinated as they've been to function as social justice warriors, and an interest group looking for free stuff from the government. And Sanders and Warren, and the rest of the denizens of the Democrats' political clown car, can't pander quickly enough to them on both fronts.

So we now have a scramble to find a "workable" delivery of free stuff to people who were intelligent enough to get into a college but not wise enough to train for a suitably remunerative career that can pay off their student loans. And when less mondaine types like Dan Crenshaw object, as the Texas congressman did on the basis that it's immoral to ask the two-thirds of the public who didn't graduate from college and generally make less than those who did to pay for free stuff for their betters with nothing to show in return, we must castigate them for their deficiency of woke.

Therefore, here is a simple solution to this problem—tax university endowments to pay for student debt relief.

As of fiscal year 2015, there was some $547 billion tied up in university endowments in the United States. Harvard, Yale, and Princeton alone accounted for $86 billion of that figure. Those institutions are essentially hedge funds with a school attached. As our Democrat friends like to tout a top tax rate of 90 percent as a wonderful tool in producing a "level" society such as existed in America in the 1940s and 1950s, let's just apply that to the endowments—particularly of the schools that boast $1 billion or more in the vault—and use the proceeds to pay off those who were cheated out of their American dream.

We all love wealth taxes these days, right?

That's only fair, no? It's sure worth it to fund a half-billion dollars of student debt relief. That would lower the burden on every student loan in America by one-third or so. But we wouldn't do that, because we'd want to make sure the wokest, brokest graduates got more relief than the ones with means. That's how we can make this *extremely* fair.

And in order to ensure that this debt relief isn't just a Band-Aid on a gunshot wound, we'll need to continue taxing those billion-plus endowments at a 90 percent rate—doing so would ensure we're not just providing a one-time delivery of free stuff but an ongoing program of reparations to the disposable income-challenged among us.

You say this isn't a workable plan? You say that it's unconstitutional to rob the university endowments and economic fantasy to believe people will continue donating to those endowments when, instead of holding tax-free status as charitable contributions they would then be taxed at 90 percent?

The obvious and correct response is that you're a bigot who hates poor people. After all, as Harvard law professor Ronald Sullivan said, after he was fired as a university dean for having taken Harvey Weinstein on as a client, "Unchecked emotion has replaced thoughtful reasoning on campus. Feelings are no longer subjected to evidence, analysis or empirical defense. Angry demands, rather than rigorous arguments, now appear to guide university policy."

Sullivan is obviously an anti-#MeToo Neanderthal, because he lacks an appreciation for unchecked emotion as a policy motivation. His brand of analysis has no place in the Democrat Party of our brave new modern age, and neither does yours if you don't like our plan to help the poor victims of our academic elites.

Attacking multibillion-dollar university endowments using alterations of the tax code is a very good way to reel in the destructive influence of elite institutions that have ceased serving their original purpose—building the best American cultural, intellectual, business, and governmental leaders possible through arming them with an understanding and appreciation of that which made this country. Instead they're building destructive wreckers of our civilization who believe we're constructed out of sin and iniquity and must be fundamentally transformed along Marxist lines.

We shouldn't pay for it. In fact, we should punish it. We need politicians and activists willing to step into the fight and force negative economic consequences on the people who broke higher ed.

Because to do so at least gives us a shot at preserving our culture against the aggressions coming out of those institutions.

CHAPTER 16

What a Revivalist America Looks Like

Now that we've established the historical framework, justification, and necessity for a new revivalist politics built on the foundations of what has worked for conservatism, how does revivalism look in practice? It turns out there are lots of examples to be found across America as it is; all we're really doing here is compiling them into a playbook.

I offer four main tenets on which to build the movement. They are:

> First, civilization is meant to make it easier to earn a living than steal one, which requires just enough government to accomplish that purpose and no more. As soon as you introduce too much government, you have given the pillagers an easier road to plunder than they could ever have through violence.

And we have far, far too much government.

Our people know that we've lost our way. We know that the nonstop COVID fear porn and never-ending inflationary government giveaways are merely symptoms of the real disease; we are both oppressed by and dependent upon the State, and it has made us less as people.

Government, in the American model we seek to revive, is meant to be merely a tool to insure liberty and security from villains and enemies.

As such, Revivalism states a specific goal of making the freest possible America for law-abiding citizens. We're for few laws, vigorously enforced.

> Second, our government is not and should never be seen as representative of the people. Rather, it is representative of the interests who have access to government. Some of those interests are popular, but most are not. President Eisenhower's famous warning about the corruption inherent in the formation of the military-industrial complex was more prescient than he could have ever realized; far from limiting that complex's scope, we've seen conservatism embrace it, leading to terrible effect in Afghanistan and Iraq, and worse, the military-industrial complex has metastasized and spread. We now have a medical-governmental complex and a media-political complex that are every bit as corrosive as the defense lobby ever was.

Therefore the State must be limited in its powers, and the Revivalist project is to pursue every avenue possible to make it irrelevant, not to give it more influence over our lives.

This is hard stuff, of course, because what it requires is the building of communities through engagement and activism. It requires service to one's fellow man. It requires nurturing and championing the civil society—churches, men's clubs, labor unions, bowling leagues, potluck dinners, and the rest.

You've undoubtedly noticed the diminution of these things. The gay and trans lobbies, among others, have destroyed the joy in forming and growing them, and now our political elite demonizes them as "super-spreaders" of the virus. Rather, they want us on our phones living our lives on social media that they control.

Revivalists demand a return of community, and we demand that government get the hell out of our way.

> Third, politics is downstream from culture, but politics has built a boat with a powerful motor. Further, politics corrodes everything it touches, and it has corroded our culture almost completely.

As culture is the foundation of society, it must be protected from those who would use it to tear us apart. Without winning that war, which conservatism sadly has never invested in doing, all will eventually be lost.

Revivalism demands that the Right engage in defending American culture, which we all recognize when we see it, specifically to elevate it beyond the touch of politics.

What does that mean? It means producing cultural content with a level of activity at least that of the Left, it means reviving beauty in the arts, and it means breaking and replacing those cultural institutions that have so clearly failed us.

Schools. Universities. Hollywood. Corporate media. Professional sports, if it won't get the message.

Start locally and move up from there. Let's write novels and plays. Let's be funny again. Let's never be canceled. And let's show the world that freedom is a lot more fun than wokeness.

And let's spare no mercy for the woke. Let's lustily subject them to all the ridicule, all the loud rejections, all the withering scorn we can summon up. Conservatism is not up to the challenge of wokeness, but revivalism is.

Even James Carville says that "wokeness is a problem," and yet the conservative movement is currently a hodgepodge of caution, cowardice, and quiet acceptance of all the key elements of wokeness. Some conservatives are, like collaborators with the SS in Nazi-occupied Europe, turning on their ideological brethren in the hope they might be eaten last. Others have modulated their speech in hopes of avoiding notice. Virtually none have been courageous enough to stand up to the woke mobs.

Revivalism says it's not good enough to silently hope that the woke fever will burn itself out. Revivalism brings the torch and the gasoline and demands the woke submit to an examination along the lines of their own standards. Revivalism insists that free speech, and the liberty to peacefully disagree without undue intimidation, return with a vengeance. Elon Musk might not be a revivalist in every respect, but his purchase of Twitter was one of the better examples of revivalism you'll ever see. And the Left's reaction, comedy gold as it's been, shows perfectly that *they can't handle a loss like this.*

> Finally, prosperity, or access to it, must be shared by all or it is illusory. The Revivalist project seeks to reopen the American and global economies to competition by independents and startups and to fight back against oligopolistic corporations. It's a very capitalist but anti-corporate philosophy.

We can defend low tax rates for billionaires on a philosophical basis all day long, but frankly it's a loser of an idea to defend Mark Zuckerberg or Jeff Bezos's income. Conservatives have done that, and what has it gotten them? The occasional think-tank donations with strings attached to push for open borders and cheap labor? Section 230 protection allowing them to play censor without consequences? Open monopolistic abuses bought-up Republican politicians are busy defending? Lucrative consulting contracts for Frank Luntz from the Sacklers of killer-opioid fame?

Conservatives have let themselves be defined as defenders of America's worst actors. Our elites make the robber barons of old look like angels, and they're all Democrats now anyway.

Revivalism offers a fresh start and a chance to stand with the American people against those elites who have foisted this dystopian 21st century upon us. Conservatism's key mantra, the one William F. Buckley so famously offered of standing athwart history, yelling "Stop," is and has always been wrong. The project isn't to stop history, it's to grab it by the throat and bend it in the direction we want.

This book isn't offering a complete policy program. It's only the first book in the revivalist series, and there is much more to come. In fact, the next book to come will, barring something unforeseen, be *The Revivalist Agenda*. So consider this just an appetizer with the entrée to come in the fall of 2022.

In 2009 a pilot voucher program was set up to offer "scholarships" (vouchers) to some 1,700 public school students in the District of Columbia so they could attend the private schools of their choice. The program cost just $15 million, which came out to $7,500 per student.

Washington, DC, spends about $15,000 per student on public schools.

There were four applicants for every one scholarship given.

By all measures the program was a success. It might have been the only thing the Bush administration did with education that actually succeeded.

Of course, the teachers' unions hate vouchers. They consider them to be the death of public education, and they say so all the time. They're not interested in competition in the least because they know what would happen if public schools dominated by the teachers' unions were ever subjected to the judgment of the marketplace.

The teachers' unions gave $56 million to political candidates in the 2008 election cycle. Ninety-six percent of that cash went to Democrat candidates.

Payment was made for those contributions when Barack Obama killed the DC voucher program in early 2009, attempting to murder school choice in its crib. An old Obama campaign quote on the issue is haunting: "Let's see if it [the voucher program] works," he said. "And if it does, whatever my preconceptions, you do what's best for the kids."

Well, that was a lie.

After the DC voucher program was spiked by the Obama administration—not only did the funding for the program get pulled amid a $3.6 trillion federal budget, but Obama education secretary Arne Duncan, who used to run the school system in Chicago Obama wouldn't send his own daughters to attend classes in, did away with the program a year early—a Department of Education report on the performance of the voucher program showed that it resulted in significant improvement in the academic performance of the participating children.

Obama had said he was willing to keep an open mind and stick to what works on education—and presented with something of clear value that did but didn't conform to his ideology and political alliances, he killed it. In the process he did damage to 1,700 families—90 percent black, 9 percent Hispanic—in the nation's capital.

You can't get a better example than this to show who today's Democrats are—heartless ideologues who couldn't care less about individual freedom and opportunity, who will reward political cronies and contributors even at the expense of the weak and defenseless.

The Republican Party ought to resurrect, and broaden, the DC voucher program. Not with congressional funding but with private donations. It ought to be done as an example of what can be done by the civil society without government getting involved.

Set up a private charity, hold fundraising events, put the arm on corporate lobbyists and the like, and fund not just private school but open-ended educational expenses, including homeschooling and other options, for all the poor families in Washington, DC, who want to escape the terrible government schools there. Show you're serious about doing something to reach out to the black community by making a gesture on behalf of the 1,700 minority kids—not the same kids, obviously, but kids from the same circumstances—that Obama consigned to some of the worst public schools in America and then shame the Democrats for not participating.

This isn't a national initiative. You'd need federal money to expand it all over, and you're going to need the House, Senate, and White House to pull that off. Maybe that can happen by January 2025; it isn't a bad bet that it will. But this project in DC could be done right now.

Figure your educational aid to these kids would amount to $10,000 apiece, thanks to Biden's inflation, and if the program you'll build is of the same size as the DC voucher program, it'll have to service 1,700 kids. That comes to $17 million.

There are more than 250 Republican members of Congress (House and Senate), but we'll just use 250 as a round number. Raising $17 million if all of them were to get behind the program would require $68,000 or so from each. These guys do that in one dinner on a good night; and raising money for a private charity to fund a free-market DC education program wouldn't be restricted by campaign fundraising limits. Seems like this would be a very easy thing to fix, and it would be a very media-friendly project. It would also be a good opportunity to cross party lines as well; I have a hard time thinking that all these well-heeled, kindhearted leftists I hear so much about wouldn't be willing to kick in a few thousand bucks to help out poor minority school kids in Washington.

You have to demonstrate that there is a better way to do things than the command-and-control method the New Deal/Great Society/Hard Left consensus of this dying third era in American politics has employed. Making an effort to do that literally in the belly of the beast by starting a privately funded program to break the hold of the Left's educational establishment in the most uniformly Democrat population in America would be such a bold strike at their hearts as to shock the world. Think of it as a Doolittle raid on the education-failure complex.

Randi Weingarten might well stroke out. What she'd definitely do is make some massive PR mistakes that would turn even more parents against the Left's education monopoly.

Out-of-the-box politics, perhaps in a bit more refined way than what Trump practiced, is key to blowing up what remains of the Third Era establishment. We need a sea change in how Republican politicians operate. An example from December of 2021, courtesy of one of the party's more recognizable revivalists, sheds some light on what that looks like.

Sen. Ted Cruz was, like most other Republicans in Washington, incensed over the Biden administration's inexplicable policy toward oil pipelines. Namely, Biden couldn't find an oil pipeline in North America he didn't despise and wasn't actively engaged in trying to shut down. He killed the Keystone XL pipeline on the first day of his new administration with Executive Order 13990. With the stroke of his pen that day, Biden canceled a project that would have boosted US gross domestic product by more than $3 billion, carried 830,000 barrels of oil daily from Canada to the United States, and directly and indirectly provided up to 26,000 jobs—11,000 of which were instantly lost. Amazingly enough, Biden even, after months of vacillating, came out against the EastMed Pipeline, which would carry natural gas from the newly discovered offshore finds in Israel to Greece and on into Europe.

Throughout 2021 news leaked about other pipeline projects the Biden administration didn't kill but entertained advocacy over destroying from the environmentalist Left. Those conversations continued to metastasize while oil and gas exploration and production dropped off throughout the year. America began 2021 as a net energy exporter and ended it with Biden begging OPEC to increase production as Canada seethed. In November 2021 the news broke that Biden was mulling the death of the Line 5 pipeline from Canada through Wisconsin and Michigan. Line 5 wasn't shut down, but it was clear the momentum on domestic energy, including the infrastructure to facilitate it, was negative.

Meanwhile, the Biden administration dropped its opposition to Nord Stream 2, the oil pipeline from Russia into northern Europe via the Baltic Sea floor—a policy choice that made little sense under any theory of environmentalism or geopolitics.

Cruz demanded a vote in the Senate on Nord Stream 2. Democrat Senate majority leader Chuck Schumer said no. So Cruz put holds on several State Department nominees of Biden's, gumming up the administration's appointments of ambassadors and driving the White House crazy.

Finally, under pressure from the administration, Schumer relented and agreed to give Cruz his vote.

What Cruz did is essentially what Jesse Jackson and Al Sharpton have made entire careers on. It's dirty, dishonest, and dishonorable, but it's absolutely appropriate to the times and very often effective, and given the utter and total bad faith of today's Democrat Party, they 100 percent deserve to have it done to them.

Placing holds on those nominees serves no particular interest of Ted Cruz. Without looking at the individuals involved, it's a good guess none of them are any good—they're almost assuredly ruling-elite twits with Ivy League pedigrees thoroughly incapable of independent or creative thought, and almost assuredly they're all angling to spend a few years in cushy Foggy Bottom sinecures on their way to even cushier sinecures with rent-seeking corporations, DC law firms, or federal contractors. America is no better or worse off with any of them in or out of office.

Would we be well served if none of these people could get jobs in the federal government? Yes. Certainly. But these people, or others just like them, will get those jobs, at least until January of 2025. Nothing can be done about that.

And Cruz knew it.

He didn't care about these people. Or at least, he didn't care about most of them.

Putting holds on them was an aggressive, hostile, unwarranted, and unproductive thing to do.

Just like recruiting an army of loudmouthed morons in yellow T-shirts to gather outside of a corporate headquarters and shout offensive accusations of racism is an aggressive, hostile, unwarranted, and unproductive thing to do.

But that antisocial behavior becomes its own currency when you're willing to trade the cessation of it for something of value—and when the party at whom it's aimed is willing to supply that consideration.

For Jesse Jackson, the take was, among other items in a long career of grifting, a beer distributorship. For Al Sharpton, it's been all kinds of things. These guys recognized that threatening white-boy corporate CEOs with bad publicity surrounding a racism beef could be an excellent business model—far more than dry cleaning or greengrocery, for example—and played it to the hilt. They're the ultimate rejection of everything Booker T. Washington preached about, but Booker T. is so out of fashion for the current "civil rights" crowd, they barely know anything about him.

Cruz was simply using what leverage he had against Schumer and Biden. Since it matters a whole lot more to them which of their DC elite leftist friends get State Department jobs than it does to Ted Cruz, maybe they'd be willing to trade something that Cruz wants as ransom for those nominees.

Of course, Schumer and Biden damned sure ought to share Cruz's position on Nord Stream 2. Especially given all the public Russophobia in which they've traded since Hillary Clinton's crooked spinmeisters brewed up the Trump-Russia hoax in 2016. That they don't share that position is suspicious enough. That Schumer didn't take Cruz's deal is even more suspicious.

Why wouldn't you impose Nord Stream 2 sanctions on Russia? Forget about the fact Russia is a bad actor seeking to become the hegemon of Europe, and the proceeds from that pipeline would inevitably fuel Putin's aims, those sanctions are simply smart negotiation. America is in the natural gas business, and the European market is one of the most lucrative in the world for it. You have to be an idiot or a traitor not to at least put Nord Stream 2 sanctions on the table as something Putin has to bargain his way out of.

When Cruz got his vote, it turned out that fifty-five senators, including five Democrats, were in favor of imposing Nord Stream 2 sanctions. Which is not to say that the bill passed—it didn't.

It was filibustered. By Chuck Schumer. At the same time Schumer was trying to kill the filibuster so he could pass an abjectly insane federal elections bill that would outlaw voter ID and facilitate ballot harvesting and letting illegal immigrants vote.

Chuck Schumer has never looked more like a schmuck than he did that day in January of 2022. You probably didn't hear a whole lot about that story, which is too bad. The GOP didn't message it as well as it should have. But we can work on that problem if we can keep a steady stream of sick burns like this one was.

Voluntarily surrendering on those sanctions, and then opposing their reimposition when Republicans ask for it, makes for interesting conversations about just how corrupted and compromised the leaders of the Democrat Party really are where it comes to Russia. Particularly given the hoax Durham's filings continue to document.

And particularly given that Putin invaded Ukraine after months of inaction as Republicans demanded a renewal of Nord Stream 2 sanctions. Nobody has excoriated Chuck the Schmuck for encouraging Putin to kill thousands of Ukrainians by employing that filibuster, which just means we need some more revivalists in the Senate willing to make that case, loudly.

Like Schumer did when he pushed that "Bush lied; people died" stuff in 2005 and 2006 after voting for the Iraq War.

If you're one of these revivalist Republicans looking to run for the county commission, state representative, school board, or Congress, tactics and maneuvers like the one Cruz managed with Nord Stream 2 are the kind of thing you had better grasp and demonstrate proficiency in.

For far too long, nice, prudent people naive enough to think the strength of their convictions, their basic competence, and their honest will to do good things would make them successful have filled up the Republican primary ballots, and very few of them understood what winning was or how the sausage gets made. And increasingly as the Hard Left has swallowed up the well-meaning liberals and taken control of the Democrat Party, those naive Republicans have been humiliated every time they've attempted "win-win" negotiations with people who don't share their values or ethics.

All negotiations with the likes of Biden or Schumer are hostile. Today's Democrat political elite are enemies. They're hostile not just to their political opponents but to American values and ideals in general. There can be no "win-win" with them, only "win-lose."

It's a zero-sum game.

And in a hostile negotiation, the way to win is to make things so uncomfortable for the other guy that he breaks.

Pressure. Constant pressure.

Jesse Jackson never brought a single thing of value to the table in any of his various extortion schemes. He never produced a widget, jot, or tittle. But he knew pressure, and he knew its use.

If you don't know how to apply it, or if you don't have the sand to bring it to bear, then go home. You won't survive out there.

Because the age of political consensus in America is over. And if the GOP is to be worthy of the power the public is clearly willing to restore to it, the party's politicians had better act accordingly.

Here's an example of that which involves education and Critical Race Theory. Old-fashioned conservatives are out there pushing bans on CRT in state legislatures and elsewhere; that's not an awful idea, but they're going to find out it's a lot harder to do than they think.

Critical Race Theory's hold on the US education and corporate systems is the poisonous fruit of a poisoned tree. To root it out will require a lot more than state and local bans. It requires of the Right exactly what the Far Left is doing: systemic thinking.

That means not taking an isolated, whack-a-mole approach that lawmakers might prefer so they can just pass some patch on the problem and send voters home with a pat on the head. It means making a comprehensive, holistic assessment of how so many of American local, regional, state, and even national leaders participate in and even condone open, government-supported racism.

Here you'll want to think about the flaws of the civil rights laws passed in the 1960s, and note that when "disparate impact" was brought into the equation as a metric for antidiscrimination laws, it was the opening of Pandora's box that ultimately led us to CRT being infused into everything.

Because if you go looking for racism, especially the amorphous "systemic" kind, you will always find it. Racism, the way the woke Left wants to define it, is a self-licking ice cream cone. It's a perpetual motion machine. And it isn't applied in good faith by the people using it.

Most people get this, and most people are disgusted by it. In Virginia, it finally became front-and-center enough to turn an electorate from solidly blue to reddish-purple. It seems well understood that this is going to happen all over the country for the next couple of election cycles because ordinary folks are tired of being lectured to by obnoxious losers and grifters like Ibram X. Kendi, Stacey Abrams, Robin DiAngelo, and Shaun King (who is white).

But what's also true is that despite the warnings from people like James Carville, the Democrats and the Hard Left in particular are most certainly not going to change their ways in response to a bad election or two. Even Carville, so you understand, is not telling his party that the use of the race card and other bad-faith anti-American political tactics has to stop. He's all for using those; he uses them himself. Carville hasn't stopped calling all conservatives racists, and he never will. All he's saying is that the messaging on things like CRT has to be more understated so the folks won't be so agitated by it.

And they're not listening to him anyway. What was the result of the electoral outcome in Virginia? Every left-wing pundit, columnist, reporter, and political hack took to the airwaves and internet to deny Critical Race Theory is even taught in schools. The point is, if they wanted the indoctrination to stop because it's bad politics and it's losing them elections, they wouldn't deny it's happening, they'd stop pushing it.

Meaning that the leftists who have infiltrated the education system from kindergarten through graduate school and control it almost completely aren't going to respect CRT bans.

If passing a ban won't work, what do you do?

Mass firings pursuant to a ban might work. But the fight to come over CRT bans will be trench warfare. The teachers' unions will go to the mattresses every time a GOP-dominated school board fires a left-wing nut who's indoctrinating kids into the idea that white American babies are little Klukkers in training. It's wrestling with a pig—you get dirty, and the pig likes it. And eventually, the anti-CRT folks will run out of gas and lose, and the Left will only intensify what they're doing.

You don't get anywhere with trench warfare. You need a blitzkrieg. What does that look like?

Well, for one thing it should be the project of the Republicans who are going to win these elections to smash the teachers' unions by whatever means necessary. The easiest way to do that is to pass Paycheck Protection laws in every state with a GOP legislature and governor. Paycheck Protection laws mean that state and local governments will no longer serve as dues collection agents for public sector unions; if the unions want to collect dues, they've got to get their members to set up direct deposit with their banks or some other kind of auto-billing, or write a check every month.

That means getting teachers to voluntarily remit dues. And everywhere it's been done, teacher union membership falls off a cliff, because most teachers aren't all that crazy about having the Randi Weingartens of the world representing them and, when given the opportunity to think about it some, they generally decide they'd prefer to keep their money rather than pay it in union dues.

Break the teachers' unions and their influence on politicians in legislative settings, and all kinds of structural improvements now become possible.

With more than 11 percent of the educational market now composed of homeschoolers of various stripes and another 12–15 percent, if not more, composed of kids in private schools, it's obvious that people with the means to escape the government-school monolith are choosing to do so quickly. How much faster do you think it'll happen if the Republican pols in Virginia and other states who see this red wave driven by education actually follow through on the perceptible public desire for money-follows-the-child education finance policy? When a quarter of the market is willing to come out of pocket for their kids' education while still paying to fund government schools, what happens if *they actually get that money back?*

And who do you think that quarter of the population votes for? A hint: it ain't Democrats.

This falls under the revivalist banner, sure, but it's really old-fashioned interest-group politics. By bringing in money-follows-the-child, your voters get to pocket thousands of dollars that are now being spent to benefit the other side's voters.

Democrats see politics in exactly this way. That's why they're for all kinds of destructive policies that clearly don't make anything better. Those policies put money in the pockets of interest groups that monolithically support the Democrats, and so they'll fight to the death to keep those policies going.

You make $5,000 per student per year available in educational savings accounts or some other similar program, and that quarter of the population escaping from public schools becomes a third, or two-fifths, or even half. Make $8,000 per student per year available, and the number could be two-thirds or three-fourths.

And what comes from that? Probably a whole lot of microschools.

Microschools are the perfect conservative response to the educational challenge. A microschool is a small business. It's a teacher or two who loves what she does but can't stand working in the Soviet-style, bureaucratized hell that a government school is built to be, so she hangs up a shingle like a lawyer or accountant would, rounds up a couple of dozen kids, and gives them individualized instruction at a space she rents in a strip mall or something.

And instead of making $50,000 per year, she starts making $100,000. And if kids in her school are disruptive, she sends them packing. No bureaucrat tells her she can't.

And by the way, if Republican policymakers really want to fly their freak flag, they'd go after the teacher certification scam that bars entry into the profession. Everybody here is aware of the fact that the education majors on practically every campus are the ones with the lowest aggregate SAT and ACT scores, right? And yet people who are actual mathematicians, scientists, engineers, writers, and so forth get frozen out of the teaching of our kids. It's insane.

Do you really think decentralization and competition, small business, couldn't fix CRT in our schools? Of course it can. If nothing else, an open, decentralized marketplace is a whole lot harder to infiltrate and capture than a closed bureaucratic system is. We talked about this earlier; it isn't an accident that the Left has gravitated so completely toward institutions that are the sole occupiers of their space—like in academia, Hollywood, and government bureaucracies. In the sectors they dominate, power is more important than competence. They're good at getting power. They're not good at anything else. So the things they run inevitably decline.

You probably didn't attach too much meaning to it when Crazy Bernie Sanders was on TV bitching about all the different kinds of deodorant on the store shelves, but when you blew that off you missed something. That was the big reveal in a little package.

What's important isn't that we elect a bunch of Republicans to Congress and to state legislatures for the next couple of years. What's far more important is that those Republicans we elect be made to understand they're being elected to move the damn ball forward. No more failure theater, and no more cowering in the face of nasty leftists like Randi Weingarten making threats about beating them in the next election.

No more standing athwart history, yelling "Stop." It's time to grab history by the throat, put a gun to its head, and calmly and politely direct it where we'd like it to go. Doing that takes a whole lot more than just winning an election or two.

Our time has come. An era is ending. The other side has achieved nearly everything it's ever wanted and can't manage any of it. They're literally choking on their success, and the country has had enough.

We just need the leaders of the Republican Party to be worthy of the success beckoning to them.

Let's demand that, and let's make it happen. Are you ready for an American revival?

ACKNOWLEDGMENTS

I've been writing about politics since 2009, when I watched it destroy my livelihood. As such, I'd like to thank Barack Obama and Nancy Pelosi first and foremost for creating me as, ultimately, the author of this book.

At the time I was working as a corporate headhunter, helping construction companies and engineering firms find construction managers and engineers. Living in Baton Rouge, Louisiana, what that meant was that the vast majority of my work involved the petrochemical industry. Up and down the Mississippi River between Baton Rouge and New Orleans are scads of oil refineries, chemical plants and other heavy industrial facilities tied to the processing of petroleum. But in the summer of 2009, the Obama regime was busily preparing to inflict the cockamamie Cap and Trade plan to regulate carbon emissions.

The narrative being sold locally then by the legacy media was that it would be great for the South Louisiana economy, because all of the plants would be forced to retool and modernize to lower emissions, and that would create tons of jobs. Initially, though I thought Cap and Trade was a colossally stupid idea, I was somewhat optimistic that maybe I'd be wrong.

I wasn't. The two stacks of paper on my desk, one being resumes and the other being jobs to fill, went from equal size to lopsided in favor of the former.

If you've ever seen Monty Python's The Meaning Of Life, you'll remember the scene in which Michael Palin arrives home to a Catholic house jam-packed with kids and says, hilariously, "The mill's closed. There's no more work. We're destitute…I'm afraid I have no choice but to sell you all for scientific experiments."

That's essentially what happened at engineering firms all over South Louisiana when Congress began debating Cap and Trade. Rather than getting excited about spending money building things to satisfy Nancy Pelosi's environmental fetishes, Dow Chemical, BASF, ExxonMobil and the other large concerns operating those plants told the industrial construction firms and engineering firms that they were canceling the projects due to come up for bid, because if the bill passed they were likely to vacate their premises and rebuild in Brazil or India or somewhere else where less political risk existed.

And the resumes of the victims of the employment holocaust that followed landed on my desk.

It's very hard to convince engineers with season tickets to LSU football to take a job in Kuwait. And in the environment Obama and Pelosi created, it was very hard for a headhunter faced with such a challenge to make a living. As politics had put me in a hole, and as I'd been in publishing before, I figured my way of pushing back was to start a blog and go to war against such people. That was the birth of The Hayride, the politics and culture site I've operated ever since. Things have progressed quite a bit since then.

So thanks, Barack and Nancy.

Thanks also to Melissa Mackenzie, R. Emmett Tyrrell, Wlady Pleszczynski and the rest of the gang at The American Spectator, who took a chance on me as a columnist back in 2012 and kept giving me more and more rope as the years went on. Thanks especially to Hannah Rowan, who's edited not just a plurality of my columns there but also edited this book for Bombardier Books. I'm biased, because Hannah and I agree on most things, but I think she did a hell of a job as always.

And thanks to the team at Bombardier—especially David Bernstein and Aleigha Kely for taking a chance on this project and for the guidance and encouragement they've offered. Thanks to Tiffani Rudder for the cool cover design as well.

This book was the project of a lot of consultation over the last few months with some terrific folks, many of whom served as beta readers for the various chapters. I hope I'm not too egregious in leaving anyone out, but among them are Rep. Mike Johnson, Louisiana Public Service Commissioner Eric Skrmetta, Mike Bayham, Louis Gurvich, Bill Stiles, Millard Mule, Mark Zelden, and the incomparable James Piereson, whose book Shattered Consensus provided the structure of America's three major political eras so much of The Revivalist Manifesto is based on.

And thanks to my folks, Ron and Susan McKay, for a whole lot more than their encouragement with this book.

ABOUT THE AUTHOR

Photo by Jenn Ocken Photography

Scott L. McKay is the publisher of The Hayride, an award-winning culture and politics site based in Baton Rouge, Louisiana, which has covered Southern and national current events since 2009. The Hayride frequently tops one million views per month in online traffic. In addition, Scott's work can be found in the pages of the conservative mainstay, the *American Spectator*, where he has been a regular columnist since 2012.